STORMWALL

OBSERVATIONS ON AMERICA IN PERIL

Michael Wilkerson

What happens to those who try to warn the present age?[1]

In a theater, it happened that a fire started off stage. The clown came out to tell the audience. They thought it was a joke and applauded. He told them again, and they became still more hilarious. This is the way, I suppose, that the world will be destroyed – amid the universal hilarity of wits and wags who think it is all a joke.[2]

– Søren Keirkegaard

Table of Contents

Preface

While a graduate student in international relations at Yale University nearly thirty years ago, I embarked on what would become a lifelong journey of interest in and study of the history of modern empires. This journey began with engagement with academic luminaries such as the eminent military historian Sir Michael Howard and Paul Kennedy, who had just published his masterpiece *The Rise and Fall of the Great Powers*. Yale's International Relations program was of particular interest to me as it sought to integrate three disparate fields of learning: economics, history, and political science, into a more integral and holistic framework in the field of international affairs. As an early 20s something, I had ideas of pursuing a career with the CIA or State Department, but it was the early 1990s, and thus *The End of History*.[3] Everyone I spoke with who was working in the sector advised me simply, "Don't go!" The Cold War is over, it's going to be boring from here on out. That may have been true for a time, but of course we know that all changed on September 11, 2001.

Life took me in a different direction in the following decades, away from academia and any idea of foreign service, first in a career as a trans-Atlantic dealmaker with Lazard Frères & Co. and then as an investor in Africa. The lessons of history and international economics acquired in those years have stayed with me, and continue to inform my understanding and interpretation of the world around me, even in times of change, uncertainty and confusion on the global stage. I have found myself in recent months clearing the cobwebs of memory and revisiting these lessons of history, and in particular of empires, to understand our own changing and increasingly perilous times.

I set out to try to explain, both to myself and others, including my two teenage boys who asked more intelligent and insightful questions that I could readily answer, what was happening in the extraordinary circumstances around us. These included the COVID-19 pandemic and related lockdowns, social unrest (ostensibly stemming from racially-charged killings by police, but belying a deeper disease related to injustice and economic dislocation), the vast disconnect between the performance of the financial markets and the harsh realities of the real economy they are intended to represent, and the increasingly loud sabre-rattling between the US and China. These developments and more seem to conspire to form a disturbing series of events leading up to the contentious and controversial presidential elections of November 2020.

I write simply as an observer of these matters, i.e. as a student and not as an economic or foreign policy expert. I write not as an economist, politician, military strategist or diplomat, but rather as a reasonably informed and experienced business leader and investor who has struggled to find meaningful, useful information in the barrage of unsettling and apparently contradictory data hitting us all right now.

While I believe my message has broad applicability for the West, I write this primarily as an American writing to Americans. I have avoided making this a detailed academic or scholarly study but rather sought to achieve a more approachable survey of the key drivers of our changing world and what I believe is a rare but inevitable turning point in history. The danger of my approach, which spans across topics touching on finance and economics, pandemics, domestic politics and foreign policy, is that I attempt to 'boil the ocean.' By saying a little something about everything I risk saying nothing about anything in particular. I have sought to avoid this by focusing on the most critical risks: the economy, the pandemic, the challenges and conflict with China and other nations, and our internal domestic strife. I've tried to focus on near-term, potentially imminent risks, not those which seem remote or long-term existential.

I wrote this in September 2020 when markets continued to gyrate wildly based on a steady stream of extraordinary events. COVID-19 cases continued to rise around the world and our daily news was punctuated with reports of protests and riots, and as the presidential debates turned bitterly rancorous and juvenile. Much of California was on fire, with clouds of smoke reaching across the continent and thousands having to be evacuated from their homes. I wrote on a very compressed timeline because I felt a sense of urgency and the need to complete the work early enough for it to be meaningful for voters deliberating on the elections. I concluded that timeliness would be more important than striving for anything close to literary perfection. I faced the fact that going the traditional publishing route would mean that the book would not come out until sometime in the first half of 2021, rendering it dated and without the relevance of the current events that we are facing. In September 2020, publishing timelines were everywhere delayed a result of printing houses being backed up from the lockdowns, and from shortages of basic items like paper stock and inks, both of which had supply chain ties to China and elsewhere outside of the US.

Given the urgency of the hour, I chose to more narrowly focus on communicating a message that would draw attention to some of the immediate challenges that we may be faced with in the coming months, and showing how they might interrelate and interact in the wake of a triggering event. A follow-up written in a post-crisis period of calm would include, in addition to the aftermath analysis of the elections, addressing the longer-term outlook and prospects for change, including potential solutions to some of the underlying and fundamental challenges that our economy and democracy faces in what will be a new world.

For my American readers fumbling through the dark as I am to understand and interpret our current times, I would hope that this book shines some light and provides some useful insights. However, this book will likely leave dissatisfied those sitting staunchly on either extreme of Left and Right who are just looking for a ready answer that supports their existing prejudices. That suits me just fine. My views do not conform with the prevailing and exclusionary orthodoxy of either conservative or liberal camps. I draw inspiration and perspectives from left, right and center, which may not please those who do not want what they already believe to be challenged. I write this for a simple purpose, which is to make the reader aware of connections that otherwise might not be obvious, and to take necessary steps where possible to prepare for what may be a very challenging time for America in the coming months.

Introduction

"Obviously, historiography cannot be a science. It can only be an industry, an art and a philosophy – an industry by ferreting out the facts, an art by establishing meaningful order in the chaos of materials, a philosophy by seeking perspective and enlightenment."[4]
– Will & Ariel Durant, *The Meaning of History*

"I learned many things from the fire, but among the most important was the unrecognizability of the unprecedented. In that early phase of crisis, I could imagine our home scarred by smoke damage, but I could not imagine its disappearance. I grasped what was happening through the lens of past experience, envisioning a distressing but ultimately manageable detour that would lead back to the status quo. Unable to distinguish the unprecedented, all I could do was close doors to rooms that would no longer exist and seek safety on a porch that was fated to vanish. I was blind to conditions that were unprecedented in my experience."[5]
– Shoshana Zuboff, *The Age of Surveillance Capitalism*

We sit at a pivot point in history where the future, arriving more quickly than many of us are prepared to admit or would prefer to accept, is unrecognizable – other than not looking much like the past. The discomforting idea that Something Has Changed comes from a confluence of several factors: suddenly diminished economic conditions and prospects: rapidly rising domestic social unrest and violence that speaks to deeper cracks in our society; and to attempts by others to capitalize on our wounds by further dividing us, increasing conflicts with China, Russia and Iran, emerging in a multitude of ways that collectively feel like the video game Cold War: Version 2.0; the most contentious and divisive presidential election in modern memory; and the ongoing COVID-19 pandemic that served as a spark to the tinder of these existing economic, social and political issues which continue to smolder and now risk burning out of control.

Turning points in history leading to seismic shifts in nations and societies are rarely recognizable – at least as to their full significance – as they happen. This is true whether they come dramatically and in a moment, or emerge slowly over years or even decades, like the Black Plague and Hundred Year's War of the fourteenth century, or the Renaissance that followed bringing the Middle Ages to a close, launching a new era of scientific and technological advancement that we are still benefiting from today, or in more modern times the challenges of Great Depression and the benefits to our generation information of the technology revolution.

Surprisingly, it seems equally if not especially true that contemporary observers fail to understand the significance even when the catalyst event comes suddenly, visibly and violently, such as happened one hot summer day in June 1914 when Archduke Franz Ferdinand, heir presumptive to the Austro-Hungarian throne, was assassinated by a Serbian separatist, ushering in the first World War. Or as came to pass that sleepy Sunday morning in December 1941 when the Japanese – after signaling for months that they were coming for us – bombed Pearl Harbor and thus finally dragged the US into that war's nearly inevitable continuation some thirty years later. A few years on, V-E Day ushered in what has since been called the New World Order, the US-led rules-based system of international institutions that saw the creation and development of the UN, NATO, the IMF and its Bretton Woods monetary system, the World Bank, the WTO, and a vast number of other many-lettered and multi-lateral governmental and non-governmental organizations, which collectively provided a lattice-like structure that prevailed as a stabilizing force over the West for 75 years, but which now seems antiquated, frail and to be gasping for its last breaths in the face of vigorous new threats from China, Russia, Iran and elsewhere, an untimely demise hastened by the withdrawal of full support from its erstwhile parent and primary sponsor, the United States. It's worth noting that despite many smaller regional conflicts and wars along the way, the fact that this period was largely peaceful, with the absence of violent Great Power conflict (the Cold War actually did work as a deterrent), is truly remarkable in the long arc of history.

Each of these triggering events ushered in a new era of history completely unlike the one that preceded it. Today, the US is facing a similar fundamental turning point for our civilization, and we don't seem to recognize where it is leading any better than those generations did in their times. We know that something extraordinary is going on, but we don't know how to explain it. We are experiencing black swan-like circumstances and events that we haven't seen before and don't recognize, and thus have no cognitive grid with which to process them. We appear to have stumbled into a potential perfect storm of concurrent economic, social, political and natural disasters.

We don't ascribe a coherent meaning to the environment we're facing, mainly because it has not occurred before in our lifetimes. But the cycles of history are long, and what we are experiencing has occurred many times over in the generations of humanity which precede us. The closest thing that comes to it for our generation are the stories we've heard from our parents and grandparents about the turbulent economic and political life of the 1930s. Similarly, today fundamental shifts are happening around us that have taken decades to develop, and yet are now suddenly breaking out, like the dam wall that finally gives way after years of a slowly expanding crack. The events around us are speaking to us now, and history has wisdom to impart ... if we will listen.

What are these seismic shifts? Ray Dalio, the founder of Bridgewater Associates (the world's largest hedge fund) and one of the best macro investors in the world, recently identified and articulated[6] three extraordinary developments that provide contour and context to what we are experiencing as a nation: 1) the long-term economic cycle: the US is nearing the end of a long-running economic cycle that has been in motion since approximately the end of WWII, and which has now reached a troubling near-conclusion as US government debt has mounted to unsustainable levels and interest rates have gone to zero, limiting monetary policy effectiveness; 2) the wealth gap: the end of that long economic cycle has resulted in three fundamentally unstable conditions in the US: i) staggering income inequality not seen in this country since the 1930s, leading to economic and political polarization, ii) the hollowing out of our core manufacturing and productive base, leaving vast swaths of our citizens unemployable beyond poverty wages in service industries, and our country now dependent on other nations for most of our consumer and capital goods, which we finance with debt funded by these same nations; iii) the rise of extremism and populisms on both left and right and its consequences in the political, economic and societal realms, including a tendency towards violence; and 3) renewed Great Power conflict: i.e. the rapid rise of China as a new Great Power and strategic competitor, leaving the US and China squaring off in what Harvard's Graham Allison labels the Thucydides Trap, which he describes as "the natural, inevitable discombobulation that occurs when a rising power threatens to displace a ruling power."[7] Throw into the mix of all of these longer-term forces the sudden and surprising emergence around the globe of COVID-19, biblical proportion natural disasters on our West Coast and elsewhere, and one of the most contentious elections in US history, and we have a very unstable and volatile cocktail in our hands.

What are the risks that the convergence of these several challenges bring to the US? The end of the long-term economic cycle means that economic growth may be muted from here, the US dollar is likely to experience a substantial devaluation, and severe- or hyper-inflation may become real risks to the US economy in the near- to medium-term. The widening wealth gap has the risk of boiling over into nation-wide social unrest, resulting in strikes, civil strife and convulsing waves of racial or class violence, and potentially even revolution or civil war. The conflict with China has already heated up into what foreign policy experts such as Robert Blackwell and Jennifer Harris of the Council on Foreign Relations have termed "War by Other Means,"[8] and risks further escalation from its current cold war-like tension into something much warmer and eventually out of control. Our internal domestic strife and contentious election process provide a fertile field for our enemies to deploy active measures in the form of interference in both.

The catalyst bringing these forces into sharp and immediate relief and urgent relevance has been the introduction of the COVID-19 pandemic and its impact on our society, which may have been hindered or helped by the patchwork of conflicting government initiatives deployed to combat it. The US government has pumped in helicopter money, increasing the Federal Reserve's balance sheet by over $3 trillion to send relief checks to individuals and small businesses, yet the gap between the haves (who can work over Zoom from the comfort of their own homes) and have nots (who actually have to show up somewhere and work to collect a paycheck) has widened and become distressingly visible for all to see, magnifying existing stresses that were present even before the pandemic. Tensions with China over trade, espionage, and the source of the virus itself have now reached a fever-like pitch.

There has been a lot of discussion in the media in recent months about why the equity markets have performed so extraordinarily well in an environment in which the underlying performance in the real economy is not keeping up. In early May, Paul Murphy of the *Financial Times* wrote a short but prescient article entitled the Zimbabwification of Wall Street.[9] As an emerging markets investor with exposure to Zimbabwe, this immediately caught my eye, and I knew what he meant before I even got past the title. The article asked the question whether what was going on with the astonishing performance of the US equity markets in the depths of the pandemic and lockdowns might not somehow be similar to what had happened in Zimbabwe in 2008. At that time, the Zimbabwe Stock Exchange started to rise exponentially, and it made no sense to most external observers. It was clear for all to see that the country's leader, Robert Mugabe, was not exactly acting sanely, there were riots on the streets, and the country was in a deep economic crisis driven by hyperinflation. The reason the Zimbabwe markets performed so well during this period was that in a time of high inflation expectations, equities serve as a reflationary store of value. Stocks become one of the better if still imperfect alternatives to a currency devaluation or a situation in which fixed income (e.g. bonds) real yields turn negative, as we are seeing in the US today. The author speculated that US investors were somehow "subconsciously or otherwise, buying insurance against inflation." The markets were seeing through the pandemic panic to recognize that the relief spending would lead to monetization of the debt (i.e. printing money) and investors were thus moving assets defensively into something that they believed would provide some protection. I think Murphy's observation was spot on. The inflation risk is one of the bigger challenges that the United States will face in 2021, and this book explores some of the causes and potential cures to avoid a severe negative impact on the dollar.

The immediate effects of the shutdown of our economy have been largely deflationary, just as they were during the Great Depression, and the global financial crisis of 2008-09. Going forward, inflation poses the greater risk to our economy as a result of several factors, including: a fundamental change in monetary policy that prioritizes employment over monetary stability; the trade war with China and in particular the "decoupling" of the two economies (if carried out); the devaluation of the US dollar, which may be in the magnitude of a loss of one-third of its value, resulting in substantial diminution of buying Americans power in world markets; and, most consequentially, the loss of status of the US dollar as the world's reserve currency. This unimaginable event would arise from the loss of confidence of the rest of the world in America's commitment to maintain a stable currency or to repay its debts, which are projected to rise to over 107% of GDP by 2023, the highest level on record. The risks of inflation are neither appreciated nor well understood by the typical American consumer, presumably because the country has not faced an inflationary environment in over forty years. US businesses and governments are no better equipped to navigate an inflationary environment for the same reason. This lack of awareness and experience may be as dangerous as the underlying issue itself.

In 1910, Norman Angell published *The Great Illusion*, a book which quickly became an international bestseller on the feel-good assertion that war between the Great Powers (incumbents Britain, France, Germany, Austria-Hungary, and emerging powers Russia and the United States) was highly unlikely because the consequences for both winners and losers were universally recognized as being disastrously high. The world had experienced over multiple decades a period of great prosperity and creativity (variously labeled la Belle Époque, the Gilded Age, or the Victorian Era, depending on whether one was sitting in Paris, New York, or London). Free trade and capital flows between countries were at levels higher than ever before seen in history. Since war had been proven by previous European conflicts to be both economically and socially irrational, and since the countries were now so peacefully integrated by travel and trade, it was popularly and widely believed even at the highest levels of society that no Great Power would be so foolish as to start such a war with another one (colonial wars were another matter). In the meantime, imperceptibly and in the shadows, "the European general staffs were quietly finalizing their war plans."[10] Within five years of the book's publishing, all of Europe was ablaze in the war to end all wars.

We are in an analogous moment. While the media and the general public seems to be talking about each of these separate challenges, there doesn't appear to be a recognition that they are interlinked and feeding off of each other, like strings of a bow resonating from one issue to another and back, creating what wave physics calls constructive interference, where each individual wave combines into one massive tsunami-like effect.

If America did not have external enemies, then there would be nothing more important for our government and its citizens to focus on than fighting our most pressing domestic enemies: COVID-19 and its economic fallout, gaping income inequality and the persistence of systemic racism, the bitter fruit of what has been rightly described as our nation's original sin.

However, the United States is one nation among many, and not all wish us well. There are nation-states around the world that are seeking to take advantage of our current frailties and civil discord by further dividing our society and distracting our government from its many threats from abroad, much as the Soviet Union did during the Civil Rights Movement of the 1950s and 60s.[11] Then and today, the Russians didn't start the fire, we created it ourselves. But they and other governments, particularly the Chinese and Iranian, are pouring fuel on it, and our own domestic tech companies have facilitated them. We have become our own worst enemy and don't seem to appreciate that American-based social media platforms, through big data and artificial intelligence, are exacerbating our divisions and separating us one from another … with Friends like these, who needs enemies? Michael Hayden, the former head of both the NSA and CIA, put it succinctly: "Covert influence campaigns don't create divisions on the ground, they amplify divisions on the ground."[12] Much ink has been spilled on the influence of Russia in the 2016 presidential election, and it is no longer a question of fact. We again, today, are experiencing substantial foreign influence, by state-sponsored actors, in the protests and 2020 presidential campaign, and this time around it's not primarily the Russians. Both China and Iran have joined the party, each with their own agenda conveniently converged around a singular event set to occur on November 3, 2020.

We have had ample warning, yet as a society seem unaware that we are in a new kind of cold war. This time around the primary actor is China and the Chinese Communist Party (though the Russians and the Iranians are happy to align by applying the old maxim "the enemy of my enemy is my friend" at least for as long as it serves their strategic interests). Like the last one, this cold war will be likely played out through trade, biological, cyber-security, financial and infrastructure attacks, proxy battles, and similar skirmishes long before it ever boils over into outright conventional war or worse. As Graham Allison points out, the fact that the Cold War conflict between the US and the Soviet Union did not result in a hot war was the minority exception to the general experience of Great Power conflicts facing Thucydides's Trap (when an upstart, rising power challenges an incumbent), where in 16 cases studied over five hundred years, war broke out 75% of the time.[13]

The Chinese Communist Party (CCP) is patient and understands the game being played much better than we do. They view history over a very long scale, and in this sense have a clearer picture of where they are trying to go and how they expect to get there. The CCP's recent successes have given them increased confidence and encouraged greater risk-taking in establishing China's dominance in the world. As Americans, it's time we became more clear-eyed and aware of the threat facing our country and our democratic values. We need to dust off Sun-Tzu's maxim and apply it to our current conflicts:

> If you know the enemy and know yourself, you need not fear the result of a hundred battles. If you know yourself but not the enemy, for every victory gained you will also suffer a defeat. If you know neither the enemy nor yourself, you will succumb in every battle.

The purpose of this book is to examine these disparate threads of concurrent but superficially unrelated forces, then attempt to weave them together into a cohesive strand, finally seeing it as a whole. History takes a long time to arrive suddenly, and then when it does, take care and take cover. We are in such a moment.

STORMWALL

Part I: The economy

1. The looming economic crisis

A recovery derailed

We are on the eve of entering into what is probably the first financial crisis in recorded history that was so willingly and knowingly precipitated by self-inflicted, proactive measures to shut down our own economic productivity over so long a period of time. We did this with the cooperative participation of governments, financial institutions, corporations and vocal individual leaders of varying degrees of qualification and expertise across the country and around most parts of the world. We did this on the expert advice of the medical and scientific community, which knew a lot about immunology and health care, but little of economics, financial markets, politics, or sociology, but which nonetheless veered wide outside of their lanes of expertise into making wide-ranging recommendations, the consequences of which would ultimately affect these areas and many more. We did this with the support and encouragement of a majority of us who as individuals, families, and households, listened to the advice of these experts. We wanted nothing more than to ensure that the horror stories being told about the possible effects of COVID-19 – and what would happen if we didn't shut everything down now – would not come to pass. This was a period of time in which fear and panic seemed more contagious than the virus itself. In the early 2020 alarm of what seemed like an unprecedented (a word both overused and incorrect with regard to the pandemic) global health crisis, our leaders reached for the nearest blunt force instrument they could find, which was to impose and enforce mandatory stay-at-home lockdowns and the shutdown of wide sectors of the economy in order to stop the accelerating spread of SARS-CoV-2.

On the eve of the COVID-19 pandemic, the private sector of the US economy was performing exceedingly well. Over the decade following the global financial crisis, the American economy had recovered and was performing among the best in the world, producing GDP growth figures averaging 4% per year since 2009.[14] Multiple sectors, including technology, health care, energy, financial services, and manufacturing, had shown significant signs of recovery from financial crisis-era lows, and were back on strong growth trajectories. It was one of the longest-running expansions on record. Over the same decade, the growth in real gross domestic private investment had averaged 6% per year, indicating that companies were strengthening their businesses for long-term competitiveness by re-investing in capital goods and research & development at a healthy pace. This was especially positive when compared with the first decade of the century, a period in which private investment didn't grow at all (annual growth was down 1% on average over the decade) and saw annual declines in growth in five of ten years of the 2000s.[15]

2019 was a great year for the American worker. Median household income grew by 6.8%, well ahead of inflation, and the poverty rate fell to 10.5%, the lowest rate on record since estimates were first published in 1959. This extraordinary result was part of a longer-term trend in which the poverty rate had declined, and the median household income for families had grown, for five consecutive years. The post-global financial crisis expansion was disproportionately benefiting women and minorities. On a percentage basis, the median income gains in 2019 were greater for Asians (10.6%), Blacks (7.9%) and Hispanics (7.1%), than they were for

Non-Hispanic Whites (5.7%). The poverty rate decreased more for Asians (2.8%), Blacks (2.0%), Hispanics (1.8%) than for Whites (1.0%). Female workers saw earnings gains of 7.8% compared with 2.5% for men, but full-time working women still earned only about 82.3% of their male peers, indicating we still had a way to go.[16] Similarly, income discrepancies still existed amongst men of different races, in that Black men earned 13% less than White men, who in turn earned 13% than Asian men.[17]

By the end of the decade, the US was experiencing one of the longest-running economic expansions on record and looked well-positioned to go from strength to strength in 2020. The unemployment rate had fallen from a high of 10.0% in October 2009 to a near post-war low of 3.5% in December 2019.[18] Additionally, the decade-long recovery had been fairly wide-spread across the nation, with each of the 50 states showing positive growth in the rate of their resident's average annual personal income (inflation-adjusted) of between lows of 1.0% (for Connecticut and Mississippi) and highs above 3.0% (for North Dakota, Utah, Washington, Colorado and Texas), averaging out to 2% for the nation as a whole. While lower than the 2.7% national average of the preceding 30 years, growth was showing an acceleration in 2019, with the US averaging 2.4%, well above the ten-year average. [19]

All of this, of course, was before SARS-CoV-2 struck the US in the first quarter of the new year, setting the decade off on the wrong foot, and ushering us almost overnight into a world we had not seen before.

While the private sector of the American economy outperformed during the decade, the public sector, on the other hand, was struggling significantly. The US government continued to face "Triple-D" challenges: Deficits, Debt, and looming Deflation inherited from previous decades and which multiplied with a vengeance in the wake of the global financial crisis of 2008-09. To these three long-standing challenges we added a fourth in 2020, which was Disease, manifested in the COVID-19 pandemic. While the economic recovery of the second half of the decade showed promise of mitigating some of these legacy government issues through increased tax revenues and lower borrowing costs, government expenditures also began to rise again, and at a high enough rate to outpace the gains in tax and other revenue. If there was any chance that the US government would be able to get back to a balanced budget, the self-imposed shutdown of the economy in 2020 eliminated any hope that the United States would be able to grow its way out of the hole. Rather, the pandemic response meant that the government would have to start deficit spending with a vengeance just to provide a stopgap solution for millions of workers required to stay home during the lockdowns. This will prove to have led to an unstable situation for the dollar and for the US government's ability to continue to finance abroad its ever-expanding losses, as we explore below.

Deficits as a way of life

The last time the US government spent less than it earned in a given fiscal year was twenty years ago in 2000 and 2001, years in which the George W. Bush administration ran modest surpluses of about $240 billion and $130 billion respectively. Since then, the US government has run budget deficits every single year, in amounts that have averaged nearly $870 billion annually.[20] This has been true of both Republican and Democratic administrations. Cumulatively, this means that the government has added over $16.5 trillion of debt in the twenty-first century to support spending beyond its means of revenue generation through taxation and other mechanisms. Of this accumulated deficit, the Watson Institute of Public Affairs at Brown University estimates that $6.4 trillion (39%) was spent on post-9/11 war efforts in Afghanistan, Iraq and elsewhere.[21] The deficit is now estimated at $3.3 trillion for 2020,[22] a trembling from the 2019 actual amount and the original 2020 budget, as the government has spent well over $2.2 trillion on initiatives related to pandemic relief. According to the Congressional Budget Office, "At 16.0 percent of gross domestic product (GDP), the deficit in 2020 will be the largest since 1945."[23] For two decades, the US government has regularly missed its budget estimates as a result of unpleasant surprises like 9/11, the global financial crisis, and now COVID-19.

Congress has continued to pass deficit budgets year after year, and year after year the government has failed to meet them. Over two decades, our congressional leaders and the various presidential administrations have, in roughly equal measure, largely ignored the issue and not treated it as a risk, in part because of our country's ability to finance the budgeted deficit at very favorable terms by any historical standards. Governments justify this spending because of a heterodox economic concept called Modern Monetary Theory (MMT). The core idea is that governments with a fiat currency[i] can run deficits in perpetuity, because they can and should print as much money as needed. Deficits don't matter because the government is not an ordinary household or firm with a budget or profit and loss statement, but the monopoly issuer of the currency which cannot go bankrupt or become insolvent so long as it can continue to print money.

---

[i] Fiat currency means a government-issued currency that isn't backed by a commodity such as gold.

As a result, MMT argues that fiscal policy should be used as monetary policy and the government should pay for all these unfunded expenses by the printing of as much money as is required to achieve the policy objective. Spending shouldn't be restrained by budget deficit levels but rather determined by whether employment is at an acceptably full level. Supporters of MMT don't deny the inflationary risks that these policies may produce, but suggest that if inflation starts to get out of hand, the government can simply use taxes as it means to control it. Stephanie Kelton, arguably the most well-known face of MMT and the economic advisor to Bernie Sanders during the 2016 presidential campaign, describes it this way (emphasis mine):

> An MMT view of the monetary system changes the way we think about it about what it means for currency issuing nations to 'live within their means.' It asks us to think in terms of real resource constraints – inflation – rather than perceived financial constraints. It teaches us to ask not 'how you pay for it?' but 'how will you resource it?' It shows us that if we have the technological know-how and the available resources – the people, the factories, equipment, and the raw materials – …
> then … *Coming up with the money is the easy part. Managing the inflation risk is the critical challenge. More than any other economic approach, MMT places inflation at the center of the debate over spending limits.*[24]

This is a dangerous idea with growing popularity; many in Washington have been following it (whether knowingly or not) for years now. Kelton is at least honest in acknowledging that under MMT managing inflation becomes the real challenge. The biggest danger in MMT is the idea that we can tame and restrain the inflationary tiger once out of its cage. History has shown that it is extremely difficult for governments to stop accelerating inflation once it gets moving and inflation expectations have embedded in the minds of markets and individuals. At some point the government can no longer practically increase taxation. With interest rates in the low single digits and now effectively zero, and willing buyers of US dollar-denominated debt around the world, it has been too easy to continue year after year to spend more than we make as a nation. However, over the long run, MMT can only go in one direction, and that is towards increased taxes, higher inflation and eroding asset values. While it may work for the government, it is devastating for its citizens. Eventually, the laws of gravity, math, and double-entry accounting prevail, and we will have a reconciling. Some would argue that we can go on for decades in this state, but there is a grave risk the current events and circumstances may soon limit our government's ability to continue to deficit spend with China's and other's money the way we have in the last two decades. If not, and domestic savers aren't willing to take up the gap left by foreign buyers, then the US government will have only one alternative left, which is to discount its notes to the Federal Reserve and thereby increase the money supply. This is inflation by definition, in that we'd have vastly increased the monetary base without being matched by a corresponding rise in the level of real underlying economic activity.

Debt becomes you

At the same time of the $2.1 trillion decline in national income in 2020, the Federal Reserve, the central bank of the United States, increased its balance sheet by over $3 trillion (an 82.5% increase in the second quarter), primarily by buying newly-issued debt of the US government, which had been raised to fund payments to individuals and small businesses under the CARES Act. This was the largest single-quarter increase in US government debt ever recorded. As recently as January 2013, the entire balance sheet of the Federal Reserve was less than $3 trillion.[25]

Looking over the same timeframe as our exploration of the deficit, US government debt stood at $5.7 trillion at the turn of the century. Going into the global financial crisis in September 2007, total US government debt stood at $9.0 trillion, and $14.8 trillion coming out of it in September 2011. Before the pandemic, in September 2019, the debt level had already grown to $22.7 trillion.[26] As of now, with more to come, potentially including over $2 trillion more in emerging debts in the fourth quarter, we're sitting at $26.8 trillion, or 81% of GDP.[27] Said differently, the US national debt has increased by nearly five times (470%) in just twenty years. That's over 8% per year, which for perspective is almost four times the average growth in GDP during the period.[28] One of the largest financiers of our debt has been the Chinese government, which now holds over $1.1 trillion of US Treasury bonds and bills.

It's worth referring to the September 2020 statements of the Congressional Budget Office itself about the near-term trends we can expect (emphasis mine):

> As a result of those deficits, federal debt held by the public is projected to rise sharply, to 98% of GDP in 2020, compared with 79% at the end of 2019 and 35% in 2007, before the start of the previous recession. It would exceed 100% in 2021 and increase to 107% in 2023, the highest in the nation's history. The previous peak occurred in 1946 following the large deficits incurred during World War II.[29]

Government debt is an indirect tax on a country's citizens. Eventually, it is the taxpayer that has to make good on its government's obligations, either through direct taxation, or through inflation and the debasement of the currency. Right now this obligation is over $81,000 per American. When compared with median household income of $68,700, or roughly $26,400 per person,[30] this means that on average each American owes over three times what they earn in a given year. If our nation were a boat taking on water in stormy seas, we have only been bailing out one bucket of water for every four or five that pours in. This is clearly not sustainable, no matter what jargon-laden economists or government lobbyists tell us, any more than it would be for a household or an individual who keeps piling on more and more debt with the hope that they will one day hit the jackpot.

The last time the US had no national debt was 1835. The US got close to paying it off again at the beginning of the 20th century, but then World War I intervened, and government spending began to increase again.[31] Some level of debt is necessary and beneficial to the economy, extending buying power in the same way that taking out a mortgage enables a purchaser to be able to take possession of a home that would otherwise be out of reach if cash were required. We have neared the point of no return, where at some point very soon, the US government will not be able to generate sufficient revenue through taxation to maintain its obligations. This leaves only two options, one of which is a default and restructuring – not very practical for a superpower and the world's reserve currency – and the other is to debase the currency and allow inflation to run, in the hopes that no one catches on for some lengthy period of time, or even if they do, they don't have any better alternative to the US dollar.

The counter-argument to this bleak scenario is that with interest rates approaching zero, the government's ability to service the debt will remain high, and not be a constraint on further borrowing. This is probably true over some period of time, assuming blue skies and smooth sailing. But it also relies on one other major assumption, which is that foreign governments continue to be willing to act as creditors to our consumption-driven economy and acquire US debt at low or negative real interest rates.[32] There are several challenges with this assumption, including that other nations continue to be willing to accept negative real rates (nominal rates near zero less whatever inflation exists). Will China, which is one of the largest creditors to the US, remain willing to support the debt of one of its primary competitors and an increasingly stressed debtor? Economically, it is still in their rational interest to do so, because financing that debt enables America to continue to acquire goods imported from China, which is still necessary to keep China's economy growing and stave off domestic unrest that could challenge the CCP's leadership position. So the Chinese do face a dilemma here that is unlikely to be resolved anytime soon. It is highly unlikely that China would push the "nuclear" economic button of halting US Treasury bond purchases, and no longer finance our economy, at least in the near-term. The Chinese should be willing to accept zero or even negative interest rates on financing that enables it to capture the profit pool on the actual trade, for the same reason a car dealer or mattress store is able to offer zero-percent financing to make the sale. John Maynard Keynes once quipped, "If I owe you a pound, I have a problem; but if I owe you a million, the problem is yours." This adage is certainly true for China in relation to the US. One the other hand, it gives the Chinese government a fairly powerful weapon in their arsenal against the

United States, for when the day comes that the world is no longer thinking in economically rational terms.

The deflationary spiral

Coming into the financial crisis in 2008, the Chairman of the Federal Reserve Ben Bernanke had one thing on his mind, which was avoiding a repeat of the Great Depression. Chairman Bernanke had spent a good portion of his career studying and thinking about the causes and effects of the Great Depression, and what the US government did and didn't do right to address the crisis. What wasn't well understood at the time was that the biggest factor driving the Great Depression were the forces of deflation at work in the economy. The monetary and fiscal actions of the US government, following the classical economic theories then prevalent, only made the depression worse by tightening credit and taking money out of the economy. What was not fully appreciated at that time, was that deflationary spirals occur when prices and wages fall in twinned response to the other. Consumers delay purchases, expecting that prices will fall, producers reduce output and start lowering prices, which results in job losses, depressing aggregate demand and leading to further price declines, which in turn leads to lower wages and employment, and the vicious cycle carries on and on. If the government tightens monetary policy, making credit more expensive, it exacerbates the situation. Bernanke brought this understanding into the position when in 2008 he faced the greatest challenge to our economy in nearly a hundred years. Bernanke recognized very quickly that avoiding a deflationary spiral was one of the primary objectives that he, in coordination with the United States Treasury and the New York District of the Federal Reserve (the New York Bank had regulatory oversight of the major Wall Street money center and investment banks) would have to focus on if there was any chance of saving the US economy, and the global financial system, from complete collapse.

One of the pernicious challenges of deflations is that debt repayments become more expensive in terms of real income. Deflation increases the effective cost to the borrower of her mortgage, car loan, student loan, credit card or other debt, as real income falls but the nominal value of debt does not. Today, with aggregate household debt in the US at $14.3 trillion,[33] or over $43,000 per person, deflationary pressures that lower household income while keeping the nominal value of debt at such elevated levels would be devastating. Once an economy is caught in a deflationary spiral, it can be very difficult to break out of that spin cycle. The best modern example of this effect is the current situation in Japan, which has suffered through nearly three decades of deflation, and despite many efforts has been unable to pull itself up into a normal and healthier low inflation environment.

During the first few months of the pandemic related lockdowns, many commentators argued a view that deflation was a greater risk to the US economy than inflation, at least in the near term.[34] This view is based on many factors, including a very long run of low inflation in the United States over the past couple of decades, the rapid disemployment of nearly 30 million workers as a result of the COVID-19 shutdowns, the steep fall in global oil prices which had occurred at approximately the same time as the beginning of the pandemic, and the expectation that consumer demand for goods and services would drop significantly as a result of the crisis.

They argued that the price increases that were seen across several categories, including food, medical supplies and other items would be more than offset by the falling demand for non-essential categories such as travel, tourism and entertainment. So far, this is indeed the case. Today, they look at the ongoing shortages in many product categories as being temporary disruptions resulting from the forced shutdowns of factories, as opposed to something more systemic in the production supply chain.

Disease

On January 14, 2020, the World Health Organization (WHO) announced that investigations by the Chinese government revealed no evidence of human-to-human transmission of SARS-CoV-2.[35] Within two weeks, Wuhan and three other Chinese cities were put on lockdown, resulting in approximately five million people leaving the city without being screened for the virus. On January 30, the WHO declared COVID-19 a "public health emergency of international concern," and a pandemic on March 11. On March 13, the crisis was declared a National Emergency in the United States, and travel, already restricted from China since January 31, was restricted from Europe. This was followed very quickly in the coming days by a patchwork of other actions, which included a progressive and increasing series of travel restrictions, stay at home orders, closing of public facilities, and similar actions initiated by the state, local or federal government. Americans working or vacationing abroad quickly booked flights to return to the US before flights were canceled. At the same time, colleges and universities shut down their campuses and sent students home to their families. These forced migrations likely widely disseminated the virus across the country as infected travelers and students returned home carrying the virus, thereby inadvertently contaminating their parents, grandparents, and other family members. By the end of March, most of the country was in a state of lockdown, grocery store shelves were bare, and businesses begin to shut down across our nation.

Over the following weeks and months, Americans, along with the rest of the world, watched fearfully from their homes as the daily rate of increase in both infections and deaths continued to rise. It appeared that hospitals might soon be overwhelmed with the number of patients in their intensive care units. The demand for respirators was being stretched beyond existing capacity, and preparations were being made to utilize stadiums, school gymnasiums, tents and other facilities in case the need for emergency hospitals should arise. The peak of initial waves occurred at different times in different regions around the world. For the United States, the beginning of the first wave came in April. Much of it was centered in the New York metro area, where at the peak over 8,000 cases per day were being registered, and approximately 20% of all tests were coming back as positive for the novel coronavirus. It was the time when hospital resource utilization peaked, including ICU and ventilator use, and human mobility hit its nadir.[36] It was however not until July that the United States experienced a peak daily rate of increase of 73,000 cases, in part attributable to better and wider testing and not necessarily indicative of worsening conditions.

Now, after about eight months of the pandemic, there have been approximately 7.4 million confirmed cases in the US and over 35 million worldwide, and daily new cases range between 40,000 and 55,000 nationwide.[37] Assuming that number still grossly underestimates actual cases, a five-fold inflator would imply 175 million cases of infection worldwide or about 2% of the global population. COVID-19 related deaths, presumably easier to track, number over 200,000 in the US and over 1.1 million worldwide as of the date of this writing.[38]

Compare this with what we know so far about the economic costs of the COVID-19 lockdowns. The unemployment rate went from a February low of 3.5% to 14.7% in April, a month in which there were 20.5 million job losses. By the worst of it in April, there were 23 million civilians unemployed in the US, compared with 6.4 million the previous year.[39] These rates are the worst since the data were first collected in 1948. Even more telling is the employment to population ratio, which has fallen from 59.7% to an all-time low of 51.3%, surpassing the previous low of 54.9% recorded in 1949, a time when women made up only one-third of the labor force.[40] Some of these losses have been regained in the third quarter, but the scale is dramatic.

The pandemic-related lockdowns and effective shutdown of a vast portion of our economy led to what we intuitively felt would be a devastating impact on our economic and social well-being. We now know that US real gross domestic product contracted in the second quarter of 2020 by an unprecedented annualized rate of 31.7%, a $2.1 trillion decline in current dollars from year-end, and the worst drop on record since the GDP statistic has been officially tracked. Within this aggregate figure, personal consumption fell by 34.1%, or $1.5 trillion, and private domestic investment fell by 46.2%, or $0.5 trillion.[41] On a year-over-year basis, the decline was 9.1%, still the largest drop ever recorded (June 2009, the worst quarter of the global financial crisis, saw a 3.9% drop).

Sweden chose to take a very different path than America and the rest of Europe, eschewing national lockdowns, without significantly worse results. We will never know what might have happened to the US economy, and to the incidence of disease, both concerning morbidity and mortality, had the economy been allowed to remain open and functioning to a larger degree with more targeted lockdowns. Trying to imagine counterfactual scenarios is rarely productive. What we can say, however, is that the decisions that were made had a severe economic impact on our country, not only to our economy, but to the social well-being of Americans, millions of whom were unable to work and to contribute productively to the economy, but rather were forced to rely on government handouts.

We are currently in the middle of a second wave, with the rise in infection rates largely precipitated by the combination of the gradual reopening of the economy and the commencement of schools and universities bringing students into close contact with one another for the first time in several months. Countries all over the world are starting to discuss the possibility of renewed lockdowns, and hot spots are continuing to develop, presenting governments with a frustrating game of whack-a-mole. The situation is clearly not under control either here in the US or elsewhere in the world.

The challenge going forward

This chapter opened by asserting that we were on the eve of another financial crisis. This may have struck the reader as curious because by many indications, there appears to be no crisis. At the time of this writing in late September 2020, equity markets remain near all-time highs, bonds and the US dollar have wobbled but not fallen over, employment is picking back up (at least in some parts of the country which have allowed more rapid re-opening), our economy appears to be re-gaining steam lost in the second quarter, and household wallets are beginning to re-open. Unlike the 2008-09 financial crisis, the banking sector does not appear to be in the middle of a meltdown. The Federal Reserve has been able to manage banking sector systemic liquidity well, pumping in more than enough money to meet demand conditions, thereby avoiding a repeat of the cascading events from over a decade ago.

So where is the problem? We indeed survived the first phase of the crisis well enough in that banks were able to meet their customer demands for liquidity. But now we have entered into a more dangerous phase where solvency – rather than liquidity – will be the primary challenge. Herein lies the problem and the reason why the crisis is likely to occur.

A test of liquidity seeks to ensure that borrowers have the ability to repay their debts and other obligations like payrolls, etc. when due, and tends to focus on the short-term horizon. A test of solvency is to confirm that the borrower has more assets than it does liabilities, to the point of ensuring that there is ultimately going to be enough value to repay that debt as it comes due. These two issues, liquidity and solvency, tend to come in pairs during times of financial distress, but not always at the same time. Typically, and as we saw in the previous financial crisis, liquidity is almost always the first issue to arise, often from a triggering event but sometimes just from a sea change in investor sentiment, the shock of which results in money being pulled out of the financial system. A chain reaction then occurs with creditors demanding repayment from borrowers when the terms of those debts allow them to do so. This can have a domino effect, as called upon borrowers then turn to their own debtors for repayment, and so on and on and on. In the most liquid markets, this can happen very rapidly and sometimes cataclysmically as was the case in 2008-09 (money markets, prime brokerage) and 1929 (stock margin lending) and beyond. In both of these cases these two issues – liquidity and solvency – played off of each other very quickly. As liquidity was pulled out of the markets, financial assets (equities, bonds, and other financial instruments) were sold to meet margin calls and other obligations, but with so many sellers and few buyers the value of all financial assets began to fall rapidly, which resulted in more margins calls for more collateral, which in turn led to dumping of assets, causing collateral values to plummet, tightening liquidity even further, and the vicious downward spiral continued until finally there were multiple interventions by the federal government of increasing size and efficacy.

A solvency issue arises when the market value of assets that were accounted at substantially higher levels prior to the start of a crisis are reduced to more reasonable levels, reflecting prevailing market conditions, while the value of liabilities (the debt) remains contractually elevated at pre-crisis levels, without opportunity for a similar downward reset (at least in the absence of the tortuous process of trying to get creditors to compromise their claims). The situation to date in 2020 has been less dramatic in that there was no abrupt liquidity crisis. However, the solvency phase is where the problem now comes in. And it will come as sure as night follows day. We are going to see a wave of defaults across both the corporate landscape and amongst economically stressed households, both of which had too much debt even before the start of the pandemic. These things always take time to develop, as defaults tend to be a lagging and not a leading indicator of financial distress. It's even worse now, as the entire banking sector has offered up numerous concessions to their borrowers in the form of moratoriums on interest payments, amortization holidays, extensions on terms, or other 'kick the can down the road' measures as part of pandemic relief programs. This effort will have the effect of hiding and delaying but not addressing the underlying issues which will continue to mount.

We can see the crisis coming for households in recent survey data from the Mortgage Bankers Association, which reported that in the second quarter of 2020 mortgage payment delinquencies nearly doubled to over 8%, the biggest quarterly rise in the survey's history and the highest overall delinquency rate in nine years. The 60-day delinquency rate is also now at the highest rate since the survey began in 1979.[42] Similarly in the corporate sector, at the beginning of July, credit ratings agency Fitch reported that in the first five months of 2020 the number of US corporate debt defaults had already exceeded the full-year number for 2019. At that rate the annual volume of defaults would exceed the record set during the 2008-09 financial crisis.[43] Moody's reported in September 2020 that default rates for high-yield debt nearly tripled from 2.4% in August 2019 to 6.4% in August 2020, having earlier projected that it could go above 13% by February 2021.[44] Brick & mortar retailers (including restaurants), energy companies (oil and gas) and asset-intensive travel-related businesses (airlines, cruise lines) will be the worst hit, as they already had too much debt before the crisis and will be the last to see benefits of the recovery.

Outside of the US, the issue is much worse. China in particular has very high leverage in its banking and corporate sectors, as does India and other markets including many countries in the southern region of the European Union. The value of China's corporate bond market is equivalent to $4.1 trillion, and analysts estimate that defaults in this market could hit record highs this year, as Chinese firms have defaulted an approximately $1.b billion (20 billion yuan) in July and August alone.[45]

All of this is creating an environment in which a financial crisis looks increasingly likely. In this case, it appears to be one in which inflation may be the most significant issue that persists long beyond the initial 'shock' phase of the crisis, even if that shock phase initially appears deflationary.

2. Inflation risk

"Inflation aggravated every evil, ruined every chance of national revival or individual success, and eventually produced precisely the conditions in which extremists of Right and Left could raise the mob against the State, set class against class, race against race, family against family, husband against wife, trade against trade, town against country. It undermined national resolution … it brought out the worst in everybody.[46]
   –   Adam Fergusson, *When Money Dies*

"The best way to destroy the Capitalist system is to debauch the currency … Men will cease to covet and hoard it as soon as they discover it will not buy anything, and the great illusion of the value and power of money on which the Capitalist state is based will have been definitely destroyed … Fortunately, the frantic financial debauch in which all governments have indulged … has paved the way everywhere …"[47]
   –   Vladimir Lenin

Why talk about inflation?

We now need to consider the possibility of a sudden shift into a highly inflationary environment. If you look at the history of severe or hyperinflations, they often start out as deflations, which suddenly – without warning or precedent – shift into an inflation that starts benignly enough and then builds up steam. While it may emerge slowly, the tail-risk is that an unforeseen event catalyzes a sudden shift for which the US is not prepared. I want to demonstrate why I believe there is such an elevated risk of damaging inflation on the not too far off horizon, but for now let me summarize some of the possible risk factors: a devaluation of the US dollar, a sustained supply-side disruption, an expansion of the money supply unable to be met by increased demand for money, war, or a combination of the above. Each of these risks appeared remote even as late as 2019, but now, as the end of 2020 approaches, have each risen in combined probability to an uncomfortable level. While many of the factors discussed in the previous chapter may appear deflationary in the short-term, in that demand suffers as the economy weakens (and indeed that was the experience coming out of the 2008-09 financial crisis), the medium- to longer-term risk lies on the other extreme.

Let's take the point on devaluation. A devaluation of the US dollar would make US exports more attractive to foreign buyers who now have the opportunity to purchase American manufactured goods at a lower cost in their own currency, which now has more purchase power against the dollar. That would have been more beneficial in the last century when America was still a manufacturing-led economy with substantial exports. But for the America of 2020, this is only partially helpful because exports are no longer a big enough part of our economy to make the difference. For imports, upon which we've become highly dependent, a currency devaluation would make everything more expensive in dollar terms. This is one manifestation of inflation.

Stephen Roach, formerly Morgan Stanley's Asia Chairman and now a Senior Fellow at Yale University, suggested in July 2020 that the dollar could lose 35% of its value "over the next couple of years."[48] He reminded us that such a decline is far from unprecedented, having occurred roughly every 10-20 years. "We had a comparable decline in the 1970s, a comparable decline for a couple of years in the mid-'80s, and about a 30% decline in the early 2000s. We're going to have another one, it's long overdue. It's 35% – it's a sharp decline."[49] If he's right, and I hope he isn't but I think he is, that means that the imported item upon which we've come to love that used to cost $10.00 will now cost over $15.00. Multiply this across tens of millions of items and one can see why this is a problem unless there is a way to simultaneously increase after-tax income by 50%.

A supply-side disruption could have the same effect. By this, I mean something that causes a breakdown in the system that normally provides easy and just-in-time access to inexpensive imported goods from all over the world, delivered straight to one's door with a click and a swipe. This breakdown could be in the form of supply chain disruptions, as were seen in the lockdowns and which are still impacting businesses and consumers six months later as factories were not permitted to operate. A disruption could result from a "decoupling" from China where other and presumably more expensive sources of supply have to be found, either domestically or from other foreign markets. Inflation would likely occur as a result of conflict with other nations that restricts international trade for some period of time. Inflation could also result from domestic causes, without reference to imports. This could result from a disruption to the food and agricultural supply chain due to a severe weather event, the outbreak of disease among a large population of livestock (as China is seeing now in food inflation resulting from an outbreak of disease among its hog population). Any of these and several other scenarios would put enormous pressure on pricing, unleashing inflationary forces that this country has not seen for a long time. I will talk later about the concept of Availability Bias, the cognitive error humans make when they take in a lot of information about something, and then overestimate the probability that it's going to occur, but with regard to inflation, the opposite issue exists. Like the turkey who comes to love the farmer that feeds and cares for him every day, he doesn't realize that everything is going to radically change for him come Thanksgiving Day. Since most Americans have not experienced severe inflations, they have no frame of reference for it and don't take the risk very seriously. Many Americans don't know what it would mean in their lives were it to occur.

For economists, tales of hyperinflations[50] are the academic equivalent of a reading of the Apocalypse in the book of Revelation. They are for the monetarily-minded a campfire story of the horrible wraith beyond the woods or the morbid fascination of an automobile crash from which one cannot turn away. The terror is understandable when one considers how severe- and hyperinflations destroy lives by eviscerating savings and wages, impoverishing pensioners and the middle classes, and ultimately undermining the fabric of society itself.

For my generation growing up in the US or Europe, hyperinflation is like a medieval fairy tale, occurring in a far-off land … full of terrifying goblins and dragons, but not real. The US and European experiences have been quite different, and both a century old. The US collective memory is marked less by inflation than by the deflation of the Great Depression and the mini-version we lived through the 2008-09 financial crisis. Europeans are shaped by the memory of multiple post-war hyperinflations, which occurred almost everywhere but which is most vividly reflected in Weimar Germany. We will explore this and other case studies, but first, let's take a quick tour of monetary history to provide background on why this matters so much.

A brief history of money

For money to be money, it generally needs to serve three functions. "Good" money needs to act as a medium of exchange and provide a stable store of value, as well as represent a standard unit of account. Modern currency, whether paper or digital, facilitates transactions between buyer and seller much more easily than trading in cows, chickens, and seashells. Similarly, currencies that are not stable (as to what they are worth, i.e. how much purchasing power a dollar or other unit of currency holds) prove to be poor stores of value over time, as it becomes difficult to hold on to purchasing power, and similarly, high volatility (e.g. Bitcoin) makes using it for exchange very challenging between buyer and seller which may have very different views on the currency's value if it changes every day.

Money has essentially moved through four stages in the modern world. For most of history, gold served as a primary form of money or, if not as the medium of exchange itself, then as the commodity used by governments to back up the value of the paper currency issued by their central and other banks. From ancient times, and through the 16th century, money usually meant physical gold and silver. This had several benefits, such as standardizing the medium of exchange and providing a unitary value of coinage (the troy ounce), but it also had severe disadvantages, such as high storage costs and security risks, a limited supply based on how much could be mined and minted, and the weight, cost, and difficulty of safely transporting it any meaningful distance.

Paper currency was first developed in China during the Tang dynasty of the 7th century, although its usage did not take off until the 11th century when it began to spread through the Mongol empire. It was discontinued, however, in the middle of the 15th century as paper notes had been issued so widely that inflationary pressures caused them to become nearly worthless. China did not return to paper money for several hundreds of years. In the West, at the beginning of the 17th century, paper currency began to be issued by banks that were backed up by gold held in reserve by the issuing banks. For a period of time, this was on a value for value basis in that each paper note represented the same value in gold specie held in reserves of the issuing bank or government, which could be drawn upon and converted to gold. This suffered some of the same challenges as using gold itself, in that the money supply could not expand more than the actual supply of gold, which placed significant restraints on the ability of credit to be extended enough to allow an economy to grow at its natural pace.

Given these limitations, banks began to issue currency notes that were only partially backed by their gold reserves. Governments moved to what is called a fractional reserve system, meaning that the gold reserves backing the currency represented only a portion, or fraction, of the nominal value of the paper currency. This enabled an expansion of credit to a significantly greater degree and reflected the fact that in ordinary times, only a small portion of customers would make claims on their gold reserves at any one time. This worked most of the time but was subject to infrequent but regular crises, as financial panics would trigger ruins on banks when everyone would demand conversion into gold at the same time. However, the fractional reserve system remained the dominant model in place over most of the twentieth century.

The 1944 Bretton Woods Agreement established a shared framework for monetary policy amongst the Western powers based on a fractional reserve system and ensured a period of relative monetary stability between its foundation and demise following 1971. Within the Bretton Woods system, member nations had a common footing for financial and commercial arrangements, which would rely upon the US dollar for settlement of cross-border transactions. The system represented a stable monetary order that required each country to adopt a monetary policy that kept its exchange rates within a certain band and tied its currency to a gold standard. It also provided that the International Monetary Fund would be able to provide a settlement mechanism to deal with any temporary imbalance of payments between countries. It was useful because it ensured some degree of cooperation amongst the countries, and limited the ability of individual nations to cheat the others in the system by 'competitively' devaluing their currencies to gain an advantage for their products in world markets. But it did place certain restraints upon its member nations, that in challenging economic times became difficult to live with and it constrained domestic economic policy.

In 1971, West Germany, Switzerland, and finally the United States left the system, breaking the alliance by ending the US dollar's convertibility to gold. The US had faced enormous exchange rate pressure against a number of the European currencies, forcing the US to play currency defense to support the dollar, thereby depleting its Treasury of gold reserves. President Nixon announced in 1971 that the US would go off of the gold standard altogether. From that day on, the dollar would no longer be convertible to gold. This effectively ended the Bretton Woods monetary era of fixed exchange rates between countries and marked the beginning of a period in which the United States dollar would be backed not by gold or silver but by the faith and credit of the United States alone, so long as the rest of the world would be willing to accept it. Exchange rates would be allowed to float freely, implicitly measuring daily the trust and confidence in the United States dollar against other currencies. It was shortly after that decoupling that the United States suffered substantial inflation in the 1970s as a result of the oil shock and the war effort in the first half of the decade.

The effect of the US withdrawal from Bretton Woods ultimately resulted in most other participating currencies also becoming free-floating. There was speculation and anxiety at the time about whether this would presage the loss of the United States dollar's status as the world's reserve currency, just as the British pound sterling began to lose its status as the world's reserve currency as it went off of the gold peg it in the wake of World War I and the depletion of the British Treasury. Due to the lack of a credible alternative, this fear was never realized, and the world adjusted in time to a world of freely floating exchange rates and increasing US monetary dominance. Ultimately, this removed the barriers and the discipline imposed on countries to manage their monetary policy within a bound tied to some underlying commodity.

So eventually, governments around the world abandoned any link to gold reserves, and began to issue currency by fiat, i.e. based solely on the credit of the government itself, rather than any underlying asset. The fiat currency system is the monetary model we live in today, and it is under strain. Since the United States went completely off of the gold standard in 1971, neither gold nor any other commodity backed the value of the US dollar or any of the other major currencies in the world. Under a fiat monetary system, money is money simply because governments say it is, and because their citizens accept that proposition. The dollar that is in one's pocket or digital wallet has no inherent monetary value. Its value is simply what purchasing power it carries as a medium of exchange, which in turn is based on its perceived value relative to other assets (whether foreign currencies or hard assets). In other words, the worth of the today's dollar is based not on intrinsic value, but rather on credit, i.e. the trust and faith that the holder of the currency places in the government issuing it to make good on the value of the currency, e.g. to accept it in payment of taxes, etc. and that in a private market exchange transaction (i.e. the buying or selling something else) it will be worth what the parties believe that it is worth.

Following the Bretton Woods period of relative discipline, the US and many of its peers began to travel a path of much more aggressive and expansive monetary policy, which over time has created an untenable situation in which budget deficits have become the normal practice, the national debt has increased every single year, and the value of the US dollar once again stands on shaky ground. The national debt burden has grown increasingly worse through successive administrations. Under President George W. Bush the national debt increased by $5.8 trillion as a result of funding the War on Terror, during President Obama's tenure, which saw the Global Financial Crisis, the national debt increased by $8.6 trillion, and now as a result of the pandemic, President Trump is on track to preside over further increases that will be perhaps double the budgeted increase of $4.8 billion in his first term.[51]

Over the past year, the balance sheet of the US Federal Reserve has grown by $3.2 trillion (82.5%) to $7.0 trillion. This extraordinary growth came as a result of the pandemic-related $2.2 trillion CARES Act, fiscal stimulus over the course of the second quarter that resulted in new money creation on an unprecedented scale. The Fed now holds $4.3 trillion in US Treasury securities, a sevenfold increase from March 2008.

A similar rapid expansion was made in the global financial crisis, with predictions of inflation accompanying, as the Fed's balance sheet grew 128% to $2.1 trillion by March 2009. However, inflation did not follow. One can observe from that experience (and from watching Japan's deflationary march over the past three decades) that the size (or rate of change) of central bank balance sheets doesn't by itself presage inflation. That particular expansion of the Fed's balance sheet was primarily the result of the Fed acquiring private market assets (e.g. bonds and mortgage-backed securities from US banks), not newly issued government debt, and as such didn't result in inflationary new money creation. Money demand grew alongside money supply, tempering inflation. This time is different. The $3 trillion expansion in 2020 was primarily created by discounting US Treasury bonds, the proceeds of which ultimately ended up as relief payments not tied to capital formation or economic activity of any kind. This was done by expanding the monetary stock. In other words, by printing money.

Some economists deny this is indicia of inflation by pointing to the slow current velocity of money (velocity refers to the rate of speed at which the money supply changes hands in the economy). Traditionally, velocity increases rapidly as inflation accelerates, as people don't want to hold on to cash that may lose value, and as such spend it more quickly on real goods or invest it in financial assets that they hope will hold value better than cash. So far in 2020, the US has not seen an increase in velocity, but rather the opposite, a decline in velocity to historically low levels as people held on to cash and didn't spend it. This may be a 'false negative' that was artificially created as a result of the lockdowns and travel restrictions. Households didn't have the opportunity to spend money on activities that they normally would have, but rather let it sit in the bank or other savings accounts. Only time will tell whether spending accelerates when the economy fully opens back up and household wallets open with it.

Velocity will certainly accelerate if inflation expectations embed (i.e. if people start to believe inflation is coming, it may tend to become a self-fulfilling prophecy) or if there is another panicked scare leading to mass hoarding. Inflation is simply defined as "too much money chasing too few goods." While US aggregate capacity seems underutilized and wage pressures are muted by high unemployment, supply chains remain partially dysfunctional with a large number of both industrial and consumer items that remain unavailable, apparently due to pandemic-related disruptions. It's not clear whether this is significant or indicative of a systemic issue, but it is a cautionary sign to be watched.

Skeptics of an inflationary scenario also point to the fact that across most categories prices have not risen significantly in 2020, and in some categories, we're seeing downward pressures on pricing (certainly true for travel and hospitality). This is a backward-looking statistic, in the sense that in the early stages of inflation the money supply typically increases for some time before prices react significantly. In other words, in the early stages of inflation, prices do not keep up with the increase in the money supply. There is a lag, but the wheels are already set in motion. It is only in later stages of the inflationary process when prices rise at an even greater rate than the increase in the money supply, based on expectations that inflation will continue to increase. That then increases the demand for money and, unless the central bank is both independent and extraordinarily disciplined, which by that stage of crisis most are not, having been "captured" by the government due to overwhelming political pressure, additional monetary expansion occurs to meet it. Inflation expectations become self-reenforcing.

In July 2020, Fitch (the credit ratings agency) fired a warning shot across the bow of the US government, placing the sovereign rating on negative outlook (Moody's had already moved its outlook from stable to negative in March) and citing "ongoing deterioration in public finances and the absence of a credible fiscal consolidation plan." Those are strong words when used against the AAA-rated issuer of the world's reserve currency. The strength of the dollar, and thus its exclusive status, is now at serious risk, especially if our foreign creditors (those who hold US government bonds) lose faith in the creditworthiness of the US, including its commitment to maintaining low inflation and a stable dollar. Holding $1.1 trillion, China is the second-largest foreign investor (after Japan) in US government debt, representing just over 15% of total debt held by foreigners.[52]

The US net national savings rate (the percentage of gross GDP) was already at 2.6% of national income before the pandemic, compared with an average of 7% since the data was first recorded in 1947. By the second quarter of 2020, the savings rate had turned negative (−1.0%).[53] We have not had a positive current account balance in this century (meaning we consistently import more than we export).[54] A negative current account balance isn't necessarily bad if the dollars held by foreigners are reinvested back in the US to finance investment in productive capital assets. But if it's financed primarily by foreign purchases of US government debt, which is then used to support deficit spending, then it is unsustainable over the long-run. It also indicates that we're spending more on consumption than on investing in infrastructure and exports. Currencies like the US dollar that are allowed to float freely play a role as a weighing mechanism against the current account balance over time. To the extent that the current account remains sustainably negative, the dollar can be expected to deteriorate.

Several of the world's most prominent investors and thinkers on the issue of the global economy and the US dollar, including Stephen Roach, Ray Dalio, Nassim Taleb, and Warren Buffett amongst others, have each come out recently suggesting or signaling (by shifts into gold and other investments targeted at inflation protection) that they believe that the US dollar has a significant risk of devaluation and that inflation is at least possible if not probable. Roach has suggested that greater than devaluation is the risk that the US could lose its status as the world's reserve currency. Taleb has also called this our most underappreciated risk.

In August 2020, at its annual Jackson Hole Symposium, the US Federal Reserve's Open Market Committee made an important announcement[55] that signaled a departure from forty years of policy and practice targeted at maintaining a low inflation rate of 2% or less. This move means the Federal Reserve is going to tolerate and even encourage inflation for the first time in over four decades. Simply put, the Federal Reserve acknowledged that with the Fed Funds rate (the rate at which the Fed lends to US banks to provide liquidity to the banking system to on-lend to businesses and consumers) approaching zero, the Fed's monetary policy toolbox (using interest rates as a lever to speed up or slow down economic growth and investment) would no longer be as effective as it had in the past. As a result of interest rates hitting zero (what the Fed calls "the effective low bound"), the Fed would no longer be able to use the lowering of interest rates to stimulate economic growth. Therefore, in order to achieve its maximum employment objective, the Fed acknowledged for the first time in a generation that it had no choice but to tolerate higher levels of inflation. The Federal Reserve's August 2020 announcement also made clear that the Fed would shift to an average inflation target over time in order to focus on the objective of maximum employment. In other words, the Federal Reserve has now made inflation official policy. The central bank will allow inflation to run for a longer period of time well above the historical target rate of 2%.

The reason that the Federal Reserve has been forced to do this is that as interest rates approach zero, and real rates turn negative, the central bank has lost one of its most important monetary policy tools, which is the ability to use the lowering interest rates to stimulate economic activity and investment. What is not readily admitted is that this shift returns the US to the policy of the 1960s, a policy that enabled annual inflation in the US to run to over 12% by 1974 and nearly 15% by the first half of 1980.

To understand the implications of the Federal Reserve's actions, it's important to understand the history of the Federal Reserve. Founded in 1913, the Federal Reserve's purpose was to provide the United States with a safer, more flexible, and more stable monetary and financial system. Today, the Fed has four primary roles, which include conducting the nation's monetary policy in accordance with priorities set by Congress, supervising and regulating banks and other systemically important financial institutions, maintaining the stability of the financial system and containing systemic risk, and providing certain services to the US government, financial institutions and others, including overseeing the nation's payment systems.[56]

In 1977, during a period of stagflation in which very weak economic growth was combined with a high level of inflation, the US Congress, through the Federal Reserve Reform Act of 1977, clarified that the Fed had three main objectives: maximum employment, stable prices, and moderate long-term interest rates. During the early days of the Reagan administration, the then newly-appointed Fed Chairman Paul Volcker placed the greatest emphasis on the stability of prices in order to break the back of the double-digit inflations that had occurred in both the first half (1974) and the second half (1979-80) of the 1970s.[57] He was successful in doing that, but at the expense of allowing unemployment to rise above 10%, which was the highest the US had experienced since the Great Depression. Chairman Volcker's strong medicine cured the patient, but not without negative side effects on its labor markets. Volcker's policy was widely maintained through multiple administrations and Federal Reserve chairs.

In 2012, then Chairman Ben Bernanke clarified the goal of stable prices by formally setting 2% as the inflation target of the Federal Reserve, which maintained the goal for nearly a decade until August 2020. One of the consequences of this policy was the preemptive tightening of the money supply (i.e. by raising interest rates) to control inflation, which has tended to have a negative effect on employment, and which was evidenced even before the pandemic took hold.[58]

So what does all of this mean? The implication is simply that the Federal Reserve is no longer going to try to put a brake on inflation. Given the priority of its commitment to maintaining employment, it will not pursue a policy of raising interest rates in order to tamp down on inflation, but rather will allow inflation to increase in order to keep the economy, and specifically employment, moving along as quickly as possible. This means that the Federal Reserve will maintain the current Fed Funds lending rate at or near zero, which by implication means that real rates (i.e. after subtracting out the inflation rate) will remain in negative territory for some time to come. This has significant negative implications for the value of bonds and other fixed-income instruments and for the purchasing power of the cash held in one's pocket or savings accounts. In this environment, a cash investment erodes in value as time goes on. At one or two percent a year decline is often not visible to the holder, but she is being slowly taxed and deprived of the fruit of her previous labor or investment. This is a time-proven strategy of governments to quietly and slowly confiscate value from its citizens, as is further described below.

The inflation tax

> "By a continuing process of inflation, governments can confiscate, secretly and unobserved, an important part of the wealth of their citizens. By this method they not only confiscate, but they confiscate arbitrarily; and, while the process impoverishes many, it actually enriches some."[59]
> – John Maynard Keynes, *The Economic Consequences of the Peace*

It is important to recognize that inflation is a hidden form of tax by governments on their citizens. Monetary expansion ('printing money') is a way for governments to raise revenue without directly increasing income or other taxes. How is this so? As the money supply increases, the value of money (i.e. the purchasing power of what a unit of currency can buy) declines. Inflation results because we then have too much money chasing too few goods. As inflation accelerates, the expenses of the government, including interest service costs on and principal repayment of its trillions of dollars of debt owed to both its own citizens and foreign governments holding treasury bonds, are reduced in real terms.

There is no reasonable prospect that government spending in the US or Europe will be reined in any time soon. Governments on both continents are now actively contemplating a second wave ... of relief spending. The US Congress is currently debating on an additional $2 trillion in additional pandemic-related spending. This expenditure will require the raising of debt or the raising of taxes, but there will be a limit on how much additional taxes the economy can afford. As a result, Congress will resort to spending money that it does not have by issuing additional US government debt, at least so long as foreign and other creditors are willing to accept it, and if not, by issuing directly to the Federal Reserve as the government did in the second quarter of 2020. To pay for its rapidly growing budget and widening deficit, the US government will begin to allow greater rates of inflation. History has shown repeated examples that this practice, once begun by governments, is an addiction not unlike crack cocaine or heroin. It is a habit that is very difficult to break once started. Eventually, the inflation tax becomes the government's only recourse to additional revenue. This is true because the government loses its ability to raise income and other tax revenue given that the real economy is not growing at a fast enough rate to keep up with expenditures, and specifically to provide sufficient revenue to the government to continue to make these transfer payments to its citizens who are unemployed and relying upon stimulus checks.

And sometimes governments, including that of the United States, dispense with the ruse altogether and confiscate the wealth of its citizens outright. This is most commonly done by imposing hefty wealth or inheritance taxes, but sometimes governments get even more creative. There is a precedent in recent American history of the US government taking actions under emergency power clauses that have the effect of breaking legal contracts with the US government and forcing the devaluation of assets held by its creditors. In the depths of the Great Depression in 1933, the US government under President Roosevelt's leadership took two extraordinary and controversial actions. The first was that the President instructed the Secretary of the Treasury to call in all of the privately held gold in the country, whether held by businesses, individual citizens, or banks. Americans were forced to sell their gold back to the US Treasury in exchange for paper dollars, and were prohibited by force of law from any form of hoarding (even keeping it under the mattress was a crime) or exporting of gold. The second shocking action that Roosevelt took, which must have caused Alexander Hamilton to roll over in his grave, was to take legislative action to invalidate the gold clauses in the US government's binding legal contracts with bondholders and other counter-parties. These clauses provided the contractual right for the holder to be paid not just in paper dollars but in gold dollars, which formed a type of insurance against inflation for the benefit of the creditor. Amity Shales noted in The Forgotten Man that this legislation forced the creditors to "accept the de facto devaluation of their assets." Noting that "deflation had hurt borrowers, and now this inflationary act was a primitive revenge," FDR's move on gold was "as an act of social redistribution, a $200 billion transfer of wealth from creditor to debtor, a victory for the populists." The creditors, i.e. the wealthy capitalist class, had the money, and (quoting Senator Thomas of Oklahoma) "'because they [the rich] have it the masses of the people of this Republic are on the verge of starvation – 17,000 on charity, in the bread line.' Now the debtor would, through devaluation, see his debt reduced."[60]

The Weimar hyperinflation and why it matters

In what is probably the most well-known modern example of hyperinflation in an advanced industrial nation – and one of the largest economies in the world –, the situation that Weimar Germany faced following its defeat in World War I still deserves attention. In identifying the historical patterns that seem to repeat across time and countries, we will find ourselves better able to assess the risks that may arise for us in the future. Lessons can be drawn not only in recognizing the elementary causes of hyperinflation but in understanding its effects on various classes of society and how the accompanying political turmoil provided the perfect landscape for the rise of extremists (on both Left and Right). A straight line can be drawn from the hyperinflation to the radicalization of Nationalist, Socialist, Communist, and labor movements that developed in the 1920s, all the way to the ultimate rise of Hitler and the Nazi Party in the 1930s. While Hitler came to power during a sharp deflationary period and political crisis in 1933, the hyperinflation years provided the fertile soil for extremist movements to grow and flourish. Once in power, Hitler resorted to printing money to pay for war materials, thus returning Germany to a new decade of inflation less than twenty years after the first had been overcome.

By Armistice Day on November 11, 1918, all of Western Europe lay in ruin. Over four and a half years, the great powers had exhausted themselves in a futile struggle that had unleashed new terrors of warfare previously unseen, unknown, and unimaginable to human civilization, with an unrelenting horror that left an entire generation (of those who managed to survive) broken, bitter and scarred, and their governments financially depleted and all but bankrupt from the process.

The war had begun in the summer of 1914 as the result of a lone assassin's bullet, an unforeseen black swan event that within weeks had drawn in all of the great powers of Europe into an abyss from which they would be unable to escape. For Germany, the potential for engagement in the war brought about an internal financial and currency crisis. Until July 1914, Germany's currency consisted of gold and silver coins, as well as paper notes that were exchangeable into gold. The value of the paper currency in circulation was not allowed to be more than two-thirds of the money in circulation, providing a legal foundation upon which trust in the currency was built. This reserve system backed by gold worked fairly well for Germany, as it did for the other Western nations, during the preceding decades of advancing trade-driven prosperity and relative financial stability.

Within the unified Germany that Chancellor von Bismark had created in 1871, the currency regime backed by gold had kept the value of the German mark stable over more than four decades, engendering the trust of both its citizens and its trading partners. But something changed in the psychology of its citizens in less than a fortnight in the summer of 1914. Hearing rumors of war in June and early July, and with the memory of inflation during the Franco-Prussian War still in collective memory, ordinary Germans started to line up outside of their banks to demand that their notes be exchanged for gold. Germany citizens had – almost immediately – lost faith in their currency, and, as bank runs tend to happen, the trickle became a flood, as individuals did not want to be last in line to get their gold out. This left the government and its central bank, with reserves already low, in a very precarious position as they watched the banking system's store of gold specie rapidly deplete over a number of days. By the end of the month, the banks had stopped converting into gold altogether, and on Friday, July 31, 1914, the Reichsbank (Germany's central bank) closed its doors and wouldn't open again until August 4th. This was the date on which a raft of emergency legislation came through that included suspending the convertibility of paper money into gold.

By this point, Germany had declared war on Russia (August 1st) and France (August 3rd), and Great Britain had declared war on Germany (August 4th). Paper currency now became the only currency in circulation, as whatever gold was in the system immediately went into hiding either as a result of hoarding by individuals or because the government was using several means to coax and coerce it out of its citizens to meet its foreign trade obligations (especially to pay for war materials).[61] By the start of the conflict, the Reichsbank had very little gold or reserve currencies with which to finance the war effort, and the situation would deteriorate over the ensuing years. It would come to pass that most of the belligerents suspended convertibility of their currency during the war years because of the inflationary pressures that the war quickly created.

Periods of war are generally inflationary for the countries that participate. The need to ramp up industrial production to produce the material of war, scarcity of goods, and the diversion of labor away from the private sector to government service all conspire to create strong inflationary pressures. It was, in fact, the onset of the Second World War, rather than the New Deal or other economic policies of the 1930s, that finally brought the United States out of the Great Depression and definitively broke the vicious cycle of price and wage deflation in America.

For each of the great powers in conflict in the Great War, inflation became a serious problem. Great Britain experienced inflation of over 15% annually during the war years,[62] while in France, the franc lost half of its value against the British pound from 1914 to 1918. In Russia, "prices doubled between 1914 and 1916, and by February 1917, the purchasing power of the ruble declined to about 30% of its pre-war value."[63] This was only the beginning. The ruble quickly collapsed under the weight of hyperinflation brought on by relentless printing of paper currency and ultimately by the terrors of 1917: the fall of the monarchy in March, the gruesome assassination of Tsar Nicolas and his family in July, and the Bolshevik revolution in November. The value of the ruble fell to nil as the country was torn by civil war in the following months. For the next several years, there was no functional currency, and workers were paid in kind. Manufacturing ground to a halt, with aggregate economic production falling by 85%. In 1914, a British pound (£1) would buy 20 rubles, by the end of 1923, £1 bought 50 billion rubles. It was only with the introduction of a new gold-backed ruble regime in 1923-4 that the situation began to improve. But that story is for another day.

In Germany, the war years saw the indexed price of imported goods rise by 47% by the end of 1917, and then by an additional 46% in the ten months to October 1918 as the war effort was clearly collapsing, such that a basket of imported goods cost 114% more in October 1918 than at the end of 1913. Prices for domestic goods fared even worse, increasing by 139% by October 1918. The amount of money in circulation had increased by 340%, and the value of the paper mark had fallen against the gold mark by over 36%.[64] But this was only the beginning. In the post-war years between 1919-23 inflation would increasingly accelerate and shift into hyperinflation until the very end in 1923, when the growth in the money supply was counted in the billions of percentage points.

With the war's end, Germany was forced to accept peace on substantively unconditional terms. Kaiser Wilhelm II had reluctantly offered the surrender of the Imperial German Army and agreed to enter into peace discussions with the allied powers that he knew were going to be unfavorable toward Germany. By this stage he and the country had very little choice, already having decimated their economy, lost a substantial portion of their youth, and depleted the resources of their Treasury. France, along with Belgium, had seen most of the fighting on its soil and had suffered great economic and human loss as a result. German industrial production had fallen by one-third, reflecting the fact that Germany had been cut off from its colonies and global supply lines and was no longer able to import from around the world a substantial portion of the products that it needed. An increased focus on the production of weapons and other materials from mostly domestic sources could only come at the cost of a very sharp decline in the production of consumer goods. Ordinary Germans, especially city dwellers, suffered enormously through the war years from a lack of food and other basic commodities. German lands remained relatively untouched, including the productive industrial base of the Ruhr Valley.

The peace process would begin around a series of meetings in Versailles, France, that became known as the Versailles Conference. The leader of the French contingent, Prime Minister Georges Clémenceau, was committed to obtaining both revenge and restitution for France's losses and was unrelentingly focused on ensuring that Germany remained both humbled (economically and militarily) and humiliated in the process.[65] The Treaty of Versailles focused on two issues, the demilitarization of Germany, affected by reducing the army to a quarter of its wartime size and by requiring Germany to surrender its warships and similar material, and the payment of reparations to the allies for the astronomical costs of the war and the damage done thereby. The final Treaty reflected a rejection of the proposal that the American President Woodrow Wilson had put forward along with his 14 points that would have represented a less punitive outcome for Germany. While the Treaty was widely condemned within Germany and would lead to a very divisive and destructive political situation, very few people outside of Germany understood the consequences or the costs and felt that Germany deserved to suffer. The one person, who was able to articulate and condemn the treaty, was the economist John Maynard Keynes, who had been at Versailles as part of the British delegation. He clearly saw from the outset that the actual repayment terms would prove to be impossible to be met by Germany and would lead to the destruction of the German economy, the dissolution of its society, and a resumption of the European war. Keynes published his condemnation of the Treaty in his 1919 book, *The Economic Consequences of the Peace*, which had the effect of opening the eyes of the rest of the world to the issue, but not enough that the allied powers would change course in their pursuit of reparations. In discussing the real objectives of its participants, Keynes wrote:

> the future of Europe was not their concern; its means of livelihood was not their anxiety. Their preoccupations, good and bad alike, related to frontiers and nationalities, to the balance of power, to imperial aggrandizements, to the future enfeeblement of a strong and dangerous enemy, to revenge, and to the shifting by the victors of their unbearable financial burden onto the shoulders of the defeated.[66]

Given the limited ability of the German government to put further burdens on its already stressed citizens, the Reichstag had determined during the war years to finance the war effort through borrowing rather than by taxation. Following the war, when the government was carrying too much debt as a result of the reparations and thus borrowing was no longer possible, the government shifted its policy toward inflationary monetary expansion, i.e. the printing of German paper marks at an increasingly accelerated rate. The government was very concerned about social unrest resulting from the now unemployed and still armed soldiers returning home from the front, most of whom did not have jobs to which to return. The only way to ensure that employment would rise was to provide very easy credit to businesses to restart and to hire laborers. This was accomplished by the same strategy of inflationary monetary expansion. "Full employment thereafter became a primary objective of both government and unions, at the mark's expense"[67] Government realized that by printing money it could keep employment high and also devalue the reparations debt in real terms. The German government may have stumbled upon this realization, but it quickly and cynically became a policy that was effectively a form of repudiation of the debt, and at the same time, passive resistance against the French occupation of the Ruhr Valley and the reparations in general. The quantity of currency in circulation in nominal millions of marks increased by well over 50% each year between 1918 and 1922, at which point the money supply began to expand to a figure approaching infinity. By 1923, the mark had completely collapsed and was essentially worthless. By this stage, it cost more money to print a mark than it was worth.

The international financial community caught onto this game rather quickly. Subsequent to 1919 it became very difficult for the German government to borrow or finance transactions of any kind based on the mark. Germany's export businesses benefited greatly as the exchange rate fell, as their goods became progressively less expensive in foreign markets. On the other hand, the cost of imports and domestic goods began to skyrocket. Frederick Taylor notes,

> Exchange rate changes became so swift and frequent that the domestic market prices found it harder and harder to keep up with them ... the rich industrialist bought and bought and got richer and richer, not so much in paper marks but in physical things. The flight into material assets became, for a minority of the German nation, a way to solid riches among the growing financial chaos.[68]

The hyperinflation produced clear winners and losers in Weimar Germany. The winners included anyone with access to foreign currency, exporters, businesspeople who could adjust prices quickly (commodities dealers, food producers), capitalists who could speculate in the stock markets, and anyone corrupt enough to play fast and loose with the various laws around foreign currency. The working labor classes did somewhat less horribly than others, as they were able to agitate (with occasional violence to show they were serious) for wage increases that at least kept up with food inflation, and kept roofs over their heads. The losers, on the other hand, included anyone in the middle class, such as professors, teachers, administrators, engineers, accountants, etc. The bourgeois and intellectual classes suffered greatly, as did government bureaucrats, employees, and anyone who was on a fixed salary and did not have the ability to increase it with daily regularity. They learned quickly that their incomes were essentially worthless and that they had to find alternative ways of survival. Sometimes this included selling of family jewels, furniture, or other assets, sometimes it was their own bodies. Those who did not find ways to attain hard currency, or physical commodities for barter, suffered enormously. Landlords struggled as laws were imposed to keep them from being able to raise rents that kept up with inflation. Banks and other creditors, savers, and any investors who depended on a fixed return lost substantially all of their value. The biggest losers of them all were elderly pensioners on fixed incomes, who came to find that their entire life's savings or accumulated value of insurance policies had dwindled to be worth less than the cost of a cup of coffee.

21st-century hyperinflations

The example of hyperinflation in Weimar Germany serves as an important lesson for us given Germany's role as one of the largest economies in the world at the time. The takeaway is that if it could happen in Germany, it can happen in America. On the other hand, one might say that it happened a very long time ago, that we've learned a great deal about how to prevent inflations, and it's not really an issue for the 21st century. Nothing could be farther from the truth. The 21st century has already seen several hyperinflationary situations in previously relatively healthy countries including Argentina, Iran, Venezuela, and Zimbabwe.

What is true is that all of these examples, Germany included, suffered political crises before hyper-inflation really took hold. While the famous economist Milton Friedman is well-known for saying "inflation is always and everywhere a monetary phenomenon ..." it is equally true that inflation is also always a political phenomenon. What Friedman meant is that inflation is driven by the supply of money ... print too much of it and inflation will surely follow, just as night follows day. He believed that inflation "is and can be produced only by a more rapid increase in the quantity of money than in [economic] output."[69] To turn Friedman's quote on its head, to say that inflation is a political phenomenon means that the decision to increase the money supply – to print money – is always driven by a government (presumably in a crisis of one form or another) trying to achieve a fiscal or employment policy objective, and coercing, cajoling or otherwise compelling the central bank to play along in the game of monetary expansion.

Zimbabwe

As an emerging markets investor, I have experienced first-hand the devastating effects of hyperinflation in Zimbabwe, a country that formerly was one of the most productive and wealthy economies in Africa. Once known as the Breadbasket of Africa, its large, highly productive agricultural sector exported food to the entire southern African region out of its surplus production. In 2000, the Mugabe government seized most of the White-owned farms effectively nationalizing them and handing them over to indigenous Blacks. This confiscation resulted in the transfer of eight million hectares of land, representing about 20% of Zimbabwe's landmass, across 4500 farms to more than 160,000 indigenous households. One of the consequences of the seizures was that between 2000 and 2008 crop production went down in Zimbabwe by nearly 80%.[70] Government mismanagement, theft, and corruption decimated the economy and brought it through not just one but two hyperinflations since the turn of the century, one in 2008 and the most recent in 2019-20.

As a result of the more recent hyperinflation, I have experienced the financial pain of seeing 90% of invested capital in a market-leading and profitable business destroyed in dollar terms practically overnight. However, the true tragedy has been observing the devastating impact on highly educated and professional Zimbabweans who watched their purchasing power go to effectively zero in a matter of months. They are now facing rampant food insecurity and the failure of basic municipal infrastructures such as electricity, water, and sewerage. Because Zimbabweans have seen this before, many businesses and individuals have applied practical lessons from the previous hyperinflation to navigate this one. However, Europe and the US have no analogous experience and remain blind both to the dangers and how to prevent it.

In hyperinflations, at some point, the government loses its ability to increase taxation, and the value of the tax revenue which is received falls to nothing in terms of its purchasing power. This limits the government's ability to provide basic services such as utilities, to acquire any goods that are not produced domestically, as foreign sellers will not accept the local devalued currency. It also leaves the government with only one remaining option, which is to continue to print money at an even greater accelerating rate to have the currency to pay its obligations in situations where it can force others to accept the increasingly worthless paper (such as their own employees and certain local vendors who have no choice but to accept what the government offers).

In Zimbabwe, "One of the many bizarre and self-defeating effects of hyperinflation was to wipe out the government's tax income totally … this forced the government to print more money and confiscate more foreign currency to replace the lost tax income."[71] As government loses its revenue, it seeks to find more and more creative ways to extract value from its citizens, often enacting new laws and rules that are impossible for otherwise law-abiding citizens to obey, and "justice becomes a matter of bribery and favors." As the CEO of a manufacturing concern in Zimbabwe put it, "hyperinflation made everyone a criminal because you had to break the law to survive. We are a nation of lawbreakers, forced on us by hyperinflation."[72]

Venezuela

Traveling to Venezuela as a young man, I found it one of the most beautiful countries that I had ever visited. Over the previous two years, my work had taken me to approximately 25 countries around the world. Yet the geography, culture, food, and music of the country, along with the warmth, beauty, and friendliness of its people, had captured my heart in a special way. Caracas felt like a magical place, and I briefly fell in love. That was the Venezuela of the 1990s, and it bears no resemblance to the place of the same name today. Run-down buildings, emaciated bodies that have lost 24 pounds on average and are now battling "higher rates of both chronic and infectious disease" as a result of malnutrition, and chronic food shortages greet the visitor who dares to travel beyond the enclaves of the political elite.[73] For nearly two decades, the man-made effects of corruption, Socialist economic policies heavily influenced by Modern Monetary Theory, wasteful government spending, rising external debt, and general malfeasance all conspired to destroy the nation. The Marxist dictator Hugo Chavez ruled the country from 1999 until his death in 2013.

The Atlantic quotes British far-left Labour Leader Jeremy Corbyn as praising the Chavista government for being an "inspiration to all of us fighting back against austerity and neoliberal economics" and eulogized Chavez for "showing that the poor matter and wealth can be shared."[74] Shortly after Nicolás Maduro took the reins from Chavez in 2013, what had for years been severe but manageable inflation quickly morphed into hyperinflation that by 2015 had grown to become the worst in the world, with inflation at over ten million percent.[75] Attempts at price controls, which never work, only stimulated the black market, leaving shelves bare and food scarce, with other goods hard to come by except through criminal networks. The government began to use food distribution as a tool to manipulate and control the population, which was an old Communist trick from the Soviet Union. Anne Applebaum writes, "The hungrier people get, the more control the government exerts, and the easier it is to prevent them from protesting or objecting in any other way. Even people who are not starving now spend most of their time just getting by—standing in lines, trying to fix broken generators, working second or third jobs to earn a little bit more—all activities that keep them from politics."[76] In the countryside, basic municipal functions like electricity and policing ceased to exist.[77]

By 2019, mass protests eventually led to a relaxing of price controls and to the acceptance of the US dollar, which, like in Zimbabwe, finally began to make a difference and end the madness. With an acceptable currency that Venezuelans were no longer acting criminally by using, store shelves began to repopulate, and businesses began to spring back to life. But the recovery has been lopsided, primarily benefitting the elite with access to dollars. For the former middle class, life in Venezuela continues to be one of misery and squalor. A university professor can barely afford to buy his dinner. Socialism and hyperinflation have led to greater inequality in Venezuela than before Maduro took over in 2013.[78] We can only hope that the dollarization of the economy, combined with the growing frustration of its people, will lead to an end to the Maduro regime.

The reader might be tempted to say, "Yes but those were all emerging economies with poorly managed and weak institutions, and failed or failing governments. This is America! We're the leading and largest economy in the world, the dollar is the world's reserve currency, we've been in deflation for over a decade, it can't happen here!" Actually, the US has been through several periods of high inflation in its short history, including during and after the Civil War (hyperinflation), both of World War I and World War II, and in the 1970s, but most Americans aren't old enough to remember it. Just because something hasn't happened recently is no indication of whether it will or won't happen in the future. The reason people call 100-year events '100-year events' is that they don't tend to happen terribly often.

How US inflation might progress

We can expect that if President Trump is successful in "decoupling" from China, specifically with regard to breaking the reliance on imports from China and moving supply chains that originate in China, inflation will result. This is a near certainty. The reason why existing supply chains with China are in place today is that over time they have proven to be both the most efficient and the most cost-effective for American companies. The benefits of those cost savings and process efficiencies have, for the most part, been passed on to the American consumer in the form of lower prices for a wide variety of consumer goods and inputs that are produced in China.

To the extent that those supply lines are broken, and new ones established, whether by import substitution, with manufacturing moved back onshore to the United States, or by sourcing new markets around the world, whether from our nearby neighbors in the Americas or otherwise, we can expect the cost of delivery to the customer will be higher, and prices will rise. So in this event, we can count on US consumers to pay more for a wide variety of household goods as a result of the decoupling.

An even more powerful inflationary effect would result from a geopolitical conflict, natural disaster, healthcare crisis, or another catalyst that results in a blockade or other stymying of interoceanic cargo. In other words, if the borders are closed, severe inflation is a certainty. In that scenario, even assuming some demand reduction of say 10-20%, we will have severe supply shortages across several categories. The result will be rapidly rising prices, or said differently, diminished value of the dollar attempting to buy the same basket of goodies.

Transitions to hyperinflations don't typically come quickly, but rather over a long period where inflationary pressures build gradually before accelerating at later stages. How does the path from more normal inflation to hyperinflation progress? Inflations typically begin when government spending starts to become a larger and larger portion of the economy. Then, the government runs up larger and larger debts over a prolonged period. Often, there is a financial crisis that forces the government's hand, where their ability to raise more debt becomes limited. At this stage, the government begins to use monetary expansion as a tool for financing its own debt and expenditures. Then, in the last stage, after running out of other options to increase revenue through taxation or otherwise, the government makes a political decision to use money printing as a primary form of financing. This eventually leads to the total collapse of the currency, resulting in a prolonged and wretched crisis that is only resolved by the imposition of an entirely new monetary, and often political, system. At this stage, the strong medicine required to cure the disease brings both fiscal and monetary austerity that is imposed at great cost and human suffering to the country. The new regime has to have the credibility to convince the various stakeholder groups that the changes are real and that the printing of money will stop, or the cycle isn't broken.

The risk of moving into an inflationary environment has multiple implications across several areas of life and business, including affecting how we should think about our household savings and investment strategies. Cash becomes worthless in this environment. In order to blunt some of the effects of inflation, it's important to keep a meaningful portion of one's wealth in so-called 'reflationary assets,' meaning that their nominal value tends to increase with the rate of inflation. Traditionally reflationary asset categories have included various degrees of effectiveness precious metals, real estate, equities, and other hard assets such as jewelry, art, timber, mineral resources, and the like.

The role of gold and other reflationary assets

Gold, along with other precious metals, has traditionally been considered the best hedge against inflation and currency debasement. The nominal price of gold tends to keep up, or 'reflate' its value inversely with the declining value of the underlying paper currency, maintaining its purchasing power in terms of other real assets. Big movements in gold and other precious or industrial metals such as silver, platinum, and the like send strong signals about what the market may be expecting regarding inflation. Since the early days of the pandemic in March 2020, the US dollar value of gold has risen by over 50%, to just under $2000 per ounce in early September 2020,[79] making it one of the best performing investment asset classes during this time.

In thinking about precious metals investment, there are tradeoffs – pros and cons – between gold and the industrial metals: silver, platinum, or palladium, as investment assets. Each of them is subject to supply constraints, in that they have to be mined and extracted from a limited and finite stock around the world. Gold is by far the largest and most liquid of the precious metals, with very deep trading markets all over the world. However, gold's actual use is limited to coinage, jewelry, and ornamentation, and has no particular industrial purpose. Silver, platinum, and palladium on the other hand, while smaller markets, each have industrial uses essential to the modern economy. This means that when the economy is growing more rapidly, these metals' industrial demand ought to rise, and when the economy slows so will demand for the commodity. The benefit is thus that silver, platinum, and palladium have alternative uses rather than just serving as fine jewelry or universally acceptable store of value. It is possible to invest in these metals through exchange-traded funds or to acquire them directly. There are pros and cons to each approach, including the additional cost, trouble, and security risk of holding the metals directly, versus the uncertainty and potential risk of third-party storage and the comfort of knowing the gold is actually there. Another point of consideration is that silver gradually deteriorates over time when exposed to oxygen, so may not be the best thing to try to pass on to one's grandchildren.

"What about Bitcoin? Is that a good alternative to holding paper currency/dollars?" My response is that I have no issue with Bitcoin as an investment, as long as one acknowledges that it is volatile and speculative in nature. While it can be a perfectly adequate medium of exchange, it doesn't yet act as "good" money as it is not a stable store of value. No one wants to store their savings, which represents both the fruit of their labor and their storehouse of value for the future, in a currency that was worth $1500 on the day they bought it, $2000 the next day, and $1000 the day after that. This isn't money in the way discussed here. That is a highly speculative and volatile investment.

Several companies around the world are working on an alternative digital currency around the idea of stablecoins, digital cryptocurrencies that attempt to deal with the price stability issue by linking the coin to an underlying reserve currency, much as was done historically by linking notes to underlying reserves of gold. In the new world of stablecoins, the most common reserve asset seems to be one of the major currencies such as the US dollar. The US's Office of the Comptroller of the Currency (which regulates certain banks and S&Ls) recently confirmed that national banks and federal savings associations are allowed to take deposits that serve as reserves for fiat currency-pegged stablecoins.[80]

The challenge is that these fiat currency backed stablecoins don't address is the potential weakness in the underlying reserve asset, i.e. the United States dollar, the primary risk which is covered here. While a US dollar-backed stablecoin might add some benefit and convenience that physical cash does not provide, and most likely avoid the volatility of a Bitcoin type cryptocurrency, it would face the same challenge that paper currencies would face in the event of a rapid devaluation of the United States dollar. However, a stablecoin that was backed by gold or other precious metal reserves might stand a better chance of actually serving the purpose for which it was intended, by creating a reflationary hedge against currency devaluation.

Part II: The pandemic

3. The origins and progress of COVID-19

"I can very confidently say there won't be another SARS incident, because [China's] infectious-disease surveillance network is very well-established. When a virus comes, we can stop it."[81]
– Dr. Gau Fu, Director of the Chinese Center for Disease Control and Prevention, 2019

"The risk of sustained human-to-human transmission is low."[82]
– Li Qun, head of the China CDC's Emergency Centre, January 2020

"Our [Chinese] government has many, many ways to withhold truth. It made sure that everyone bought the theory that the seafood market in Wuhan was the problem, but it was a big lie."[83]
– Dr. Li-Ming Yan, Virologist and Former Research Fellow at the University of Hong Kong, September 2020

Origins

In February 2020, senior executives and invited guests of the drug company Biogen traveled from all over the world to gather in Boston for the company's annual leadership conference. Over several days, meeting participants huddled together to discuss their businesses' performance and prospects, as well as trends impacting the industry. The attendees sat with one another in lecture and small group settings, ate together, hugged, kissed cheeks, and shook hands. They remained indoors to avoid the chill of the New England winter. They carried out their business as all the world did in the days before its awareness of COVID-19. The hundreds of attendees departed for their homes and families without the least bit of awareness or concern that they had just participated in one of the initial "super-spreader" events that would facilitate the mass propagation of the virus across the country. Over the following weeks, tens of attendees of the conference carried with them a version of the virus that would ultimately end up infecting hundreds then thousands of people not just in the Boston area, but across the United States and to locales as far-flung as Luxembourg and Senegal. By mid-July, the particular variant of the virus present at the conference had been found in about one-third of all the cases sequenced in Massachusetts and 3% of all those studied in the United States.[84] How did all of this begin? And where is it going?

There are two questions about COVID-19 that are extremely important to the broader topic of America's relationship with China, and yet which remain unanswered and hotly debated: Where did SARS-CoV-2 come from (its genomic origin) and how did it initially spread (i.e. to and from Patient Zero and beyond)? These questions have both a scientific and an intelligence community aspect, and the answers may have significant diplomatic, military, and/or economic consequences.

The first of these two questions is primarily scientific and remains highly polarized between the view that SARS-CoV-2 is completely naturally derived, i.e. without human interference, and the possibility that it is either man-made or modified from a natural (i.e. animal-derived) source in a lab such as the Wuhan Institute of Virology (the "WIV") or another Wuhan-based facility. It turns out that this is less clear cut than it would appear on the surface, and that there are legitimate challenges to the assumption that the virus was completely naturally derived.

It has been nearly impossible to get accurate information out of China about the origins of the coronavirus, which has rebuffed substantially all international investigative or medical assistance. During the early days of the outbreak in Wuhan, after a period of saying nothing or downplaying the situation, the Chinese government put forward a narrative that was quickly picked up and accepted as gospel by the media, which suggested that the disease originated in a wet market in Wuhan and spread from there. In January, Gao Fu, the Director of China's Center for Disease Control and Prevention (CDC), claimed twice that the virus came from wild animals sold at the Wuhan market.[85] This has now been disproven and is no longer propagated as a theory even by the CCP itself.[86] In the meantime, between January 1st and April 4th, 2020, the Chinese government criminally charged close to 500 individuals for speaking out about the coronavirus's existence, its risks, challenging the wet market theory, and the role of the CCP in the government's cover-up of the disease.[87] In March, China expelled American journalists working for *The New York Times*, *The Wall Street Journal*, and *The Washington Post*, which incidentally were the same sources aggressively pursuing the coronavirus story and the cover-ups in China in January and February.[88] Further reacting to the increasing pressure, China then changed its story and went on the offensive. In a spy-novel worthy propaganda move endorsed by the Ministry of Foreign Affairs, China promulgated a false story that a US soldier originally brought the coronavirus to Wuhan, rather than Wuhan exporting the virus to the world, as part of an American conspiracy against China.[89]

In April 2020, Chinese virologist Dr. Li-Ming Yan fled from Hong Kong, where she was formerly a research fellow at the University of Hong Kong, to take refuge in the US for fear that her life was in danger from the Chinese authorities. On safer ground, she has since written a 26-page scholarly paper entitled Unusual Features of the SARS-CoV-2

Genome Suggesting Sophisticated Laboratory Modification Rather Than Natural Evolution and Delineation of Its Probable Synthetic Route.[90] In other words, she claims that there is sufficient evidence to assert that the virus was engineered and manipulated by humans. She asserts that while it may have originated in nature, there are features of the virus that suggest it was modified in a lab. This has not been well-received by the scientific community, which points out that the paper has yet to be peer-reviewed and makes some unsubstantiated claims. Dr. Gkikas Magiorkinis, assistant professor of hygiene and epidemiology at the National and Kapodistrian University of Athens says, "the paper by Li-Meng et. al. does not provide any robust evidence of artificial manipulation, no statistical test of alternative hypotheses and is highly speculative" while Daniel Altmann, professor of immunology at Imperial College London takes a more moderated response, saying the study is "interesting, but perhaps an outlier opinion."[91] Other experts are at least willing to consider the possibility that she is speaking the truth. Yanzhong Huang, a global health expert at the Council on Foreign Relations acknowledged the claims should be explored further:

> Given the moral antipathy and the secrecy surrounding any
> biological weapons program, and given the difficulty of
> differentiating a naturally occurring outbreak and a
> deliberately caused one, it is not entirely invalid or illegitimate
> to suspect the virus was man-made. I don't challenge Dr.
> Yan's credentials in making such bold arguments.[92]

Dr. Li-Ming has written multiple peer-reviewed scientific articles on subjects to virology[93] and does appear to be a credible witness for this highly controversial and subversive view. It is hardly surprising that the scientific community and mainstream media have had a negative visceral reaction, and indeed should be somewhat skeptical, as the implications are vast. But the claims should not be dismissed out of hand as if uttered by a crack-pot conspiracy theorist. Dr. Li-Ming had this to say on the situation:

> I'm working on the second scientific report to show the world scientific evidence ... the people who I have worked with in the past months have been lying to the public about the origin of the virus, thereby ignoring the safety of the world at large. Now even when I put my scientific report out, the top experts in the field, lie. And people believe them because they are experts. For example, from the 19th January, Lu De's broadcast channel in Chinese helped me deliver a message that the virus was man made and important people in the government listened to that which went against the Chinese Communist Party. When the authorities watched the broadcast, they knew someone inside delivered the truth outside so that's why they admitted that there was indeed a transmission going on, it was human to human and that the cases had already tripled, were taking place all over China not only in Wuhan. Just a few hours after the broadcast, the Chairman Xi Jinping published the first Chairman statement of 2020 to upgrade the SARS 2 disease at the same level as SARS 1, as a very serious infectious disease. But despite us pushing to help people, this government allowed people to go all over the world, and WHO said that masks do not work, there's no need to be scared, there won't be pandemic, to not impose PHEIC (Public Health Emergency of International Concern) on China ...[94]

Since Dr. Li-Ming published her article, Twitter has suspended Dr. Li-Ming's account, cutting off her 60,000 followers from accessing this report. This seems inconsistent with Twitter's policy of – rather than suspending accounts – labeling content about COVID-19 that is disputed or controversial to "provide additional explanations or clarifications in situations where the risks of harm associated with a tweet are less severe but where people may still be confused or misled by the content." No explanation was given by Twitter for the decision to suspend Dr. Li-Ming's account rather than simply labeling her content as being disputed or controversial.[95] As this book went to print, reports had begun to circulate that Dr. Li-Ming's mother had been arrested by the CCP in mainland China.[96]

In June 2020, Sir Richard Dearlove, the former head of Great Britain's MI6 intelligence service, told The Telegraph that he believed the coronavirus pandemic "started as an accident" when the virus escaped from a laboratory in China.[97] In a very controversial pivot, many Western intelligence and government officials in the US and the UK have in recent months provided additional support to this view, suggesting that they believe it is likely that the virus made its way through the WIV.[98] This shift has been documented by Lt. Col. (res.) Dr. Dany Shoham, a microbiologist and an expert on chemical and biological warfare in the Middle East, and a senior research associate at the Begin-Sadat Center for Strategic Studies. As both a scientist and former senior intelligence analyst in the IDF and the Israeli Defense Ministry, Shoham has an expert and credible perspective on the subject which should be taken seriously.

The implications of this allegation are fundamental to the West's relationship with China. We already know that the Chinese government lied, hid, and denied facts about what was going on in Wuhan during the last quarter of 2019 and early on into 2020.[99] We also know that "the WIV was involved in the improper dispatch of highly virulent viruses from Canada to China" in 2019.[100] If the intelligence community in the US and UK is now saying that there is a probability that the COVID-19 virus came from or at least through the WIV, broader questions remain, including why? and how? What was the nature of the work being done on the virus, and how did the 'accidental' release from the laboratory occur? We have to consider the possibility, which the intelligence community probably knows but won't be able to answer publicly, of whether SARS-CoV-2 was part of a biological weapons program and what was the nature of the release into the human population in Wuhan.

At the risk of swerving dangerously into the lane of speculation here, it is not beyond the realm of possibility for the CCP to have infected some of its own people in a biological experiment run amok. One doesn't have to look further than the Chinese government's treatment of the Uyghur minorities in Xinjiang, including imprisonment (over one million people held in detention centers), widespread torture, forced sterilizations, abortions, and murder, to realize that this possibility cannot be ruled out of hand.[101] An independent tribunal is to convene in London in 2021 to consider whether the Chinese government's treatment of its own citizens in Xinjiang constitutes genocide.[102]

Given its track record of disregard for human life, it is not beyond the pale that the CCP intentionally infected human subjects. This possibility takes two forms: that the infection was intentional, but the leak and widespread contagion were not; or, more troubling, that the leak and contagion were anticipated but at some point, the process got out of control in terms of severity and breadth. The World Health Organization is charged with an independent investigation into SARS-CoV-2's origins. But one has to ask how independent the WHO can be when it is substantially funded by China (and the US, to be sure) and whose work will rely on the cooperation of Beijing, which has every incentive to keep what really happened in Wuhan under wraps for as long as possible.

At a minimum, it cannot be denied that governments, especially including the Chinese, hid or minimized critical information about the emergence and spread of the virus and in so doing made the pandemic worse, and may have served national strategic interests counter to those of the United States. We will return to the learnings and implications of this issue in chapter six when we discuss the biological threat that the United States continues to face.

Progress

While the origins of SARS-CoV-2 may remain opaque for some time, we now know something about the impact of COVID-19 on human health. As previously mentioned, after approximately eight months of the pandemic, there have been approximately 7.4 million confirmed cases in the US and over 35 million worldwide.[103] COVID-19 related deaths number over 200,000 in the US and over one million worldwide as of the date of this writing.[104] There is reason to believe that while the number of US deaths presents a reasonably accurate picture, that the statistics coming in from the rest of the world, especially from its most populous nations of the world including China, India, and elsewhere substantially under represent both infection and death rates.[105]

To contextualize the COVID-19 numbers in the US, let's consider influenza. The CDC estimates that each year since 2010, influenza causes 9 to 45 million illnesses, 140,000 to 810,000 hospitalizations, and 12,000 to 61,000 deaths in the US, at an annual cost of over $10 billion.[106] In other words, to date, there have been three to five times the number of deaths from COVID-19 than is typical for the flu in any given year, and we're not out of the woods yet. So a serious issue to be sure. On the other hand, of the confirmed and probable COVID-19 related deaths for which there are age data, 58% of deaths have been of individuals over 75 years of age, and 79% of deaths have been of individuals over 65 years of age. Only about

5% of all confirmed and probable COVID-19 related deaths have been amongst the under-50 age cohort, even though that group represents nearly two-thirds (64%) of COVID-19 cases. Whites make up the substantial majority of the elderly (over age 65) deaths, while Blacks and Hispanics each comprise about a third of the deaths in the 18-29 cohort (68.3% combined vs. 32% of the population[107]). Deaths among Blacks between ages 65-75 are also represented at twice the population (26% vs. 13%), although deaths within the 75 and older group align more closely with demographic distribution by race. Infections and deaths among Asians are at 3.3% and 4.9% of the respective totals while comprising 5.9% of the population.[108] Amongst healthcare workers, many of whom are presumably attending to these same elderly patients, there have been approximately 700 identified deaths since March.[109]

There is a lot of noise in these data because each state collects them in their own particular way, and the numbers may not line up exactly on the same basis, but directionally the information tells a pretty clear tale. Based on all we know after six months, COVID-19 appears to be primarily killing the elderly, most of whom have pre-existing conditions, and not youth or working-age adults in large numbers. The majority of deaths have come from the 75-year-old and above group, the vast majority of which – with some hale and hearty exceptions – were presumably already either at home, in nursing homes or other care facilities, or in hospitals, as opposed to being out and about working in the marketplace.

Looking across the Atlantic to the United Kingdom, the patterns are the same. Those over 80 years of age represent 53.4% of COVID-19 related deaths, and those over 60 years of age represent 91.4% of COVID-19 related deaths. Of the 8.6% of deaths that have occurred amongst those under 60 years of age, 87.9% had pre-existing conditions. In other words, of the 29,705 COVID-19 tagged deaths in the UK as of this writing, only 308, or 1%, have occurred amongst healthy youth or working-age adults.[110] Even these figures overstate the mortality rate based on the way the data are gathered in the UK. If you died in a car accident yesterday but had COVID-19 in March, yours was counted as a COVID-19 related death.

This raises the possibility that the lockdowns did not directly benefit those most vulnerable to the virus, but rather perversely kept the most productive and apparently resilient element of our society on the sidelines of the economy. This is not the narrative that we are being told by most of the media. We seem to be in a world of panic and exaggeration of the issue, and it's distracting us from other concerns. Like our jobs and livelihoods.

Furthermore, the lockdowns and resulting shutdown of the economy are exacerbating pre-existing wealth and income inequality issues. Job losses harm minorities and working-class Americans more severely than the affluent. Approximately 13% percent of Black workers and 10.5% of Hispanic workers were unemployed in July, compared to 7.3% of White workers.[111] While workers in creative industries (and the knowledge class more generally) can more easily work remotely, service and factory workers, laborers, and those dependent on the gig-economy more often have to be on location. Most of the jobs lost in the lockdowns have been in low-paying jobs. While low-paying sectors account for 30% of all jobs in the US, they represented 51% of the jobs lost from February to July.[112] Harvard University's Raj Chetty, an applied economist who has tracked the data nationwide since the beginning of February, shows us that by August, high wage employment had essentially returned to its pre-lockdown levels while low wage employment remains 16% below pre-lockdown levels, disproportionately impacting low-income families. His data have shown that employment losses have been the worst in highly-affluent areas such as Manhattan, where low-income workers depend on the spending patterns of high-income residents.[113] Chetty has been quoted as saying that "the recession has essentially ended for high-income individuals" while the bottom half (by income) of American workers constitute almost 80% of the jobs still missing.[114]

Beyond the US, the World Bank estimates that 40-60 million people globally may be pushed into extreme poverty as a result of the slowdown of economic activity around the world.[115] While women appear to be taking less of a direct hit from COVID-19 then are men, with lower rates of infections and death – presumably due to the relative prevalence of underlying conditions and men's shorter life expectancy generally –, the indirect impacts of the pandemic fall disproportionately on women and children. According to a recent article in The Lancet, "the lockdown and school closures mean that just as their access to paid work diminishes, women face an increase in their unpaid labour."… "Domestic duties, things like childcare, preparing food for the extra youngsters who would normally be at school, and looking after sick family members, these responsibilities fall disproportionately on women." The article further notes that "women are staying away from healthcare centres partly because of the measures put in place to control COVID-19 and partly because they are worried about contracting the disease. As a result, we are seeing an increase in the rates of severe acute malnutrition in children; usually, that can be discovered at an earlier stage but these days kids are presenting much later with other complications."[116]

In addition, an estimated 24 million students from impoverished families may never return to the classroom. UNESCO and UNICEF estimate that over 1.6 billion students from 192 countries around the world have been impacted by closures, noting that the impact "is particularly severe for the most vulnerable and marginalized boys and girls and their families. The resulting disruptions exacerbate existing disparities within the education system but also in other aspects of their lives."[117] Today, after nearly nine months since the beginning of the year and outbreak in China, "872 million students – or half the world's student population – in 51 countries are still unable to head back to their classrooms."[118] For nearly half a billion people around the world, there is no such thing as remote or online learning, and as of today, nearly one in four countries surveyed do not have a date set for when schools will reopen. Many millions of students are already being pushed into child labor as their families are unable to generate sufficient income in the downturn. Left unchecked, shattered aspirations represent a powder keg of future social unrest.

In September 2020, as infection rates have begun to rise again in various parts of America and elsewhere around the world, the debate has resumed about how to balance the risks of this second wave with the economic and other consequences. Questions of returning to lockdowns, extending or reimposing travel restrictions, the safety and efficacy of a rushed release of potential vaccines, and other matters are both divisive and not easy to follow. The following chapter explores these topics and provides some recommendations.

4. The ongoing health challenge

Canst thou, O partial sleep, give thy repose
To the wet sea-boy in an hour so rude;
And in the calmest and most stillest night,
With all appliances and means to boot,
Deny it to a king? Then, happy low, lie down!
Uneasy lies the head that wears a crown.

· · ·

Then you perceive the body of our kingdom
How foul it is; what rank diseases grow,
And with what danger, near the heart of it.

· · ·

O God! that one might read the book of fate,
And see the revolution of the times ...[119]
– William Shakespeare, *Henry IV*

How should leaders decide?

When Shakespeare had King Henry IV sleeplessly mutter, "Uneasy lies the head that wears a crown," the Bard was speaking a human truth that resonates across centuries and cultures to anyone in leadership whose responsibilities entail decisions that affect human lives and livelihoods.

Today, around the world, national, regional, and local political leaders, along with their corporate and business peers, are facing in COVID-19 a leadership test unseen in generations. These leaders' constituencies, and the experts advising them, all have opinions about what should be done. Ultimately, though, it is the leader who must absorb, incorporate, and sift through the information, and choose a course of action. They and their constituencies will have to live with the consequences of these decisions for a long time to come.

The mythic figure of Justice has often been represented blindfolded, holding a weighing scale in one hand and a sword in the other. Symbolically, the blindfold represents impartiality, the scales a fair balance of the rights of the individual against the needs of society, and between the conflicting interests of one individual against another. The sword is the enforcing power behind these lofty ideals.

Today, our leaders hold the scales and, blindfolded or not, must weigh in the balance the human impacts of COVID-19 against all of the economic, social, emotional, and healthcare costs of extended lockdowns of people and commercial activity, travel restrictions, and school reopenings. Now, these leaders must also consider the question of renewing lockdowns ahead of an election and into the winter months. In the first pan, the scale holds COVID-19 mortality, morbidity and the related costs of, and strains on, the health care system. In the other pan sits the sum total of consequences of the Great Pause and its lockdowns.

Most of these costs fall into the quadrant of 'known unknowns.' We know what the categories are — soaring unemployment, extensive bankruptcies of small- and medium-sized businesses, the disempowerment, disfranchisement, and potential radicalization of classes of workers who are dependent upon regular and weekly paychecks, the potential disappearance of entire industries and global supply chain breakdowns – but we find it impossible to estimate their total cost.

No leader, whether in the political or business realm, will be able to act with the idealized impartiality of a blindfolded Justice. Each will have their constituency and will ignore them at their peril. Leaders can, however, attempt to estimate and communicate the costs and consequences of various choices, and make courageous decisions accordingly. Decision-makers have to choose among unappealing options with imperfect information. The costs of a second wave of infections, deaths, and overwhelmed healthcare systems must be weighed against millions of lost jobs, mass bankruptcies, rising rates of depression, untreated illnesses, and higher rates of suicide stemming from economic misery, and importantly, the risk of widespread social unrest much worse than anything we've seen to date.

Perspectives on lockdowns

Several polls taken in the second quarter indicated at the time that a majority of Americans believed that lockdowns should continue (April) or be renewed (June) for as long as necessary to prevent deaths and impede the rise of a second wave.[120] The problem is that for many moderate and lower-income Americans, and for our economy as a whole, this path has proven to be financially ruinous. In September 2020, some voices in the debate began calling for "more complete lockdowns than were previously implemented" in the United States, for "six to eight weeks with a goal of reaching no more than one new case per day per 100,000 people," and even then continuing with more targeted and localized lockdowns for as long as needed until a vaccine is broadly and successfully deployed.[121] This recommendation conveniently omits reference to the fact that such a move, if implemented timeously, would cut right across the Presidential elections. The recommendation also makes the convenient – if only it were true – assumption that federal and state governments can continue to pay individuals and small businesses to stay closed indefinitely. There are two very important questions that should always be asked: *qui bono*? who benefits? And who pays the price? The timing of this recommendation, coming just a few weeks before the most contentious election in history, does not appear coincidental. It is a fantasy to believe that the US federal, state and local governments can continue to spend trillions of dollars (that would have to be created out of thin air) to compensate businesses and individuals, without wreaking enormous havoc on our economy, and storing up even worse problems in the years to come that ultimately will have to be reconciled.

While a second wave of infections may yet create circumstances dire enough to warrant a renewed round of lockdowns as infection rates rise over the winter, we are not there yet today. While the reimposition of lockdowns would never be an easy decision to be made, our leadership has to take extraordinary care at this moment in considering whether to take any action before the elections. Anything that could be perceived as impinging on individuals' civil liberties and ability to vote, or otherwise viewed as tampering with the election prior to completion of the process, risks inviting chaos and mayhem. Which may be exactly what the Marxists and Anarchists – or the extreme Right, for that matter – want. It is in the Communist playbook after all.

The purpose of the lockdowns was not to eliminate COVID-19 from the population. That may not happen for months or years, and perhaps never. The intention was to "flatten the curve," i.e. to avoid a sudden surge that would overwhelm our healthcare systems. That mission has made real progress. The lockdowns were also meant to buy time to expand the capacity of the healthcare system and the means to test, track and monitor potential spreaders of the virus, so that society can better cope with probable future waves of the pandemic as confinements are eased. In this regard, substantial progress has also been made. The medical community has gathered significant information from learnings about the best treatment methods, pathways of transmission, and mitigation strategies. At the same time, the health care infrastructure has had time to rebound from the first wave of the crisis that strained peak capacity, and health care leaders have been able to plan and put in place better systems, processes, and surge capacity strategies should it be needed. To the extent new lockdowns are required, they need to be approached more thoughtfully, and with the benefit of experience, than the last time around. The first round of lockdowns was brute force application of a tool not well suited to the task. Any new lockdowns need to be much more targeted, limited to high-risk areas and highly sensitive populations and prioritized based on a number of factors including protecting essential workers in our economy, and with an eye to proactively ensuring that these policies don't unfairly discriminate against the poor and already economically challenged amongst us.

Sweden did not go through national lockdowns. Sweden's government, with support of its iconoclastic state epidemiologist, Anders Tegnell, took the country in a very different direction, which while it's still too early for a final judgment, may have been correct. Tegnell's view on lockdowns ("It's really using a hammer to kill a fly") and face masks ("Face masks are an easy solution, and I'm deeply distrustful of easy solutions to complex problems") have annoyed and irritated the establishment, but resonate with more practically-minded people. While Sweden was loudly and widely condemned (*The New York Times* called Sweden a "pariah state" and "the world's cautionary tale"[122]) for not following the rest of the EU (and the world, for that matter) in implementing nationwide lockdowns, we know six months later that Sweden's per capita death rate has, at least to date, been lower than the

US, the UK, Spain, and Italy, [123] each of which implemented lockdowns, some of them draconian. Sweden's rate of new infections is now also lower than the rest of the EU and the UK.[124] Not only have health care outcomes been better to date, but Sweden and its Nordic neighbors are expecting much less worse outcomes for their economy this year then for the rest of the European Union. Specifically, the Nordic region expects declines in GDP of 4%, compared with 8% for the eurozone in 2020. Sweden also took a proactive step to address one of the sectors of the economy most likely to be negatively impacted by the pandemic. The Swedish government created a rebate plan targeted at shopping malls and other property owners that provided funds to reimburse landlords for 50% of any relief reduction rent relief given to tenants.[125]

On the other side of the globe, many countries in Africa took the opposite approach, going well beyond their northern hemisphere peers in implementing very draconian lockdown protocols and shutting down their borders to all travel and trade, and closing vast sectors of their economies for several months. The severity of the lockdowns and other restrictions in places like South Africa, Kenya, and Nigeria were disproportionate to the risk these countries faced at the time. As a result, the impact on their economies has been severe. For example, South Africa announced that its gross domestic product (GDP) fell by over 16% between the first and second quarters of 2020, implying an annualized decline of 51%, as a result of the government-mandated lockdown of all citizens, and the shutdown of any non-essential economic activities, including development projects within the energy sector, even though energy security is a greater long-term threat to South Africa than is COVID-19.

Lockdowns in large African cities are not the same as in China, Italy, or the United States. Housing settlements are informal and population densities are higher. Food and other essentials must be bought and consumed daily – often from open-air markets and kiosks, with cash earned the same day. Social distancing is impossible when five or more household members sleep in one poorly ventilated room. Washing hands frequently is difficult when the water has to be fetched from an unprotected community source down the road. Eventually, however, hunger will speak louder than government edicts. Most African workers are involved in primary agriculture and must be able to plant, harvest, and process their crops. After all, there is no point in living now only to starve later.

African leaders will continue to look abroad for support. Many African governments, having tilted easily and early to the Chinese sphere of influence, have begun seeking alternatives elsewhere. But China will seek to capitalize on the crisis by extending its reach in Africa. For example, China has offered financial, medical, and other assistance, as it did earlier with Italy. China's aggressive and decisive actions to combat the pandemic at home will be seen by many as a paradigm for Africa, given Europe and America's disjointed and slower responses, which has created a credibility gap with some African leaders.

Africa should emerge from the pandemic with less lasting damage than many fear. Leaders have learned important lessons from earlier epidemics, notably Ebola. Warm climates, a mostly young and rural population, and lower rates of regional travel seem to be slowing the spread of the virus and holding down its mortality rate. African institutions are too frail and under-resourced to cope with the pandemic and its economic fallout, and the continent's medical systems are woefully unprepared if things get worse. But financial and institutional support from European and US development institutions will help mitigate the harm, particularly if solutions focus on delivering education, supplies, and infrastructure to where the needs are greatest.

Within the United States, of the eight states that never imposed state-wide lockdowns or shelter in residence orders, half of them have virus reproduction rates[ii] at or below 1.0, consistent with the national numbers including states which had the most aggressive lockdowns (24 of 50 at 1.0 or below), indicating that lockdowns may or may not have made as much of a difference in more rural states with lower population densities than in urban areas.[126] If nothing else this is another example that one-size-fits-all solutions are not appropriate. We have to be more targeted in high-risk areas.

Like Sweden's government, President Trump and the US administration received a great deal of criticism domestically and on the international stage for what was labeled a failure of national leadership to implement lockdowns and other stricter measures comprehensively across the US, and sooner than was actually done. But what these observers and critics consistently ignore is that constitutionally, the Federal government was limited (under the 10th amendment as part of the Bill of Rights) in what it could do without drawing on emergency powers based on 'urgent and exigent' circumstances. One can imagine how the country would have reacted to this perceived usurpation of dictatorial power. Unless the

---

[ii] The virus replication rate, or Rt, "represents the effective reproduction rate of the virus calculated for each locale. It lets us estimate how many secondary infections are likely to occur from a single infection in a specific area. Values over 1.0 mean we should expect more cases in that area, values under 1.0 mean we should expect fewer."

requested power was explicitly provided by the constitution to be in the hands of the Federal government, only the States could implement such laws and regulations. This indeed left the United States more vulnerable, more disorganized, and with slower response times, than the more authoritarian regimes such as China and Russia, which governments were able to move quickly using the coercive power of the state to lock down cities, limit all travel and impose several other very restrictive constraints on the civil liberties that we take for granted in America. Democracy is messy, and in this case, just as in our attempts to prepare and mobilize for the world wars, America required more time and coordination to get to the desired outcome than would have been the case in an authoritarian regime.

Federalism, the model of government practiced in the United States, bifurcates authority and power between the states, which have authority for every power that is not otherwise provided by the constitution to the federal government, and the federal government, which has the authority for which the constitution provides, and several others which have been accumulated both through amendments and precedents established through decades of practice. With so much power embedded in the states, it means that it may take longer for the US to get there, and require a lot of engagement and collaboration.

The question of states' rights, with corresponding challenges to the jurisdiction and authority of the federal government to override them in questions of national interest, is as old as the republic itself. Since the founding of the nation, there has been a constant tug-of-war like tension between the states and the federal government, which tension has been taken up by both conservatives and liberals at various points in history depending on the underlying issue. It was the framework of states' rights that gave the ostensible legal and political cover for the Southern states' intransigence over the question of slavery, which ultimately led to succession and the American civil war. Some of those same states, including Alabama and Mississippi, again used states' rights to face off against the US government in the 1960s on civil rights-related issues of segregation and voting rights, and protection of the participants of the civil rights movement themselves. Today, it manifests in the highly divisive and fundamental questions of abortion rights and gender assignment or identity. Is a very old and thorny issue around which much American fraternal blood has been shed throughout our republic.

It is within this context, with so much power devolved to the states, that we have seen significant conflict between the federal government and some of the state governments over the implementation of policies and the nature of assistance provided for preventative and health care solutions during the pandemic, and in response to the protests and riots that have torn our cities and our citizens apart over the past several months. This conflict has largely fallen out on party lines. Generally, the Republican governed states took a less restrictive approach to the implementation of lockdowns, travel restrictions, and other measures to address the pandemic, and welcomed the support and intervention of the federal government, including the National Guard, when faced with substantial social unrest. The Democratic-run states, on the other hand, took more stringent approaches to the lockdowns and COVID-19 related restrictions, and at the same time have resisted US government assistance to help keep the protests and demonstrations free of violence while maintaining the right to peaceable assembly provided under the constitution.

Our country is now entering into renewed debate and discussion around the question of whether lockdowns should be re-implemented. We are already seeing localized versions of this issue manifest in our system of universities and colleges, many of which abruptly reversed course in recent weeks and moved everything back online. In what could be perceived to be a bait and switch tactic, the schools' administrations took in tuition payments from students and their parents, brought all of their students back for the start of the academic year, only to then announce the change to remote-learning and restricting movement and access to campuses just a few weeks later.

This controversy surrounding the question of renewed lockdowns is certainly not isolated to just the United States. Today, in democratically run countries like France, Spain, and the United Kingdom, there is significant debate, and – unlike in March – organized resistance, to the idea of going back into lockdown in cities like London, Paris, Madrid, and Marseilles. This resistance is being led by individual citizens and small businesses, labor unions, and political parties, which are aligned against the reimposition of arbitrary and universal lockdowns that would once again throw their economic and social lives into havoc. Anyone who's tried to homeschool their children while simultaneously working from home and carrying on with their ordinary responsibilities understands this concern. One of the main arguments for those now resisting the renewal of lockdowns is the question of whether there's any real evidence that the lockdowns actually work in achieving their intended objectives.

On the other hand, I have been in several ethereal conversations recently with a number of otherwise intelligent and rational people who have said, in effect, that they want no actions taken by the government to save the economy that would put their elderly parents or other loved ones in any increased danger. The practical implication, when talked through logically, is their belief that the lockdowns should continue, for months if necessary. This view seems to reside primarily among white, wealthy, and privileged classes who have an existing store of wealth, are still making money and who don't know what it means to go hungry or to not be able to pay their rent or provide for their children with a basic education because they didn't work that day. When I speak to ordinary Americans: former (because they're not working) house cleaners, small gym owners, Ubër drivers, cooks and waiters, airline crewmembers, daycare workers, and barbers ... they just want to get back to work to be able to make a living and provide for their loved ones. Even with limited government support, they are not making ends meet, and are running out of time to survive. I appreciate and share the view that we love our family members so much that we would do anything we could in order to protect them and keep them from harm. This is fundamental to human nature and to our civilization and is a good policy at the family or household level of decision-making.

This sentiment cannot, however, be the basis for national or even regional policy decisions. The implications of these choices go well beyond one's own family and loved ones to impact our communities and our nation as it struggles to recover economically from the pandemic related lockdowns. The weight of true leadership requires that our government and business leaders are able to look beyond their own personal interests and take the common good and the life of the nation into account as their top priority. The significance of this is that choices will have to be made that have mortal consequences, decisions that will result in life and death.

This is the weighty crown of leadership of which Shakespeare spoke. It is a high calling that should not be taken up lightly, coldly, or with a view to personal reward. For those who are charged with such leadership responsibilities, it should be viewed as a sacred duty and trust for which one will be held accountable. As every leader who has faced this kind of challenge knows, part of the responsibility will come with the inevitable backbiting, complaints, criticisms, and personal attacks that the leader has to learn to filter for truth (that should be acted on) while discarding the rubbish. This takes a thickness of skin and focus that has been absent in much of our leadership, but which can be developed and strengthened even in a crisis. As soon as leaders are distracted by all the noise of the critics around them, they start to engage in the wrong battle and lose their focus on the main mission at hand. As we know from business and life, there is no surer way to deplete the energy and vitality of a mission-critical effort than to get sidetracked by arguments, irrelevant obstacles, committees to discuss forming a committee, and other sideshows.

Travel bans, mask-wearing, and other shuffling of the deck chairs

Are the travel restrictions and upon-arrival quarantines that are still being imposed by certain states being politicized or implemented for reasons unrelated to health and safety? I don't know, but I do observe some uncomfortable patterns in the data for the Tri-State region (New York, New Jersey, and Connecticut, each with Democratic governors). As at the date of writing, of the 28 states on the Tri-States' shared travel advisory list,[127] 19 of the states with travel restrictions (68%) are Republican governed, compared with nine, or 32%, Democratic governed states. Of those 19 travel restricted Republican governed states, 14 of them actually have estimated virus reproduction rates below the estimate for New York itself, including 11 which are estimated at below 1.0 (the estimated effective reproduction rate below which the virus should be going down in that area) so it is hard to see how these travelers are actually endangering public safety or facilitating the spread of the virus in a manner greater than travel generally or within the region.[128] Indeed, as at the date of this writing, Connecticut has the fourth-highest virus reproduction rate nationally, and New Jersey has the seventh.

As other observers have recently pointed out,[129] these same states in the Northeast (i.e. those inside the Tri-State's approved bubble) are now showing the worst unemployment in the nation, with five of the states above 10% in August, including Massachusetts, New Jersey, New York, Pennsylvania, and Rhode Island. This compares with August unemployment rates in Florida of 7.4%, Texas at 6.8%, Arizona at 5.9%, and Georgia at 5.6%. These states have been on the hit list as being too open and risky and indeed did see big spikes coming out of the lockdowns in early summer. But they have taken action. Today, Texas has one of the lowest virus reproduction rates in the country at 0.82, and each of the other three is below 1.0 (compared with 1.04 for New York and 1.15 for Connecticut). These states have prioritized getting their economies moving again, and it does not yet appear to be at a cost of compromising aggregate health outcomes.

My conclusion to all of this is that the inter-state travel restrictions are not necessary, do not add any real public service benefit such as improving public safety or reducing transmission, have political overtones when the data are mapped, and are self-defeating as part of a broader set of policies for the economic recovery of the region. And finally, virus reproduction rates are higher within the travel bubble than without. Perhaps it should be the rest of the country protecting itself from the Tri-

State area by restricting travel from the Northeast, not the other way around.

If only it were that simple. New York City, my beloved home for over twenty years, is falling apart because of the decisions being made by state and local governments. "By June 2020, the New York metropolitan region had experienced more infection, death, and economic destruction than anywhere in the world."[130] Over 6000 businesses have already closed, bankruptcy filings are up by 40%, and it's only going to get worse from here.[131] Employment declined by 20%, or 921,000 jobs through April, before seeing a modest recovery of 3.4%. New York City is projecting a budget shortfall of over $8 billion in the fiscal 2021 year, which it hopes to bridge by 2.8 billion and savings proposals, in using another 2.8 billion of reserves. For the remainder, it hopes to receive additional funding from state and federal governments.[132]

In September 2020, over 170 business leaders of large New York City area firms and companies that collectively employ millions of people, wrote an urgent letter to the mayor, with a cc: to the New York state governor, desperately appealing for some semblance of leadership in the city to address the chaos that had erupted over the summer:

> Despite New York's success in containing the coronavirus, unprecedented numbers of New Yorkers are unemployed, facing homelessness, or otherwise at risk. There is widespread anxiety over public safety, cleanliness and other quality of life issues that are contributing to deteriorating conditions in commercial districts and neighborhoods across the five boroughs.
> We need to send a strong, consistent message that our employees, customers, clients and visitors will be coming back to a safe and healthy work environment. People will be slow to return unless their concerns about security and the

> livability of our communities are addressed quickly and with
> respect and fairness for our city's diverse populations.
> We urge you to take immediate action to restore essential
> services as a necessary precursor for solving the city's longer
> term, complex, economic challenges ...[133]

The issues that prompted the letter included increasing concern on the part of business leaders in New York City over the substantial deterioration in public services including essential services, a substantial rise in shootings and violent deaths over the summer, and other issues that appear to be deteriorating the working and living conditions in both commercial and residential neighborhoods across the city.[134] The city had also suffered from the nation-wide riots and looting in June. These riots occurred in multiple neighborhoods and faced ineffective resistance from law enforcement. Storefronts and other businesses were still boarded up several weeks later. Vagrancy and panhandling had increased over the summer, and essential services such as garbage hauling seemed to be neglected.

As a perfect example of a red herring issue that has been politicized, there has been much controversy around the question of mask-wearing. I have observed more than once individuals who have walked mask-less into stores talking about their civil liberties and constitutional rights, while they video the manager try to gently but firmly shuffle them out the door after they've refused for the Nth time to put on a mask. What is the point? Any traveler who has observed armies of TSA agents standing idly around airport security checkpoints has probably paused to consider the actual efficacy of those hordes, and come to a similar conclusion that may be true of mask-wearing. Whether or not they are improving public safety, if nothing else, face masks do provide a sense of safety and the comfort that at least something is being done. They are on the face reminder of the need for ongoing caution, vigilance, and distance. There is absolutely no point in acting the rebel by refusing to wear face masks in public establishments. My civil liberties are not more infringed upon here than by the custom and law (in most places) that I wear pants in public.

Masks clearly do no harm, and there is some reasonable likelihood that the current scientific community thinking is correct. The operative view is that the primary vector for SARS-CoV-2 transmission is through aerosolization (i.e. through droplets from sneezes, coughing, and the like), which may or may not be able to travel even beyond the six-foot distancing recommendations. A September 2020 article concluded that recent scientific research supported a view that "both surgical masks and unvented KN95 respirators, even without fit-testing, reduce the outward particle emission rates by 90% and 74% on average during speaking and coughing, respectively, compared to wearing no mask, corroborating their effectiveness at reducing outward emission," but was unable to confirm whether cloth, homemade masks made any difference.[135] Nonetheless, if wearing masks reduces the expectorated viral load of a cough, sneeze, or heavy sigh by even 40% to 50%, then we're likely reducing the probability of transmitting infection by upwards of 75% to 90%. It's too early to know for sure, as unfortunately, we have not yet learned enough about the true nature of SARS-CoV-2 and its transmission. Until we understand more precisely how the virus works, masks are a very minor, painless, and increasingly creative and humorous, inconvenience. Let us embrace it for now. There are bigger battles to fight.

While new cases will continue to unfold, and hotspots re-emerge, we must press on towards restoration of our economies and a vast improvement in the provision of healthcare including massive investment in various technologies that will allow societies to better cope with the next, inevitable, pandemics or other health care concerns. And the government, business, labor, and community leaders have a once-in-a-generation opportunity to address both the health care infrastructure gaps that the surge revealed, and beyond that the structural imperfections in our societies that the pandemic has exposed.

Beyond the immediate questions of mask-wearing, lockdowns, travel restrictions, and the implementation of vaccines in a safe and effective manner, we need to look ahead and consider the longer-term implications of the pandemic and its indirect consequences. Throughout history, plagues and pandemics, like wars and other disasters, have tended to lead towards upheaval and substantial shifts in the social fabric of nations. This destabilization can lead to very rapid change, some of which may be good and some of which may be very bad. It is probably too early to know what kinds of impact COVID-19 will ultimately have on our society, but it's important to carefully observe what we see going on around us, and try to draw some inferences from the past.

Pulitzer-prize winning historian Barbara Tuchman wrote in her book *A Distant Mirror: The Calamitous 14th Century* that the Black Plague shifted the balance of power from the landowner to the peasant, sparking a revolution, which over time benefitted labor and the working-classes, and may have been the "unrecognized beginning of modern man."[136] Daron Acemoglu and James Robinson point to something similar in *Why Nations Fail*, which is that "the Black Death would create havoc and further strengthen independent cities and peasants at the expense of monarchs, aristocrats and large landowners."[137] So far, the conditions of the current pandemic appear to be poised to lead to an opposite and regressive outcome for the poor and disenfranchised. Many of the lockdown measures imposed in countries around the world are clearly regressive and penalize the poor and marginalized in society, including in Singapore, where over 300,000 of the city-state's migrant workers who make up most of the low-wage workforce continue as at this writing to be confined to their residences.[138] The impact on the marginalized may yet worsen unless there is rapid and extensive intervention by governments and businesses around the world. Governments should act, even if not for reason altruistic motive, then pragmatically to prevent the kinds of social unrest, revolts, and revolutions that could destroy all that passes in their wake. However, this has to be done in a way that is not just throwing money that does not exist at the problem, but rather ensuring that the poor and disenfranchised are integrated into employment, housing, and other sustainable long-term solutions. Out of tragedy can emerge hope, but only if societies come together to acknowledge the challenge and work together to develop better solutions. As Tuchman put it: "An event of great agony is bearable only in the belief that it will bring about a better world."

Part III: The external threat

5. The rise of China and inevitable conflict with America

A phenomenon noticeable throughout history regardless of place or period is the pursuit by governments of policies contrary to their own interests. Mankind, it seems, makes a poorer performance of government than of almost any other human activity... Why, to begin at the beginning, did the Trojan rulers drag that suspicious looking wooden horse inside their walls despite every reason to suspect a Greek trick?[139]
– Barbara Tuchman, *The March of Folly*

"Never in history has one government controlled so much wealth. As China's economic might has grown, so too has its ability and temptation to us this power to advance geopolitical ends ... It is ... the major reason regional and global power projection has become such an economic (as opposed to military) exercise."[140]
– Blackwell & Harris, *War by Other Means*

A shotgun tour of fifty years of Chinese economic development

The rise of China is THE story of our generation in terms of world affairs. As recently as 1993, China accounted for less than 2% of world GDP, [141] and up to that point, observers had been more focused on Japan as the presumptive economic challenger to the United States (by the early 1990s there were dozens of books on the subject of Japan's imminent takeover of the US).[142] In less than 30 years, i.e. by 2020 or perhaps 2021, China will represent around 20% of world GDP.[143] Today, China's influence is felt from Asia to Africa in trade and finance, in a more muscular foreign policy, and in a substantial military buildup, all of which is challenging the US position as a global hegemon in ways unimaginable at the turn of the century.

From a US-centric perspective, the resumption of America's relationship with modern China began in 1971 when then-Secretary of State Henry Kissinger undertook on behalf of President Richard Nixon his secret diplomatic mission to China. The strategic purpose in reopening the relationship with China was to put pressure on Moscow in the midst of the Cold War and a failing military entanglement in Vietnam. This trip initiated a new era of diplomatic engagement with China that the US had not had since the establishment of the People's Republic of China (PRC) in 1949, following the defeat of the US-supported Nationalists (who fled to Taiwan). The United States chose to formally recognize the government in Taiwan, and as a result lost diplomatic contact with the mainland for over two decades during the depths of the Cold War. Over the following twenty years, the US came into conflict with China primarily through proxy wars in places like Korea and Vietnam. Since China and the USSR viewed each other with suspicion, and since China had turned inward to deal with its own domestic issues, the US was able to focus most of its attention on the Soviet Union.

At the time of Kissinger's visit, China was in the middle of the Cultural Revolution, which featured a revival of ideological communism (Maoism), a purge of capitalist and traditional influences, and the reconsolidation of power under Chairman Mao Zedong. Mao had been briefly side-lined in the mid-sixties following the devastation wrought by the Chinese Communist Party's Great Leap Forward, a misguided attempt at industrialization that moved farmers into communes to produce steel. This action produced the inevitable and unsurprising result: very bad steel. But it also resulted in national economic failure and the worst famine in recorded history. This, in turn, led to death, mostly by starvation, of at least 30 million and potentially up to 45 million Chinese. In 1971, China remained largely backwards, agrarian, and still isolated from the West and indeed most of the outside world. The country was poor and not relevant to the world economy, with a total GDP of $100 billion, and GDP per capita of $113, compared with US GDP of $1,164 billion and GDP per capita of $5,234 at that time.[144] One of the biggest threats to Mao's leadership remained the instability and poverty of the millions of rural peasants who were feared as a potential source of revolt against the government and the Chinese Communist Party (CCP). While millions have been lifted out of poverty in the last few decades, alongside mass urbanization, this fear of revolt haunts the CCP and remains a motive force for many of its domestic policies even today.

Following Mao's death in 1976, reforms led by de facto national leader Deng Xiaopeng, which progressed through the 1990s, resulted in substantial political liberalization and economic progress, including opening China to foreign investment and world markets for the first time. The United States formally recognized the PRC in 1979 in acknowledgment of these reforms. The new relationship benefitted from the progress Nixon, Kissinger and their successors had made through shuttle diplomacy over the course of the decade. Deng, and his generation of more moderate and reform-minded leadership who had turned away from many of the more extreme ideological views of the previous generation, promoted "socialism with Chinese characteristics." This set the stage for the acceleration of China's economic growth and entry onto the world stage. Growth really began to accelerate in earnest only after 1993 under the leadership of Party General Secretary and President Jiang

Zemin and Premier Zhu Rohgji, who presided over GDP growth of nearly 10% per year over the following decade.[145]

In the 50 years since Kissinger's visit, China has grown its GDP at double-digit rates each year, reaching $14.2 trillion in nominal GDP and $27.3 trillion in purchasing power in 2019, or $19,520 per capita PPP.[146] Comparatively, the US grew by an average of 6% in nominal terms over the same period, reaching 2019's level of $21.4 trillion of purchasing power and $64,767 per capita PPP.[147] China is now either the largest or the second-largest economy in the world depending on how it is measured. By many metrics, China is now outpacing the US economy especially if aggregate purchase power is counted. This story, if not the statistics, is well known and has been the focus of most observers of the international economic scene for two decades now.

What has been less appreciated is how the benefits of this growth have been expropriated by the ruling class, and not shared by ordinary citizens, as the living standards of ordinary Chinese have grown far less than China's gross domestic product. "The share of Chinese GDP consumed by Chinese households fell by 15% between the late 1980s and the bottom in 2010. As of 2018, Chinese households still consume less than 40% of Chinese output – a lower ratio than in every other major economy in the world, by far."[148] The Chinese Communist Party has pursued a policy of growth that has favored the elite and in particular the owners and shareholders of export-driven businesses, at the expense of workers and the middle class. At the same time, untold millions have been lifted out of the abject rural poverty so endemic to China in the mid-twentieth century. There can be no reasonable doubt that the vast majority of Chinese people are substantially better off today.

A peculiarity of the modern Chinese economic system, somewhat like the Soviets in the mid-twentieth century, is that growth in GDP is an annual target set by the central economic planning committee. This is in contrast to how we think about measures of our economy in the United States and the West, where GDP is an output resulting from the actual bottoms-up performance of various sectors of the economy, including private consumption, business investment, and government spending, as a way of keeping score of how we're doing. In China, however, government officials determine and proclaim by decree that this year, growth will be X%. This mandated objective filters down into the various industrial segments of the economy and geographic regions of the country where the banks, corporations, local governments, and other entities then go about playing their part in fulfilling the mandated growth objective. As one would expect, and as University of Chicago economist FA von Hayak pointed out decades ago in *The Fatal Conceit*,[149] this kind of centralized, top-driven economic policy results in two gigantic systematic distortions.

The first is massive and wide-spread falsification of data and reported statistics in order to look good in front of the central authorities. This deception occasionally results in arrests, purges, and executions on charges of corruption and fraud, but usually as a ruse for taking out political enemies since it isn't the actual fudging of the numbers that is offensive to the CCP. For the CCP, it's policy.

The second distortion is exorbitant domestic spending on investment projects with no real benefit or use, corresponding underinvestment elsewhere, resulting from the mismatch of production and investment objectives with actual consumer demand. This distortion has led to the creation of the infamous ghost cities of China – massive developments without inhabitants –, highways to nowhere, and bank balance sheets bloated with bad loans that will never be repaid, but which carry an implicit guarantee from the Chinese government. As a result, these loans are never written off the way in the way they would be in the West. This perpetuates significant distortions in the Chinese domestic economy that eventually will have to be reconciled. There are only three possible ways to do this. The first is for the banks to recognize the losses, creating massive capital holes that the government would have to fill with fresh capital, much the way the US government had to do through the TARP and other programs in the 2008-09 financial crisis in America, but on an even more massive scale. The second is to allow the banks to go into default, bankruptcy, and ultimately liquidation. As neither of them is at all appealing to the Chinese Communist Party, we should expect that nothing will be done anytime soon and that these imbalances will continue to grow. The path actually chosen is to pretend the problem doesn't exist, and instead to make talking about the problem illegal, and subjecting to arrest those who do. These are the conveniences of a totalitarian state, but eventually, truth will out and there will have to be an accounting with reality. When it does, look out below!

The biggest tool that China has used to pursue its growth objective is through international trade and exports in particular. Trade accounts for approximately 40% of China's GDP compared with 28% in the United States. In many ways, China has more to lose in the deterioration of the trade relationship with the US than the US does. China's exports to the US grew to be over $500 billion by 2017, representing 20% of its exports. At the same time, the United States exported $130 billion to China, of which nearly 40% were services such as intellectual property and transportation, tourism, and other services, rather than tangible products. "The bottom line is that US exports to China amount to barely 1% of US GDP and 8% of total exports, while China's to the US amount to 4% of Chinese GDP and one-fifth of total exports."[150]

Like a co-dependent relationship, the two countries have come to depend on one another for economic growth and to achieve domestic political objectives, but this relationship has brought systemic distortions to each economy. These negative effects – 'externalities' in econ speak – will be discussed further below.

Externalization of Chinese economic power: the BRI & the new Scramble for Africa

The Silk Road is the ancient network of trading routes that connected China with the Middle East and Europe. It was the route through which paper and gunpowder came to Europe, and that Marco Polo traveled from Italy to China to visit the Mongolian emperor Kublai Khan in Xanadu in 1275. Established in the second century BC, it remained a primary trade route until the 15th century, when it fell into disuse as ocean-going travel increased in the Age of Exploration. The Silk Road and surrounding areas of Central Asia later became the setting for the 19th century 'Great Game' of geopolitical intrigue and conflict between the incumbent power, Great Britain, and the emerging challenger, Russia, as they vied for control of the region and in particular access to the wealth of India.

In 2013 Xi Jinping announced China's intention to rebuild the ancient Silk Road, connecting up to 70 countries in Asia, Europe, and North Africa, and reaching over four billion people through an initiative called One Belt, One Road. Officially known as the Silk Road Economic Belt and 21st-Century Maritime Silk Road Development Strategy, or in short, the BRI (Belt & Road Initiative), China's commitment to the BRI is estimated to be as high as $1.3 trillion towards development of a vast network of highways, railways airports and related infrastructure across much of Asia moving westward towards Europe. The Chinese sponsored Asian Infrastructure Investment Bank (AIIB) is expected to provide a substantial source of debt funding. BRI is a centerpiece of the Chinese Communist Party's foreign policy, which sees this as the primary tool through which to push back on the United States 'Pivot to Asia' announced under President Obama. The BRI is also a means for China to gain geopolitical control and economic power over a much wider sphere of influence beyond its borders in Eurasia. Specifically, China sees the BRI as an opportunity to press neighboring nations into accepting Chinese investment, project development, and ultimately, Chinese made products and services.[151] This has raised alarm bells in Washington and the capitals of Europe as concerns grow about China's increasing political, military, and economic power in the region. Graham Allison is more explicit about China's intention behind the BRI, which he argues "will allow China to project power across several continents. [BRI]'s promise to integrate the countries of Eurasia reflects a vision in which the balance of geostrategic power shifts to Asia."[152]

According to the Washington DC-based Institute of International Finance, China has lent over $730 billion to date to overseas investment and construction contracts in over 112 countries around the world. In addition to investing in projects in countries along the BRI routes, a significant portion of China's overseas investment has been deployed in Africa.

I have been actively involved in deploying capital in Africa for well over a decade through both nonprofit organizations and as CEO of a publicly-listed company focused on investing in high-quality businesses in Africa. One of the markers of the African investment landscape in the 21st century has been the ubiquitous presence of China across much of the continent in multifaceted roles. These roles have included as lender to governments and the commercial sector, as developer of critical infrastructure including transportation, energy, logistics, and telecommunications, as entrepreneur and as customer, especially in the context of extraction of natural resources for its domestic market. China is estimated to have made over $300 billion of investment in Africa to date since 2005.[153] There are an estimated 10,000 Chinese companies operating in Africa with over one million Chinese businessmen on the ground in African today.[154]

To be sure, much of this investment and development has been good for Africa and its people. However, it has also come with strings attached that extends beyond financial returns into a projection of power into regional affairs and in influence with governments. Much of Chinese investment in Africa has been made on purely nationalistic lines that do little to benefit the economies of these nations or to provide job opportunities and poverty upliftment for African workers and their communities. Rather the opposite effect occurs, which is exemplified in the way that Chinese imported products squeeze out domestic production and damage local industry. A common feature of Chinese investment in Africa has been to insist that Chinese labor be used for infrastructure projects that are funded by Chinese banks, meaning that it is not uncommon to see Chinese labor crews working on roadways or other projects in the urban or peri-urban areas of African countries where the local unemployment rate remains upwards of 50%.

China has been very focused on developing and maintaining dedicated supply lines of basic commodities for its home market. As such, Chinese contracts often come with clauses that provide for preferential treatment for export to China before supplying other nations or domestic markets. I experienced this firsthand in 2013 when we competed for an investment against other bidders backed by the government of China. We were interested in investing in a leading and publicly-listed agricultural company focused on increasing food security across Africa. We believed that the company had expertise in agricultural infrastructure that could be deployed more broadly across the continent to build up these countries' domestic food supply, reducing their reliance on import markets and thus alleviating the grave food insecurity that still plagues many nations in Africa.

While sub-Saharan Africa has more than 60% of the world's remaining arable land, which along with abundant rainfall and other conditions should allow for high productivity in agriculture and food production, logistics and infrastructure remain underdeveloped, posing challenges to distribution and storage. Many countries in sub-Saharan Africa still rely on imports for over 90% of their food supply. In our particular situation, the target company received alternative proposals at the same time as ours, including from a leading Chinese firm backed by the Chinese government. Ultimately our bid was to prevail, not because we were willing to pay substantially more than other parties (we weren't), but rather in part because the Chinese proposal insisted on a right of first refusal over the offtake from the more than eighty-grain silos the company owned across its markets in Africa. The Chinese bidder intended to be able to export as much as of the offtake of the silos as they might need to service the Chinese market. The South African government, in particular, recognized that this preferential right would put their country and the entire Southern region of Africa in a dangerously insecure position with regard to its food supply in periods of drought, pestilence, famine, or other stress. It was very clear to those involved in the situation that the Chinese were intent on strengthening food security for their own rapidly growing population, and were willing to do so at the expense of Africans. I believe that this situation illustrates a type of commercial arrangement that is not uncommon in Africa.

The other very common aspect of Chinese investment and business activity in Africa is the widespread use of bribes and payoffs to win contracts and facilitate business transactions. The United States, the United Kingdom, and the European Union each have very strict laws prohibiting the bribing of government officials and similar acts, which laws are actively enforced, including imposing harsh penalties on businesspeople who violate them. There is no similar enforcement of anti-bribery or anti-corruption laws in the Chinese context, but rather an implicitly understood expectation of how Chinese firms do business in Africa. China's motives for investment in Africa extend beyond economic benefit and guaranteeing the provision of critical commodities and other items to China. The role of China in Africa represents an illustration of the CCP's broader projection of political and military power and presence around the world.

China's focus on Africa represents a new era of colonialism similar to Europe's 'Scramble for Africa' in the 19th century. African leaders are aware of this, but face a daunting combination of carrots and sticks and limited viable alternatives. While France, in particular, has maintained an active interest in its former colonies in Africa, the US – never an African colonial power – has treated Africa as an afterthought from the end of the Cold War until recently. This outlook changed when the United States government seemed to wake up to the significance of what China was doing on the continent. As the geopolitical challenge came into a clearer view, the US increased its focus on Africa and sought to better engage on a level footing with China. This pivot included changing the name and mandate of the Overseas Private Investment Corporation (now rebranded the U.S. International Development Finance Corporation) to enable equity investment and other more flexible forms of investment and involvement in Africa and other emerging markets around the world to better compete with the state capitalism practiced by China in these regions.

Flexing the muscles: projection of Chinese military and political power

Alongside the remarkable economic growth described above, China has in parallel been working very aggressively to build up its military power and the ability to project it globally. China now has the largest Navy in the world, at least as measured by fleet strength if not firepower. Boasting of 350 ships in its 2020 fleet, up from 335 in 2019, China's navy is today about 55% larger than it was in 2005. Compared with a fleet of 293 ships for the United States, China has ambitions to further build its navy to over 500 ships, while the US ship count has been stagnant in recent years. According to the retired head of intelligence for the US Pacific Fleet, Captain Jack Fanell, "The biggest challenge for US national security leaders over the next 30 years is the speed and sustainability of [China's] national effort to deploy a global navy."[155] China now has between 25,000 and 35,000 marines, a significant increase from about 10,000 in 2017, according to US and Japanese estimates. One defense analyst recently explained the motive behind the build-up: "Ten years from now, China is almost certainly going to have marine units deployed at locations all over the world ... Beijing plans to send military units wherever its global strategic interests require."[156]

Since the 1970s, China has been on a path to regain territory in broader Asia, most intensely in the South China Sea. In 1974, China seized control of the Paracels Islands from Vietnam, and then took control of the Scarborough Shoal from the Philippines in 2012. China has effectively redrawn the map of the South China Sea and asserted exclusive ownership over what observers have called the 'South China Lake.' To strengthen and re-enforce its ownership claims, China has developed military outposts and other projects throughout the Spratly Islands and reclaimed more than 2900 acres of land. China has built airstrips, deep-water ports, installed radar and other surveillance equipment, and erected supporting facilities to enable China to expand the reach of its naval ships and military aircraft. Chinese and American naval forces regularly come into dangerously close proximity as they each assert their conflicting and, at least as their governments see it, mutually exclusive rights over the waterways of the South China Sea.

Perhaps most concerning are China's recent and aggressive moves towards Taiwan. Couched in the form of military drills, in early September 2020, nearly two dozen Chinese military aircraft and naval ships maneuvered in an area within Taiwan's air defense identification zone located between a Taiwan-controlled atoll and Taiwan's southwestern coast. The Taiwanese government called it a "severe provocation," saying they believed this was part of a broader Chinese plan operate freely in the area surrounding Taiwan going forward. A former senior Taiwanese military official said the move was "the most serious threat to Taiwan security since 1996" when China landed missiles in the waters surrounding Taiwan. China has long claimed Taiwan as part of its sovereignty and has threatened to use military force to control the country if Taipei refuses to submit.[157]

The ongoing China challenge

In many ways, the large challenges that are facing China today are mirrors of similar issues in the United States. China is enmeshed in a very large debt trap, where the role of government in supporting its banks and shadow banks places great strain on the government and the economy over the longer run. While government-sanctioned statistics show China's debt to GDP at 259%, a figure which is amongst the highest in the world and compared with a first-quarter ratio of 108% for the US,[158] according to the IIF China's actual ratio of debt to GDP had grown to 317% as of the first quarter of 2020.[159] Between 2005 and 2016, China accounted for almost half of all new credit created worldwide, which stood at a global total of $233 trillion in late 2017.[160] On the other side of the ledger, China is now the world's largest lender to low-income countries. In total, other countries now owe China $5.5 trillion, representing 6% of global GDP, up from $875 billion in 2004.[161] China and the United States now find themselves in a new arms race that drains resources from other parts of the economy.

Likely, one of the reasons the Trump administration has been focused on unwinding many of the multitudinous military commitments that have accumulated over the past several decades is a recognition of the high cost and limited benefit of sustaining a military presence in over 70 countries, including several of limited geostrategic purpose such as Afghanistan, Iraq, and Syria in which US troops have been engaged in conflicts and lost a large number of lives, without, I think it's fair to say, a tangible sense of victory or even evidence that the environments have sufficiently stabilized. This is not an indication of a lack of commitment to protecting American interests abroad, but rather a recognition of the need to concentrate the United States' national military resources on a much stronger and more formidable adversary.

Paul Kennedy, in his seminal work *The Rise and Fall of the Great Powers*, summarized the challenge and cost of maintaining the status of global hegemon this way:

> Wealth is usually needed to underpin military power, and military power is usually needed to acquire and protect wealth. If, however, too large a proportion of the state's resources is diverted from wealth creation and allocated instead to military purposes, then that is likely to lead to weakening of national power ... In the same way, if a state overextends itself strategically – by, say, the conquest of extensive territories or the waging of costly wars – it runs the risk that the potential benefits ... may be outweighed by the greatest expense of all – a dilemma which becomes acute if the nation concerned has entered a period of relative economic decline. The history of the rise and later fall of the leading [Great Power] countries ... currently the United States – shows a very significant correlation ... between productive and revenue raising capacities on the one hand and military strength on the other.[162]

In the course of the last 50 years, China has gone from being viewed primarily as a foil for US engagement with the Soviet Union to becoming an increasingly important trading partner and sometimes viewed as a competitor, to being primarily viewed as a competitor and now as an adversary of America. While it may not yet be correct to describe China as an enemy, China is certainly now the biggest strategic threat that America faces as a nation. The challenges that China presents spans across economic, military, and political fronts. Over the past several years, America and her leadership have been slowly waking up to this reality. There still seems to be a high degree of skepticism in certain quarters ... or ignorance around the issue, as to whether China poses a real threat to the US. Some suggest that new leadership should seek to restore the US to its position in a multi-polar world as it existed before MAGA and Trump's poking a sharp stick at the Chinese dragon. The complexity of the relationship with China, and why decoupling is so difficult, is exacerbated by the US corporate sector's now almost complete dependence on the trade relationship with China in order to maintain its growth and profitability, which has benefited from this relationship over several decades. That relationship has resulted in short-term gains for shareholders at the cost to American workers, and in the long term leaching away of our technological and scientific leadership. The disruption caused by the Trump administration's confrontation with China was a necessary albeit unpleasant consequence of the strong medicine needed to bring the patient back from the brink of economic sepsis.

While it should be obvious, I need to point out that the threat we face as a nation is not from Chinese-Americans or the Chinese as an ethnic group. Any suggestion otherwise is a misleading lie intended to imply racial bigotry and throw us off of the scent of the real issue. The challenge we face is not with China as a nation or the Chinese as a people, but with the current Chinese government which is indistinguishable from the CCP, which remains Marxist in ideology (with some modifications) and is actively seeking to supplant the US in scientific, technological, military and economic leadership, regularly using illegal and underhanded methods to do so.

To facilitate our short-term commercial interests, we turned a blind eye to the essentially totalitarian and evil nature of the Chinese Communist Party. We see examples of it in the treatment of the Uyghur minorities in Xinjiang province in the west, in the repression in Tibet, in the squelching of protests and any form of democratic movement within their own country, the harassment and imprisonment of Christians trying to worship in their own homes, the complete censorship of the press and media, both traditional and online formats including social media, the 'disappearing' of journalists and activists, and most recently in the repression and lockdown of Hong Kong, which represents a disavowal of the treaty China entered into with Great Britain undergirding the 1999 handover.

This same Chinese leadership is encouraging large distortions within their own economy that are benefiting the ruling elite to the detriment of their own people. In their recently published book *Trade Wars Are Class Wars*, Matthew C. Klein and Michael Pettis point out that the CCP's policies have placed enormous burdens on both the United States and China's own middle and lower classes, and unfortunately, some large American firms doing business with China Inc. have been complicit here (emphasis mine):

> The Chinese people are not the enemy. Rather, there is a conflict between economic classes within China that has spilled over into the United States. Systematic transfers of wealth from Chinese workers to Chinese elite distort the Chinese economy by strangling purchasing power and subsidizing production at the expense of consumption. That, in turn, distorts the global economy by creating lots of manufactured goods and by bidding up the prices of stocks,

bonds and real estate. Chinese underconsumption destroys jobs elsewhere, while inflated asset values lead to devastating cycles of booms, busts, and debt crises. Chinese policies do not just hurt Americans – they also harm ordinary Chinese workers and retirees … *Some combination of falling employment and rising indebtedness outside of China was the inevitable consequence. Americans have borne much of these costs thanks in part to the collusion of US business interests with Chinese politicians and industrialists.*[163]

Like the US, China will be faced with the thorny question of whether to use inflation and currency devaluation to reduce the real cost of its debt. Inflation statistics for China are even less reliable than for debt and GDP, but analysts generally believe that actual inflation runs several points higher than the official CPI estimates, which stood at 2.7% in July, driven by a 13% increase in food prices.[164] As the debt challenge grows larger, China will have a more difficult time keeping its currency stable. While the Chinese government strongly desires that the renminbi will become a global reserve currency, some of these economic issues and structural barriers will impede acceptance for transactions other than with the Chinese government itself. China also has very significant demographic issues to face over time, including a very large population that is aging more quickly than the population in the West.

What is Xi's vision for China? In the words of Graham Allison, "To make China great again." Allison boils this down to four objectives: returning China to the predominance it had in Asia before the West intruded; re-establishing control over the Greater China territories, including Xinjiang, Tibet, Hong Kong, and Taiwan; recovering its historic sphere of influence on its borders and sea lanes so that lesser powers give it the deference befitting a great power, and commanding the respect of other great powers. He goes on to describe the word view of senior

Chinese officials as of those who "recall a world in which China was dominant and other states related to them as supplicants to a superior, as vassals came to Beijing bearing tribute."[165]

Why did we tolerate the lopsided relationship with China for so long? Barbara Tuchman provides a framework for understanding our self-deception in her work *The March of Folly*, which chronicles how governments throughout history have regularly and repeatedly pursued policies contrary to the self-interest of the constituency or state involved. Looking as far back to the ancient Trojans, who foolishly took the wooden horse within their walls, to the Renaissance popes whose refusal to change brought about Protestant secession, to the British empire's loss of America as a result of an unwillingness to yield on small, initially inconsequential matters, through America's self-betrayal in Vietnam across four administrations each of which privately admitted the war to be unwinnable. Tuchman shows how nations continue to pursue self-defeating policies 1) even when those policies were known to be counter-productive in its own time (i.e. not merely by hindsight, 2) when a feasible alternative course of action was available, and 3) when 'wooden-headedness,' or self-deception plays a significant role in government. Wooden-headedness "consists in assessing a situation in terms of preconceived fixed notions while ignoring or rejecting any contrary signs. It is acting according to wish while not allowing oneself to be deflected by the facts ... Wooden-headedness is also the refusal to benefit from experience."[166] Is hard to imagine a more accurate description of the US's shortsighted and self-defeating engagement with China over three decades on such grossly unfavorable terms, which ultimately cost us so much in terms of loss of technology, intellectual property, and competitive position in the world.

6. The war by any other name

War between the US and China … is not just possible, it is
much more likely than currently recognized.[167]
– Graham Allison, *Destined for War*

"Winter is Coming" became a widely recognized phrase from the popular TV show Game of Thrones. It is also the appropriate title of an important if polemical and somewhat finger-wagging book by Garry Kasparov on Putin's rise to power and the West's ongoing complacency in the face of what Francis Fukayama called our "greatest foreign policy challenge." Written in 2015, Winter is Coming presented for the first time a roadmap outlining the diabolical nature of the Putin regime, detailing what actions and active measures had been taken to undermine Georgia and Ukraine, and pointing out the risks to Europe and the US going forward.

Winter is Coming should now also be a thematic phrase for America as we head into our national election season alongside a resurgence of the pandemic in our cities and economic hubs, surging unemployment, widespread social unrest, and a host of fundamental and largely ignored threats, such as the increase in state-sponsored cyber-attacks seen in 2020.

One of the great things about America and Americans is that we tend to take our entrepreneurial spirit, our optimism, and our faith in our institutions and ideals, including both democracy and capitalism, into our engagements with the rest of the world. On the whole, this is a good thing in that much of the American Dream, and our aspirations for life, for liberty, and for prosperity have been a bright and guiding light to many nations and millions of individuals around the world over the years. One of the downsides of our approach, however, is that we tend to assume that other nations and their leaderships look at the world the way we do. We assume that they share our outlook, dreams, and aspirations for a better world in accordance with the same principles of liberty, democracy, and free-market capitalism. We conveniently forget that many of the nations with which we are engaged do not share our values, do not share our ideals, and do not share our rules-based institutions. The mistake we make is to believe that governments around the world, whether it be China, Russia, Iran, or otherwise, look at the US the way we look at them, and we assume that they are as well-intended as we are. This is a fallacy and blindness that has kept the US from appreciating that these governments and their leaders often do not share our values, and it becomes especially apparent with regard to human rights.

While many of the former Communist nations have adopted a more Capitalist orientation, it is of a very different form and flavor than what we understand in the West. Labeled state capitalism, it is a mixing of certain market principles within the context of an authoritarian regime whose primary objective is to retain power and to accumulate wealth within the confines of that power structure and government regime. Ultimately, these nations see America not as a benign trading partner, with whom one can conduct business in such a way as to make both better off, but as a competitor in a zero-sum game, where one's win will only come at the other's loss and vice versa.

While the ruling party in China has retained the name Communist, its objectives are no longer purely Marxist ideologically. What matters to the leaders in China also includes traditional Chinese aspirations for regional and global economic, political, and military power, combined with a very materialistic drive for personal wealth that doesn't align with Maoism. Most large enterprises in China are not owned and controlled by institutional and individual investors the way they are in the West, but rather directly or indirectly by the Chinese government, and heavily influenced by the CCP. Through both legal (e.g. acquisitions) and illegal (e.g. espionage) means, China has been implementing a long-term plan to compete with and overtake US industry. They do this by taking advantage of our openness to foreign investment and strategic partnerships while keeping their own market tightly-controlled and closed off to US and other foreign ownership and control.

China is the foremost adversary, but other nations including Russia, Iran, Turkey, North Korea, and others are increasingly aligned and coordinating with China against US interests.

By mid-September 2020, there were over a dozen substantial flashpoints between the US and China,[168] including privacy concerns which have focused on TikTok and WeChat, immensely popular social media and financial services payment platforms respectively. These have come under criticism from the US as being potential backdoors for information security leaks in which the Chinese government can create behavioral profiles of Americans. At the same time, US platforms Facebook and Twitter have long been banned from the Chinese market. Disputes over Hong Kong-based on new national security laws that unwound many of the rights and privileges of the citizens of this special autonomous zone led the US to revoke Hong Kong's special trade status and place sanctions on several of its leaders. There have been diplomatic skirmishes around classic espionage, in which the US and China have begun to accuse the other's diplomats and representatives in a tit-for-tat game reminiscent of the Cold War, culminating in the US's closure of the Houston-based Chinese consulate in June 2020 on charges of systematic spying and stealing state secrets from the US government and private sector. Providers of critical IT and telecommunications infrastructure have been targeted, especially Huawei, which the US has not only banned but is trying to move its allies away from the use of the Chinese company's equipment for 5G networks on security concerns. Media companies generally are implicated on both sides, and each country has blocked or flagged the other's media outlets for censure. The US, UK, and European Union governments have each accused the CCP of inhumane treatment of the Muslim minorities in Xinjiang province, including the detention and imprisonment of over a million Uighurs and even occasional torture and murder, and in the Tibetian disputed autonomous region. The treatment of one another's citizens on foreign soil is worsening, with arrests, detentions, targeted sanctions, and travel blocks. Territorial claims and challenges, both in the South China Sea which have resulting in naval tensions and dangerous confrontations,[169] and the ongoing diplomatic and military feints associated with Taiwan. We have seen high-level accusations by senior officials in the US government of Chinese complicity in the coronavirus pandemic, and have discussed this issue in some detail. Tariff and trade wars, as described further below, have become one of the most critical issues facing the relationship between the countries today.

There should be no illusions here: the strategic objective of the Chinese government is to supplant the United States as the world's leading economic, military, and political power. As US Senator Ben Sasse wrote for *The Atlantic* in January of this year (emphasis mine),

China intends to reestablish its place, not as one political
power among others, but as the world's preeminent power. We
are witnessing the return of the Middle Kingdom. While the
Middle East remains a hotbed of violence and instability that
threatens American lives and interests, we cannot allow our
primary focus to move from the unique, long-term, and
existential threat that is Beijing. *This is the defining national-
security challenge of our age.*[170]

China will pursue this goal by any means possible, including by
seeking to destabilize and disadvantage the US economy, diminish,
degrade or disable its military presence and power, especially in Asia, to
discredit and denigrate it in diplomatic and political matters, and to
undermine it in domestic affairs. We have entered stage of the conflict in
which we can expect an escalation in this new cold war to include more
active measures previously viewed as off-limits, and we should expect that
China will solicit help from its allies of convenience, those countries like
Russia and Iran who share a mutual interest in the demise of the United
States and the liberal democratic ideal of the West, just as the Soviet Union
did during the Cold War through proxy nations such as Cuba and conflicts
in Central America, Southeast Asia or elsewhere. The following sections
explore some of those potential measures and the risks they pose to the US
and the West.

The trade war has been the first battleground

> "No one could deny that China had been a major, perhaps the biggest, beneficiary of globalization over the last 20 to 30 years, and yet this interpretation of China as the champion of globalization and free trade was naive, even rather sycophantic. … [Trump] is right to call China out on substantive issues such as China's import tariffs, inward investment rules and regulations, protection of local businesses and enterprises, and now straight state driven innovation strategies, all of which put foreign firms at a disadvantage."[171]
> – George Mangus, *Red Flags*

When President Trump came into office in January 2017, he began to implement a fundamental shift in the commercial relationship between the United States and China. For decades, the policy of US engagement with China on economic matters seemed best summarized as quieta non movere, essentially, "don't rock the boat." Upsetting the apple cart of thirty years of diplomatic, political, and economic appeasement of Chinese encroachment, Trump began a process of disruption and confrontation with the Chinese government based on his campaign promise of 'America First.' Led by Secretary of Commerce Wilber Ross, US Trade Representative Robert E. Lighthizer, and Peter Navarro, Assistant to the President, Director of Trade and Manufacturing Policy, each of whom has been in their respective roles since early 2017, the administration set out on a policy course under the America First banner that soon showed to not be just patriotic electioneering. While much media attention has been paid to executive office turnover in the Trump administration and to perceptions of incoherence in foreign policy, this core team of economic advisors, importantly along with Secretary of the Treasury Steven Mnuchin, have been with the administration since the beginning. This team formed the administration's core positions on trade and economic policy during the 2016 campaign, and their essential strategy toward reforming American trade policy has not changed. The application of this principle resulted in the US exiting or renegotiating key trade agreements, beginning with NAFTA in 2017 and then the repudiation of the Obama-era Trans-Pacific Partnership, among others.

Presidential candidates Trump and Biden each now seem to be going out of their way to establish who will be tougher on China.[172] In recent weeks, President Trump has escalated the trade war rhetoric to describe a "decoupling" of the US trade relationship with China, implying that American companies will bring jobs and manufacturing back to the US or find other supply chains outside of China. According to President Trump, "Whether it's decoupling, or putting in massive tariffs like I've been doing already, we will end our reliance on China, because we can't rely on China."[173] He has described Biden as a pawn of Beijing, ridiculing previous comments attributed to Biden that "The United States welcomes the emergence of a prosperous, integrated China on the global stage because we expect this is going to be a China that plays by the rules."[174] Not to be outdone, presidential candidate Joe Biden, using more Trump-like and less diplomatic language than in the past, called Xi Jinping a "thug" during a Democratic primary debate in February,[175] and has threatened to impose swift economic sanctions on China if needed to protect US interests. He wrote an essay in Foreign Affairs in early 2020, saying "The United States does need to get tough with China. If China has its way, it will keep robbing the United States and American companies of their technology and intellectual property. It will also keep using subsidies to give its state-owned enterprises an unfair advantage – and a leg up on dominating the technologies and industries of the future."[176]

So at least in words, both candidates are now acknowledging the existential threat posed by China, and the challenges that have floated to the top of the pile of issues the country is reflecting ongoing into the November elections. If indeed the United States' engagement with China is one of (if not the most) important strategic priorities for the country going forward, then the question of which candidate will be more effective in navigating the United States' foreign policy options, including economic, diplomatic, and military engagements with China, becomes the paramount question for voters coming into the November 2020 presidential elections, amidst several other urgent priorities around the pandemic and a vaccine, social unrest, and the domestic economy.

This process began what now appears to be a sea change not only in the United States but in Europe, Africa, and Southeast Asia, as other nations reconsider the economic terms of their engagements and relationship with China. To date, this has culminated in each of the United States[177] and the European Union[178] separately declaring within a few days of each other in September 2020 their intention to pursue a more independent path and to decouple their trade relationships with China. This was a massive policy shift which was both necessary and late in coming, and which was neglected by several presidential administrations prior to the current.

Practically speaking, it's going to be quite difficult for the United States to decouple from China. Since 2014, China has been the United States' largest trading partner, and that relationship is deep and very well-integrated. It will be very nearly impossible for the thousands of American companies operating in or sourcing goods from China to move operations or change existing supply chains without substantial cost and complexity. The reason that these trade relationships exist, and that so much of the industrial and consumer goods consumed in the US are manufactured or assembled in China, is because this has proven over many years to be the most cost-effective and efficient source of supply in a remarkable period of history in which companies were free to look all over the world to source their products. Should the 2021-24 administration be successful in forcing American companies to establish other supply chains, new relationships, and/or to re-onshore manufacturing back in the US, the consequence will certainly be higher prices, and the inflationary pressures described previously will increase significantly. The United States may take the view that this negative impact on prices may be worthwhile in order to support a higher level of employment and wages for American workers.

However, just because the trade relationship between China on the one hand, and the United States, the UK, the European Union or Japan on the other, are so deeply integrated and vast in scope, does not mean that they cannot be disrupted and unwound in a moment in a war-like crisis. Lest we forget, all of Europe went from somnambulant peace to a state of general war within five weeks of the assassination by Serbian nationalist Gavrilo Princip of Archduke Franz Ferdinand, the one leader who probably could have kept Austria-Hungary from declaring war on Serbia, thus setting the whole horrific chain of events in motion.[179] Keynes reminds us that, in 1914 on the eve of that Great War, Germany was as much or perhaps more greatly and tightly interconnected by trade and capital flows with its soon to be mortal enemies than we are with China today:

> The statistics of the economic interdependence of Germany and her neighbors are overwhelming. Germany was the best customer of Russia, Norway, Holland, Belgium, Switzerland, Italy, and Austria-Hungary; she was the second best customer

of Great Britain, Sweden, and Denmark; and the third best
customer of France. She was the largest source of supply to
Russia, Norway, Sweden, Denmark, Holland, Switzerland,
Italy, Austria-Hungary, Romania and Bulgaria, and the second
largest source of supply to Great Britain, Belgium, and France.
[Great Britain] sent more exports to Germany than to any
other country in the world except India, and bought more from
Germany than from any other country in the world except the
United States. There was no European country except those
west of Germany which did not do more than a quarter of their
total trade with her.[180]

This goes to the point that a disruptive decoupling and resulting

process of deglobalization, which seemed so completely unimaginable just

a year ago, is not beyond the realm of possibility as conditions continue to

deteriorate in the relationship between the US and China. Even though it

would not be in the rational economic interests of any of the countries, at

a certain stage other factors come into play: a potentially legitimate view

that the targeted country is being pushed out of its rightful place in the

global economy; the irrational, or at least questionable, human

psychological forces of perceived national prestige, the hubris or ego of

individual leaders; and underlying domestic political realities including

internal strife that needs externalization to generate domestic unity, even

if for a time. Author Margaret MacMillan, in *The War that Ended Peace*

describes this all too human element in the leaders careening recklessly

towards war in the summer of 1914:

Products of their backgrounds and times, with deeply
ingrained beliefs in prestige and honor (and such terms were
going to be used frequently in those hectic days), they based
their decisions on assumptions which they did not always
articulate, even to themselves. They were at the mercy of their
own memories of past triumphs and defeats, and of their hopes
and fears for the future.[181]

While nationalistic ideals of national prestige and honor, and the revenge occasionally required to satisfy them, doesn't seem to have much place in a vast portion of America in 2020, these are ideas that remain core to the unifying messages of the leadership of China, Iran, and Russia. The risk we face is that the process of globalization in which the world has been engaged since the beginning of the New World Order in 1945, could just as dramatically and rapidly put itself into reverse. Rather than simply rebalancing and finding a new equilibrium that addresses some of the inequities that have arisen with China, the entire structure could collapse in the face of accelerating hostilities. Much of what has taken over 70 years to be built could be undone in less than a year should the right combination of escalating crises and confrontations present themselves.

Whatever the reader might think of President Trump, whether as a person or as the leader of our nation, is almost irrelevant. There is one thing that is without dispute, and which probably matters more than almost everything else, and that is the fact that President Trump was the first Western leader to pull the facade off of the Potemkin village of our relationship with China. Gone now are the placards of smiling faces and waving hands, the propaganda that belied the underlying realities of the geostrategic competition in which we have been engaged with China since its opening to the West in the 1970s. Previous administrations, both Republican and Democrat, failed to do this timeously and as such did their nation a great if unintentional disservice. Our nation's leaders, both in the public and private sectors, allowed trillions of dollars of critical intellectual property and technology slip through our hands and into the minds, coffers, and toolbox of the Chinese Communist Party. That the CCP undertook this heist through appendages made to look like Western corporations that we would recognize should not have fooled us. But perhaps it didn't really fool us. Rather it was our greed, both as corporations for short-term profits and as consumers for cheap plastic goods providing the illusion of abundance, that blinded us to the reality. No longer.

The trade wars have been the visible, active, and tangible aspect of America's confrontation with China. As we observe the increasing number of flashpoints of engagement, whether economic, militarily, or otherwise, and consider the risks for the US, there are some other aspects of potential conflict that should be considered.

The biological threat has already manifest

A biological attack, which is the intentional release of a biotoxin or pathogen used against humans, domestic animals, or plants, is a particular threat that has received renewed focus with the introduction of SARS-CoV-2. For an attack against humans, they are several pathways through which a biotoxin or pathogen might be introduced, including aerosol dissemination, contamination of food or water sources, or by human or animal carriers including insects, or physical distribution such as we've seen in attempts to send poisonous substances through the mail to the White House.

The power of biological agents to bring our country to its knees has been warned about for years by experts, and largely ignored by government and society – until now. The advent of SARS-CoV-2 has raised substantial awareness among the general population about the biological threat that bio-toxins or pathogens pose. We have previously discussed the question as to whether the Chinese or other government actors created, modified, or intentionally spread SARS-CoV-2 for nefarious purposes, but regardless, the case has been proven to anyone who might have been curious – the US is vulnerable to biological attack.

It should now be plain to all Americans that our country is open, fragile, divided, and hurting, and thus in real eventual danger of an intentional, coordinated, and even more deadly biological attack. There is a material risk that COVID-19 will prove to be but a trailer to a full-length horror movie yet to come. If nothing else, the pandemic has proven to our enemies, whether state actors or other non-state aggressors, terrorists, and jihadi just how effective biological warfare can be to disable a nation's economy and undermine its society. This is especially true if, like in the case of COVID-19, a perpetrator can't be found.

The Russian government, led by President Putin, has been actively using biological weapons against its perceived enemies and political opponents for several years. Most recently Russian opposition leader Aleksandr Navalny was poisoned while on a campaign trip in Siberia. Russia continues to deny that it used poison against Navalny, but the evidence provided to the German investigative authorities is overwhelmingly clear. Navalny was poisoned by a nerve agent called Novichok, a compound developed by the Soviet Union as part of a secret chemical weapons program and known to be used by the Russian security forces today. Poisonings have become a characteristic feature of the Putin regime. In Ukraine in 2004, opposition leader and presidential candidate Viktor Yushchenko was poisoned with dioxin, leaving him disfigured. Later that year, investigative journalist Anna Politkovskaya fell suddenly ill and lost consciousness after drinking a cup of tea while flying to the Russian city of Beslan during the school siege there. She survived but was shot dead two years later, on Putin's birthday, a symbolic gesture to ensure that the significance of the message would not be missed. In 2006, Alexander Litvinenko, a former officer from Russia's FSB security service turned critic, died after being exposed to polonium-210, a radioactive isotope slipped into his tea at an upscale hotel in London. A UK public inquiry concluded that Putin had likely personally ordered the assassination. Another former Russian intelligence officer was nearly fatally poisoned In 2018 in the English town of Salisbury.[182] The poison was identified by British investigators as Novichok, the same nerve agent used on Navalny. A pattern emerges. In places where Russia is fighting proxy wars, it does not always have to resort to poisoning and other biological weapons. Sometimes it uses good old-fashioned intimidation and coercion by security apparatus, such as recently when masked security forces loyal to autocratic president Alexander Lukashenko detained Maxim Nzak, one of the leading opposition figures in Belarus, kidnapping him from his office in broad daylight in September 2020.[183]

The financial system threat may be next

Like the plumbing behind the walls of our homes, we often lose sight of the importance of the basic infrastructure that enables our global economy to work. The US is in imminent danger of being undermined in global financial markets through the loss of control of the basic infrastructure of global funds flow. The Russians and Chinese are working together, along with at least India, Iran, and Turkey, to create an alternative for SWIFT,[184] the international money transfer network over which secure messages related to more than half of high-value cross-border transactions occur. SWIFT has become a sore spot for our national competitors, as the US government routinely monitors transactions over the network and has used SWIFT as a tool for threatening and enforcing sanctions against Russia, Iran, and others by cutting off their banks from the network, imperiling their import and export markets. Most US dollar transactions utilizing SWIFT are routed through US banks, which enables the US government to seize payments – even between banks and parties completely outside of the US. Finding an alternative is a top priority for the participating governments. There are a large number of private companies that have received funding, including from China and Russia, to create alternative multi-currency cross-border transaction mechanisms that avoid the US nexus of banking relationships. The risk is not being taken seriously enough by the United States.

Whoever controls the flow of traffic, whether on rivers, sea lanes, telecom towers, over the internet, or through financial networks, has the power to exclude an individual, a group, a company, or a nation, or at least hold them up for ransom. The Chinese, Iranians, and the Russians understand this full well from over a century of dealing with the British Empire. As Philip Zelikow et.al. recently put it, "they seem to appreciate how the empire's power did not rely solely on soldiers or warships; it came, rather, from the empire's control of ports, canals, railroads, mines, shipping routes, telegraph cables, commercial standards, and financial exchanges."[185] The US wields this power today, but it is slipping away through both our own neglect and the active measures of others.

The Asian Infrastructure Investment Bank (AIIB) was specifically sponsored and established by China in 2016 as a means to create an alternative to the World Bank and other development finance institutions nurtured under US leadership. Launched with nearly $100 billion in subscribed capital,[186] 87 countries signed on despite vigorous attempts by the US to discourage participation amongst its allies. One of the US's primary concerns was that China would use the AIIB as a tool for engagement with and funding of totalitarian countries where human rights are ignored, and whose governments or leaders would not pass the anti-corruption, anti-money laundering, or other governance standards required by the World Bank or other western institutions. Additionally, the US has been concerned that China would use the AIIB as a tool of influence in recipient nations, on conditions that were more political or military than financial in nature. By accepting loans and other financial assistance, China would expect that these nations would accept, or at least ignore, China's rapid military build-up and expanding presence in the region. A good example of this is India, which has been the largest recipient of AIIB funding, with fourteen projects approved through January 2020, over twice as many the next most often funded country, and nearly 25% of the total number of approved projects.[187] At the same time, India has been a vocal opponent and boycotter of China's Belt and Road Initiative,[188] and Chinese and Indian troops are engaged in hand to hand melee and skirmishes over disputed boundary lines in the Himalayas.

The financial system in the US faces specific risks from cyber-attacks, a broader topic which we address in more detail in the next chapter. However, within the framework of our financial institutions' infrastructure, there are at least four categories of typical risk. The first is a single point of failure attacks, where breaches of trading platforms, depositories, payment and settlement systems can have significant consequences for the financial institutions and their customers, with the risk of losing both money and sensitive confidential information. Secondly, a very common means of attack which has plagued both financial institutions and corporates has been distributed denial of service attacks, i.e. attempts to overwhelm the network with tens of millions of rapid-fire data requests. These kinds of attacks have happened to most of the large banks in the US, including in 2012 when several were attacked simultaneously, including Bank of America, Wells Fargo, JP Morgan, Capital One, and others. The SWIFT system described above has increasingly come under attack in recent years by hackers trying to break into the system to divert flows of funds. Unfortunately, some of these attacks have been successful, giving fuel to the argument that an alternative infrastructure and system is needed. Finally, as new security technologies emerge, those novelties actually create new risks from hacking, at least until those technologies are tested, vetted, and probed over a longer period of time.[189]

The critical infrastructure threat

The pandemic has revealed that our food and medical supply chains are inherently fragile. Decades of progress in the efficiencies and cost savings of just-in-time inventory have left the US vulnerable to both foreign powers and to the vagaries of nature. Global famine, a scourge from what seems like the ancient past, may again become a real threat as climate change and extreme weather patterns become more severe. This is not even on the radar of most policymakers as a serious threat, and – just as in the recent pandemic – we are woefully unprepared should it occur.

Further, the past six months have made clear that we are deeply dependent on our high-speed internet and mobile communications networks to function remotely. Our government and private sector servers and network infrastructure – including those that control our energy, water, power, and telecoms utilities – are particularly vulnerable to systemic attack. There have been dozens of confirmed significant cyber-attacks against key US resources and its allies by state actors in recent months, a shocking pattern largely ignored by mainstream media.

In the high-profile case of Huawei, the CCP controlled company has already been charged with multiple counts including espionage, theft of trade secrets, fraud, and obstruction of justice. In January 2019, the US Department of Justice laid out 23 criminal charges against Huawei, centered primarily around the theft of intellectual property and violation of sanctions of export of controlled items to North Korea and Iran. In 2017, a jury found Huawei liable for stealing robotic technology from T-Mobile. In addition to questions of theft of intellectual property in violation of sanctions, the bigger prevailing issue with Huawei today is whether its 5G technology provides the Chinese government with a backdoor of information gathering and surveillance over the data networks of the company.

In addition to the threat posed by mobile telephony, the electrical grid is of equal or greater concern. The electrical grid in the United States is of particular risk due to its age, scope, and heterogeneous complexity. In North America, there are three grid systems: one for the East, one for the West (including western Canada and a part of Mexico), and one for Texas (presumably keeping their independence options open).[190] As of five years ago "more than 70% of the grid's transmission lines and transformers are 25 years old; add nine years to that and you have the average age of an American power plant."[191] The numbers have only gotten worse since. Today, the average age in the US of a gas steam turbine is 50 years, a coal plant is 40 years, and a combined cycle gas plant is 14 years. Notwithstanding the progress renewables have made, and the hype surrounding the greening of the grid, we still rely on coal and gas for nearly two-thirds of our power, and an additional 20% comes from nuclear, which plants are on average 37 years old.[192] A study by the Congressional Research Service reported that the US has the highest number of blackout minutes per customer per year of any of nine developed nations. The next worse country, Spain, had less than half of the US number.[193] These interruptions cost Americans $150 billion per year on average, and one singular event, the 2003 Northeast Blackout, resulted in an estimated $6 billion economic loss for the region.[194]

Gretchen Bakke, in her 2016 book *The Grid*, tells the story of how that one event, the 2003 Northeast Blackout, which was "the largest blackout in our nation's history, and the third-largest ever in the world, swept across the eastern half of the United States and parts of Canada, blacking out eight states and 50 million people for two days."[195] Bakke relates the fascinating backstory of how, like the kingdom lost for want of a horseshoe nail,[iii] this epic disaster was triggered by a single tree that had been allowed to grow to 50 feet.

This is an unacceptable height around power lines and one that represented about a decade of not being adequately trimmed back by the privately-owned utility responsible for the lines. It turns out this is a very common issue, and that trees, not terrorists, are the greatest daily threat to

---

[iii] For want of a nail the shoe was lost.
For want of a shoe the horse was lost.
For want of a horse the rider was lost.
For want of a rider the battle was lost.
For want of a battle the kingdom was lost.
And all for the want of a horseshoe nail.
– Anon

the grid. What made this situation unique and near-catastrophic was what happened next. As fate would have it, there wasn't only one tree that got in the way of civilization's progress that steamy August afternoon, but three trees located across Ohio, each of which within a matter of seconds had brought lines down. This commenced a ripple effect that began to cause outage after outage, and within a few minutes, four high voltage lines were lost. That, in turn, began a domino-like effect of self-preservation and shutting down of other points along the system as circuit breakers began to trip and the entire system became unbalanced. This created a wobble across the system, as certain other areas were immediately drawn upon for additional electricity that was essentially sucked out of neighboring regions. This escalation wasn't helped by the fact that at this time there were two regional generating plants that were down for maintenance.

At some point within the first quarter-hour, over twenty-five high and medium voltage lines were down before the utility control room began to notice or react at all. A later investigation concluded that this wasn't due to an operator's untimely coffee break or other negligence, but rather a software bug that had the effect of both failing to refresh the control room's computer screens as well as silencing its alarms. So just like the falling of trees, this part of the breakdown wasn't caused by terrorist cyber-attack, malware, or virus, but rather by a few lines of badly written code hidden away and unobserved for years. The operators "were blind to the blackout that was coming. And because they didn't see it neither did anyone else."

Keep in mind that all this is happening in a matter of minutes, as the current, traveling near the speed of light, courses through and now around the now disabled portions of the grid. So soon we've got a real problem on our hands. The still localized issue began to expand into a regional imbalance of electricity, wherein some sections it appeared there wasn't enough current to meet demand, and in others too much, a rapid-fire wobbling confusion that resulted in operators in Albany and quickly then other parts of New York, Pennsylvania, Michigan, Ontario and other states beginning to defend against what was happening in the system. Running out of options, and time, and rapidly becoming overwhelmed, they begin isolating themselves from what was going on in Ohio. This created a system of surpluses and deficits that led to significant imbalances that were extremely dangerous and impossible to control or manage. From there the blackouts begin. The author will soon walk down 62 flights of darkened stairs from the top of 30 Rockefeller Center into the hot and muggy midtown Manhattan afternoon. Nothing would move again, including several of the nation's busiest airports, for nearly three days.

What commenced in an instant and occurred over a matter of minutes, took days to restore and years to understand. Each of these small starting points – apparently insignificant glitches in vastly complex networks –, an overgrown tree, some poorly written software, ultimately cascaded into a systemic crisis that took down the grid for a substantial portion of America for days. This is, of course, a cautionary tale, not only of the ongoing fragility of our electrical grid, but of the nature of black swan events themselves, however small and innocuous their origins may be, and just how quickly they can cascade and how potentially catastrophic their effects.

An EMP attack may be how the escalation manifests

Electromagnetic Pulse ("EMP") attacks intended to disable our critical electrical and communications infrastructure poses one of the most plausible risks in the cold war dynamics already in existence as we consider more imaginative speculations of what a "warm" war might look like. A possible scenario of disruption includes the possibility of a low-grade, non-nuclear electromagnetic pulse ("EMP") attack.

Electromagnetic pulses are disturbances (a lightning strike is an example in the natural world) that can damage, destroy and/or disable, sometimes permanently, electronics equipment including computers, phones, power grids, generators, appliances, vehicles, and aircraft. In other words, everything that we use on a daily basis that distinguishes our existence from our ancestors in the Middle Ages. Disruption of our electrical, telecommunications, and computer networks would be a powerful offensive tool to effectively disable our economy.

The US government has recently increased its focus on the risk posed by an EMP attack and has devoted additional resources towards 'hardening' both public and critical private sector communications infrastructure. Specifically, in March 2019, President Trump signed an executive order entitled Coordinating National Resilience to Electromagnetic Pulses, which establishes resilience and security standards for US critical infrastructure as a national priority initiative.[196] A follow-on report in June 2020 authored by Dr. Peter Vincent Pry, the Executive Director of the EMP Task Force on National and Homeland Security, opens with the following statement, worth quoting in full (emphasis mine):

China has long known about nuclear high-altitude electromagnetic pulse (HEMP) and invested in protecting military forces and critical infrastructures from HEMP and other nuclear weapon effects during the Cold War, and continuing today. China has HEMP simulators and defensive and offensive programs that are almost certainly more robust than any in the United States. China's military doctrine regards nuclear HEMP attack as an extension of information or cyber warfare and deserving highest priority as the most likely kind of future warfare ... Chinese military writings are replete with references to making HEMP attacks against the United States as a means of prevailing in war ... China's military doctrine closely associates cyber-attacks with nuclear HEMP attacks, as part of a combined operation in what they call Total Information Warfare.[197]

Short of nuclear HEMP, smaller-scale EMP events can be created by non-nuclear technologies such as High Power Microwave (HPM) with batteries or chemicals which have been known to be in possession in weaponized form by China, Iran, and terrorist nations for over a decade.[198] The very real risk we face is that the efforts of the US government to more systematically address the issue over the past two years have come too little or too late to prevent wide-scale damage from such an attack. If such an attack came on November 3rd, or January 20th, our defensive shields may yet not be ready.

Unlike information warfare and cyber-attacks, an EMP attack would move the nations very quickly from cold war engagement to something much hotter, and governments would surely calculate that risk before acting. However, I do not believe that it can be ruled out as a possibility. Therefore, swift and urgent attention has to be paid, not only by our government but by the private sector (and individual citizens as well) to ensure that proper defenses are in place and risk and recovery scenarios are well-understood.

Today, North Korea already has the capability to launch a HEMP attack against the US today with its existing missile or satellite capabilities. According to Pry, who considers North Korea an existential threat, says that the rogue state is testing a new generation of advanced short-range missiles ... that fly on a flattened "hypersonic" trajectory that could defeat US THAAD missile defenses based in South Korea ... Pyongyang, Beijing and Moscow hope that nuclear-armed North Korea will undermine the credibility and upset the whole strategic calculus of US security guarantees to Pacific allies—and eventually make the US retreat from the region."[199]

An EMP attack represents a particular kind of threat that we face as a nation, but it speaks to means, not to the desired ends. The purpose of such an attack would be to disrupt our electrical and communications grid, the consequences of which would be the loss of power across a wide region or even nationwide. While an intentional EMP attack is one form of threat to the grid, there are other more mundane and naturally caused events that could wreck similar damage. These potential threats include natural disasters such as massive electrical storms, hurricanes, wildfires, and earthquakes, each of which we are seeing an increasing incidence of in recent years or a coronal mass ejection which is essentially a giant burst of energy in the form of plasma from our own sun.

The topic of the EMP threat speaks to a broader issue of the vulnerability of our critical infrastructure and the risk it poses to our economy and society. Our electrical infrastructure is a highly complex system that we have come to depend on for every single aspect of our lives. It is the very air of life inspired by the modern world. Even though there is by some estimates a 70% to 90% probability of a regional or nationwide blackout at some point in the next few years, very little attention is paid to it by government other than a few experts, and I'm fairly certain that it rarely enters the mind of the vast majority of the American people.

In a 2013 report entitled Solar Storm Risk to the North American Electric Grid,[200] the catastrophic risk insurer Lloyd's of London summarized the issue as follows:

- A Carrington-level[iv] extreme geomagnetic storm is almost inevitable in the future.
- The risk of intense geomagnetic storms is elevated as we approach the peak of the current solar cycle.
- As the North American electric infrastructure ages and we become more and more dependent on electricity, the risk of a catastrophic outage increases with each peak of the solar cycle.
- Weighted by population, the highest risk of storm-induced power outages in the US is along the Atlantic corridor between Washington D.C. and New York City. Other high-risk regions are the Midwest states, such as Michigan and Wisconsin, and regions along the Gulf Coast.
- The total US population at risk of extended power outage from a Carrington-level storm is between 20-40 million, with durations of 16 days to 1-2 years. The total economic cost for such a scenario is estimated at $0.6-$2.6 trillion.
- Storms weaker than Carrington-level could result in a small number of damaged transformers (around 10-20), but the potential damage to densely populated regions along the Atlantic coast is significant.

Only just last year, in a 2019 article written in Energy, Sustainability and Society entitled *An Assessment of Threats to the American Power Grid*, authors Weiss and Weiss noted among other things that high voltage transformers remain the weak link in the grid. There are

---

[iv] The September 1859 geomagnetic storm (also known as the Carrington Event) was a powerful geomagnetic storm during solar cycle 10 (1855–1867). ... A solar storm of this magnitude occurring today would cause widespread electrical disruptions, blackouts and damage due to extended outages of the electrical grid.

30 of them are "critical," the loss of nine of which in certain combinations could cripple the grid nationwide. If they were custom-built domestically, they could be replaced within 12-24 months "under benign, low demand conditions." However, since the US had offshored most of its manufacturing capabilities, there is a risk that delivery from overseas could take up to three years. The authors went on to assert that as of the time of their writing there had been no effective hardening of the grid. [201]

While a sustained power outage and lack of electricity would wreak great havoc across several aspects of our lives, from transportation to communication to health care and otherwise, one of the direst and immediate effects would be the impact on food security.

Large cities would fare the worst. At the beginning of the 20th century, only 10.2 million, or 38.6%, of Americans lived in urban areas,[202] while the majority still lived on farms or rural areas. By 2019, 270.7 million, or 82%, of Americans live in cities and only 47.3 million, or 17.5%, live in rural areas.[203] In good times, the modern-day benefits of large cities are enormous, and the quality of life, unlike anything that we have seen in all recorded human history. With the power out over a sustained period, urban-dwellers immediately become the most vulnerable and far worse off than their rural cousins. This is in part because under these circumstances we should expect a collapse of the water delivery and purification infrastructure in most of our large cities. Cholera outbreaks would occur and similar water-borne illnesses would follow. While primary food production would continue, and while those who live on or around farms and in rural areas would manage to find access, those hundreds of millions of people who live in large cities far away from the source of food production would be challenged severely by the inability to access food and to maintain refrigeration at warehouses and other distribution points as food stock travels over highly sophisticated, modernized, and centralized distribution networks from farm to table. Even for non-refrigerated items, trucks would not be able to take on fuel without the electricity to pump it. This is perhaps the most critical aspect of the threat to our power supply, in that it would mortally affect such a broad swath of our population. Our nation is very heavily urbanized and relies on efficient, just-in-time food supply to restock our local Whole Foods, Wal-Mart, or Krogers several times a week. In the absence of electricity, and thus refrigeration and fuel, the entire system will break down in a matter of days. People (who would already be sick from dirty water) will start to starve in many weeks. And when that happens, we will see riots and violence on our cities' streets on a scale like nothing this country has witnessed since its founding. Sub- and peri-urban areas will not be any safer, as marauding mobs move through them en masse towards rural farming areas, as was seen in Weimar Germany at the depth of the hyperinflation.

While we've just taken significant time to describe how an EMP event that disables our electrical grid, telecommunications systems or otherwise is possible from naturally occurring phenomena, be forewarned that if such an event occurs in the next few months in any proximity to our national elections and inauguration day, it was almost certainly not a cosmic coincidence of bad timing. If something happens during this timeframe it will not have been because of a solar burp or a misplaced asteroid, but because one of our nation's enemies found a way to slip through our half-ready defenses and intentionally set off a weapon of war to destabilize our country and destroy our economy.

7: Total information warfare

Man's ingenuity often overcomes geological handicaps: he can
irrigate deserts and air conditioned the Sahara; he can level or
surmount mountains and terrace the hills with vines; he can
build a floating city to cross the ocean, or gigantic birds to
navigate the sky. But a tornado can ruin in an hour the city
that took a century to build; an iceberg can overturn or bisect
the floating palace and send a thousand merrymakers gurgling
to the Great Certainty.[204]
– Will & Ariel Durant, *The Meaning of History*

A national emergency

As the reader is aware, on May 15th, 2019 the President of the
United States declared a national emergency. Remember?

If you are like me, you don't recall there being a national
emergency in the months before COVID-19, and you certainly don't
remember what the emergency was if one had been declared. You are not
alone, as the media really didn't talk about it that much at the time, and it
did not capture the public's attention in the way that the pandemic has as a
clear and present danger. In fact, the top news stories, tweets and social
media chatter of that day[205] were about Alabama's passage into law of a
bill limiting almost all abortions,[206] two-time Presidential candidate Bernie
Sanders tweeting in response that abortion is a constitutional right[207] (I'm
going to have to look that one up), the usual sparring amongst political
parties and between Congress and the administration,[208] and a Rick and
Morty animated clip.[209] However, the formalized declaration of a national
emergency resulted from a conclusion reached by the administration that:

"foreign adversaries are increasingly creating and exploiting
vulnerabilities in information and communications technology
and services, which store and communicate vast amounts of
sensitive information, facilitate the digital economy, and
support critical infrastructure and vital emergency services, in
order to commit malicious cyber-enabled actions, including
economic and industrial espionage against the United States
and its people."

In the view of the Administration, the risk posed "potentially catastrophic effects, and thereby constitutes an unusual and extraordinary threat to the national security, foreign policy, and economy of the United States."[210] The executive order which accompanied this declaration explicitly prohibited certain types of transactions such as

"the acquisition, importation, transfer, or use of any
information and communications technology where the
transaction involves any foreign country and poses an undue
risk of sabotage to, or subversion of, information and
communications technology … [or] poses an undue risk of
catastrophic effects on the security or resiliency of United
States critical infrastructure or the digital economy of the
United States."[211]

Finding this Act to be insufficient, in August 2020 the President specifically called out China as the intended target of the 2019 Order: "The spread … of mobile applications developed and owned by companies in the People's Republic of China continues to threaten the national security, foreign policy and economy of the United States," and, in what was a head-scratcher for many, addressed one mobile application in particular – TikTok – that many adults may only have been aware of if they had preteen or teenage children. The effect of this order was to put TikTok on a 45-day ticking clock to find a new home – an owner that would not be as offensive to the American government as were the current Chinese owners. This caught the world's attention amidst a din of criticism and misunderstandings of the issues at play.

The most prevalent form of cold war in which we are already engaged with countries around the world is information warfare. There are at least three branches of information warfare that comprise the suite of active measures that the enemies of the US can be expected to deploy: (dis)information campaigns, intended to sow division and discord within and between citizens and the US government; cyber-attacks, including online espionage (for data collection or data theft) and sabotage; and other active measures focused on telecommunications, information and utility infrastructure.

With regard to China, United States National Security Advisor Robert C. O'Brien, in a recent speech on China's ideology and global ambitions, referenced John Garnaut, author of *Engineers of the Soul: Ideology in Xi Jinping's China*, who expressed it this way:

> "In Classical Chinese statecraft," Garnaut has noted, "there are two tools for gaining and maintaining control over 'the mountains and the rivers': the first is wu (武), weapons and violence, and the second is wen (文), language and culture. Chinese leaders have always believed that power derives from controlling both the physical battlefield and the cultural domain." "For Lenin, Stalin, Mao and Xi," Garnaut writes, "words are not vehicles of reason and persuasion. They are bullets. Words are for defining, isolating, and destroying opponents."[212]

(dis)Information campaigns

In an article I wrote in June 2020 warning about the threat of foreign interference in our domestic social unrest and political process, a key message was that we should expect foreign actors to interfere as we head into the November elections. This was not a particularly outlandish prediction given what we now know about Russia's interference in the 2016 presidential elections.

The Select Committee on Intelligence of the US Senate, in Volume 2 of its report *Russian Active Measures, Campaigns and Interference in the 2016 US Election*, came to a definitive conclusion that "Russian operatives associated with the St. Petersburg-based Internet Research Agency ("IRA") used social media to conduct an information warfare campaign designed to spread disinformation and societal division in the United States." What was the objective of this campaign, which the Committee determined was sponsored by the Kremlin itself? "… to polarize Americans on the basis of societal, ideological, and racial differences, provoke real-world events, and … [provide] covert support of Russia's favored candidate in the US presidential election." Some of the findings of the report are worth quoting in detail (emphasis mine):

> … Russia's targeting of the 2016 US presidential election was part of a *broader, sophisticated, and ongoing information warfare campaign designed to sow discord in American politics and society.* Moreover, the IRA conducted a vastly more complex and strategic assault on the United States than was initially understood. The IRA's actions in 2016 represent only the latest installment in an increasingly brazen interference by the Kremlin on the citizens and democratic institutions of the United States.

> ... while the Russian information warfare campaign exploited the context of the election ..., the preponderance of the operational *focus, ... was on socially divisive issues-such as race, immigration, and Second Amendment rights-in an attempt to pit Americans against one another and against their government. ...* IRA influence operatives *consistently used hot-button, societal divisions in the United States as fodder ... to stoke anger, provoke outrage and protest, push Americans further away from one another, and foment distrust in government institutions.* The divisive 2016 US presidential election was just an additional feature of a much more expansive, target-rich landscape of potential ideological and societal sensitivities. [213]

While then-presidential candidate Hillary Clinton was the main target of the attacks, the committee found that the IRA also targeted Republican candidates including Senators Ted Cruz and Marco Rubio, as well as Jeb Bush, and, in terms of audience, "no single group of Americans was targeted by IRA information operatives more than African-Americans." It should by now be apparent that the Russians were exploiting the very real wounds and grievances of African-Americans to create division, sow chaos and foment anger. Blacks in America are being targeted and used by foreign actors which are preying on the legitimately felt and unhealed wounds of racism.

Volume 2 of the Senate Committee's report focused on social media, but the fifth and final volume of the Senate Committee's report, only recently published in August 2020 looks at many aspects of the counterintelligence threat posed by Russian influence operations. [214] This gives a roadmap of the tactics and tricks used at the time, and the threat posed to the US going into November 2020. We can only hope that it also provides our intelligence community and the large social media platforms such as Facebook and Twitter with a comprehensive view and tools that will translate to better defense going forward. Although we can be sure that the vector of attack will change, the motives and objectives are now more apparent.

In September 2020, Microsoft reported that an internal investigation had confirmed that "Russian, Chinese and Iranian hackers have stepped up efforts to disrupt the US election by targeting the campaigns of President Donald Trump and Democratic nominee Joe Biden." Microsoft reported that over 200 organizations tied to the US election have been targeted, noting that "multiple cyber-attacks have been aimed at political parties, advocacy groups, academics and leaders in the international affairs community."[215]

But beyond deploying trolls and bots with leak and hack campaigns on social media, how else might an unfriendly state interfere in our domestic political processes? If one were an enemy actor, where would one apply one's efforts? A clever subversive power noticing our social unrest and community protests would send agitators (in person and through online influence) in equal measure to both the extreme Right and extreme Left. Unlike the Cold War era of the 1960s, which pitted the ideological forces of Communism and Totalitarianism (represented by the USSR and its proxies) against Democracy and Capitalism (represented by the United States and encapsulated all over the free world in the ideal of the American dream), today there appears to be no overarching ideological agenda, but rather the simple and singular objective of the subversion of the United States and its leadership in economic, political, and military realms in the world today. Neither is there only one singular power which along with its proxies would be interested in such an outcome, but rather several: China (as first amongst its confederation), Iran and Russia to name a few, who depending on the agenda may act independently or in concert to further their joint and several goals. The chaos and mayhem created by the social unrest within the US provide fertile soil for the seeds of discord, division, distrust, and escalating violence, and the presidential elections provide an attractive target to focus foreign actors' efforts around a specific date and event.

In the 1960s, the protest movement was broadly aligned around two specific yet interrelated issues: opposition to the Vietnam War and civil rights. Over time, the view of mainstream elements of American society shifted on both of these issues as the latest technology (television) was able to bring the realities of these situations into the living room of American families for the first time in history. Why this was successful in influencing and ultimately changing the views of millions of Americans was that there still existed some degree of trust that what the networks and national papers were showing and describing were approximations of truth. Not only is today's unrest much more fragmented and kaleidoscopic (although racial injustice and police are providing a rallying point), there is no longer even a modicum of trust left in the now much more greatly diffused media to provide a fair, moderate and balanced view of the facts and circumstances unfolding around us, but rather echo chambers that are amplifying back to us our own prejudices. This inherent lack of trust had been growing for years but was furthered by Russia's interference in the 2016 campaigns. In that sense, Russia succeeded in the mission that the Kremlin set out to accomplish.

US officials have asserted that China, for its part, has been focused on "subnational diplomacy" by reaching out to engage with and influence state governors and mayors of key cities.[216] With so much attention on the Fake News element of the election campaigns and Russia's now exposed and fully detailed involvement, Russia and Iran appear to have shifted their focus to cyber-attacks, which risks are outlined below.

Cyber-attacks are rising dramatically

Our nation's shared experience of work-at-home confinement in 2020 made it clear that we are deeply reliant on our high-speed internet and mobile communications networks to function remotely. We are today completely and obsessively dependent on our mobile phones, laptops, and a plethora of other interconnected devices in our homes and cars which help get us throughout our day. While a pre-existing reality, this became increasingly apparent in the era of lockdowns and working from home with the use of video conferencing. It has been true for several years now that most of our personal and work-related data are stored remotely in the Cloud, a great productivity and efficiency enhancement, as long as it works. At the same time, our government and private sector servers and network infrastructure – including those that control our energy, water, power, and telecoms utilities – are both rapidly aging and yet increasingly interconnected and thus vulnerable to systemic attack.

As early as 2018, the World Economic Forum identified cyber-attacks as one of the leading threats to the global economy in the wake of the WannaCry attack, which in 2017 affected more than 200,000 computers across 150 countries and caused upwards of billions of dollars in damage.[217] The attack was ultimately attributed by the US, UK and Australian governments to hackers connected to the North Korean government.[218]

One consistent form of cyber-attack practiced by China for several decades has been industrial espionage against military and economic targets in Western governments and the private sector.[219] The US, UK, Australia, and New Zealand finally formally and publicly called out China on this practice in 2018, after years of complaining about it privately through diplomatic channels, but turning a blind eye publicly, carrying on with business as usual. More recently, in July 2020, the US accused China of attempting to steal information related to the development of a coronavirus vaccine.[220] The US Intellectual Property Commission report *The Theft Of American Intellectual Property: Reassessments Of The Challenge And United States Policy* estimated that "the annual cost to the US economy continues to exceed $225 billion in counterfeit goods, pirated software, and theft of trade secrets and could be as high as $600 billion."[221] Over a decade, this adds up to as much as $6 trillion of lost income to the US, equal to nearly one-third of our entire national debt. As of February 2020, the Federal Bureau of Investigation had over 1,000 open investigations into cases of Chinese economic espionage.[222]

Since the outbreak of COVID-19, the incidence of cyber-attacks has increased dramatically, especially following the increased tensions which have grown in 2020 between the US, China, Russia and Iran.[223] Specifically, in the first eight months of 2020, there were over 70 significant cyber-attack incidents logged by the Center for Strategic & International Studies.[224] Dozens of confirmed significant cyber-attacks against key US resources and its allies by state actors is a shocking pattern that should have caught our attention, but it has been largely ignored by mainstream media.

For emphasis, and to understand the nature and extent of the problem, I've included in an Appendix a selective sampling of just a few of these attacks. These incidents clearly point to a state-sponsored and coordinated effort by the Chinese, Iranian, Russian, and North Korean governments to infiltrate, burglarize, undermine and sabotage the data networks and critical infrastructure of the US and other western governments and private sectors. This is one of the clearest examples that these governments are committing Acts of War towards the US and her allies in the West.

Why target TikTok and WeChat?

As a mobile app very popular amongst teenagers, the social media platform TikTok has an extraordinary reach, including an estimated 170 million downloads of the application in the US and a billion around the world. It is not the size that is the concern for the government of the United States. Nor is it the fact that its users create and share short videos that mostly seem to involve a lot of awkward dancing and karaoke with special effects that these kids will probably come to regret later in life. The US government's concern is a view that TikTok's Chinese parent has access to and collects extensive data on TikTok's 100 million US user base, which the administration believed would be visible to and accessible by the Chinese government. The thinking went that the CCP would be able to use this information in several nefarious ways, including for espionage, tracking, blackmail, to spread misinformation and propaganda, or to censor politically sensitive content.

The censorship concern was cited by a US senator who noted the remarkable dearth of any TikTok video clips related to the ongoing upheaval in Hong Kong, at a time when that subject seemed to predominate the content of most of the other social media platforms. Another US official noted "[TikTok] accounts criticizing CCP policies are routinely removed or deleted."[225] TikTok came into Chinese hands through the 2017 acquisition of musical.ly by the Beijing-based Chinese internet company ByteDance, which in addition to local Chinese investors has some prominent foreign shareholders including private equity and venture capital firms KKR, Softbank, Sequoia Capital, and General Atlantic. Globally, ByteDance's apps reportedly have 1.5 billion monthly active users and 700 million daily active users, with a valuation approaching $80 billion. [226] The Committee on Foreign Investment in the United States (CFIUS) took up a retroactive formal review of the 2017 musical.ly acquisition at some point in 2019 as these concerns began to resonate throughout various branches of the US government.

WeChat was added to the threat list by a second Executive Order[227] issued later on the same day as the TikTok Order (on August 6, 2020). WeChat is a social media, messaging, and payments application owned by Tencent (a leading Chinese internet company deeply connected with the Chinese government and the CCP). WeChat is the primary communications application used by over a billion people worldwide, and by 19 million people in the US. WeChat is also one of the primary means for Chinese students and workers residing in the US to communicate with their relationships in China.

The United States Commerce Department put the enforcement wheels in motion six weeks later on September 18th, 2020. Secretary of Commerce Wilbur Ross explained, "While the threats posed by WeChat and TikTok are not identical, they are similar. Each collects vast swaths of data from users, including network activity, location data, and browsing and search histories. Each is an active participant in China's civil-military fusion and is subject to mandatory cooperation with the intelligence services of the CCP. This combination results in the use of WeChat and TikTok creating unacceptable risks to our national security."[228]

Two days later, a San Francisco based US magistrate judge blocked the order that Apple and Alphabet remove the app from their stores, stating in a 22-page order "certainly the government's overarching national-security interest is significant. But ... while the government has established that China's activities raise significant national security concerns — it has put in scant little evidence that its effective ban of WeChat for all US users addresses those concerns."[229] The Department of Commerce immediately challenged the order, stating "prohibiting the identified transactions is necessary to protect the national security of the United States, and the Department expects to soon seek relief from this order."[230] The inclusion of WeChat was a similarly large and disruptive move by the US government, and the ban will have larger implications than TikTok itself given WeChat's ubiquity in the Chinese community in America. We can expect this drama to continue to play out in the coming weeks before the elections.

The role of CFIUS (the Committee on Foreign Investments in the United States) as a deterrent agent has increased substantially during the Trump administration. In the previous seven years between 2010 and 2016, there were a total of 367 CFIUS investigations, or 52 per year on average, and only one Presidential action blocking a covered transaction. During the first three years of the Trump administration, there have been 443 investigations, or a trebled average of about 148 per year, and five Presidential actions.[231] Finance, information, and technology have been the clear areas of CFIUS's focus. Of the covered transactions since 2017, China has been the focus of 20% of them, with Japan (14%) and Canada

(11%) the runners-up. However, the number of proposed transactions involving Chinese acquirors fell from 60 in 2017 to 25 in 2019, as relations between the countries deteriorated. In 2019 eight transactions were withdrawn because the parties were unable to identify mitigation measures that sufficiently addressed CFIUS's concerns.

Notable recent cases in which the CFIUS process has blocked or resulted in failed transactions with Chinese acquirors include: Beijing Kunlun Tech's proposed acquisition of gay dating site GrindR, presumably on concerns about the ability of the Chinese government to blackmail gay American men using their personal data including HIV status; iCarbonX's acquisition of PatientsLikeMe, which according to law firm Gibson Dunn "claims to have tens of millions of 'data points about disease,' and its partners range from large pharmaceutical companies like Biogen to non-profit health organizations …", which uses the site to find patients for clinical studies and research. The 2017 deal was designed to marry the Chinese company's artificial intelligence technology for improving healthcare with PatientsLikeMe's customers and data sets;[232] a proposed JV between Ekso Bionics, a US company manufacturing robotic exoskeletons for medical and industrial use, and two opaque Chinese parties. Law firm Cleary Gottlieb noted "given Ekso's past work for the Defense Advanced Research Projects Agency (DARPA), among others, on military exoskeletons, this result would not have been surprising had it been a Chinese acquisition of Ekso. But, [as reviews of foreign JVs had not previously been part of CFUIS's mandate, it] potentially signals a significant expansion of CFIUS's asserted jurisdiction."[233]

The proposed tech transactions that President Trump himself blocked included a Chinese private equity group's bid for Lattice Semiconductor Corp. and Broadcom's $117 billion bid for Qualcomm, both targets being substantial semiconductor industry players. The Trump administration has been clearing transactions at about a 60% approval rate compared with 95% for the Obama administration.[234]

TikTok and WeChat have been of particular concern for the US government given the vast amount of personal user data they access, collect and store, the close relationship with the Chinese government and the CCP, including party members and senior officials within management and on boards, and the risk that this data was going to be used for belligerent means, either now or in the future when conflict between the countries increases. This signals that the decoupling of the relationship between the United States and China that President Trump has articulated is extending rather quickly to the world of data and Internet communications.

We know that for years China has, through what has become known as The Great Firewall, placed significant restrictions on its citizens' access to western social media and other web sites, censored vast amounts of news and information and that the Chinese government systematically surveils its own citizens' online presence and activity, with a particular eye towards politically-oriented content and most importantly anything critical of the CCP.

Is this the end of the internet revolution? It is possible that this action marks a new era, one in which the Internet is no longer globally ubiquitous and free, but operates in at least two different spheres of influence, one explicitly controlled by the Chinese government and the other implicitly influenced and shaped by the US government's and its western allies' response to the challenge. A better alternative to the banning of specific applications or companies based on foreign ownership or other firm-specific criteria would be the application of legislation, along with enforcement tools, regulating the use, storage, and transfer of personal data, that could be applied universally across all technology companies operating within the United States. According to Samm Sacks, Senior Fellow at Yale Law School's Paul Tsai China Center and a Cybersecurity Policy Fellow at New America:

> "Instead of playing a game of whack-a-mole against a rotating cast of Chinese tech companies, the US would be wise to spend more time developing legislation and standards for how all companies, regardless of country of origin, protect online privacy and secure data. No company should have access to and retain sensitive data in the first place that could then be transmitted to a government that could use it to do harm or be hacked by state actors."[235]

The one-off targeting of TikTok may do very little to address the underlying cyber-security challenge that the United States faces across a multitude of platforms. Given that TikTok will likely end up in the hands of another large US tech company, the forced sale increases the concentration, size, and power of the existing big data companies within the US. We need more diverse digital competition at this moment, not less, as the next chapter illustrates.

Part IV: The internal threat

8. The enemy within

"… the destruction which has overtaken a number of
civilizations in the past has never been the work of any
external agency, but has always been in the nature of an act of
suicide. We are betrayed by what is false within."[236]
– Arnold Toynbee, *A Study of History*

What is happening here?

Ask almost anyone today and they would agree that something is terribly wrong in America. The agreement would stop there, as everyone seems to have a different understanding of what is the problem and what is required to fix it. We have spent time looking at the external threats that we face as a country today. At the same time, we recognize that we also face several domestic challenges, some of which we began to touch on in the discussion of our economy and COVID-19. These challenges don't necessarily require external forces to damage or even destroy the fabric of our country as a free and democratic nation. Yet beyond these issues, something intangible seems to be slowly undermining us as a society, some symptoms of which we see and can describe, and some of which is less obvious and below the surface. An unseen devourer is slowly eating away at the infrastructure of our democracy, like termites hidden in the walls of a stately but old house in need of repair and restoration. Some of these divisive issues are not hard to spot and have been touched on: a growing wealth gap, increasingly strained race relations, each of which is tied to unjust policies or outcomes, and political polarization facilitated by the rise of social media, Fake News, and its pernicious effects on free speech and democracy. These issues are then channeled and reflected as what appears to be Two Americas, sometimes labeled as Red States and Blue States, Left and Right, Black and White, or other misleading and divisive but convenient labels.

The widening wealth gap is evidenced in growing income inequality. Returns on capital grow, benefitting from loose monetary policy, while returns on labor continue to fall as a consequence of three decades of poorly pursued trade and other policies. Persistent or renewed racism is exacerbated by economic stress, injustice in how we treat the poor and disenfranchised and reflected in the criminal justice system. There is a sense from a too large portion of our population that they don't belong to America or America to them.

A related problem arises in how we know what we think we know about these issues. By and large, we are now filtering the information we receive to support our existing views, ensuring that the process of cognitive bias cements and amplifies our divisions and misunderstandings within our communities and in the nation as a whole. A new risk that has emerged is that manipulation of information may come from the large social media companies themselves. Now under pressure from all sides, these platforms are increasingly choosing to censor content, block accounts, or otherwise eliminate material that they may deem to be bot-generated, offensive, overly controversial, or tending towards social unrest or violence.

The obvious issue here is that rather than protecting us, the censorship restricts our access to information and violates our first amendment rights to freedom of expression and freedom of the press. Russia, China, and others may not need the IRA or equivalent if their work can be done for them by Facebook, YouTube, Twitter, and the like, or more accurately by the corporate advertisers behind them.

This chapter explores the challenge of the wealth gap and widening inequality in America, discusses the role that social media has played in affecting our culture and our public discourse, and seeks to understand the impact it may be having on our society and our democracy.

Widening inequality in America

The last time we saw income and wealth inequality in the United States as bad as it is today was the 1930s. That did not end well. We are familiar with the Great Depression scenes of bread lines, windswept dustbowl prairies, and iconic photos of desperate and starving Americans by Dorothea Lange and others sent out to visually chronicle the tragedy. What is less memorialized and thus remembered is that it was a time of violent social upheaval within the United States. Unions, Communist and Anarchist agitators, the KKK, and home-grown Fascists regularly organized, demonstrated, and occasionally rioted in the streets of our cities and towns.

The extremely difficult economic conditions of the Great Depression hit the large cities of the United States particularly hard, as the working class was faced with diminishing wages, widespread layoffs, and the growing unaffordability of foodstuffs more readily available to rural Americans still living on or close to farms. The unemployment rate hit levels never seen before, peaking at just under 25% in 1933,[237] and unemployment offices were overflowing with men and women desperate for any kind of work.

This environment became fertile soil for the Communist Party, which on multiple occasions organized rallies in large cities such as New York, which often escalated into riots of tens of thousands of violent participants. For example, in March 1930 the Communist Party organized an unemployment rally in Union Square which brought out over 35,000 people. The demonstration "transformed in a few moments from an orderly, at times bored, crowd into a fighting mob" which proceeded to march on City Hall. The violent throng was ultimately broken up by the police after several hours of fighting, and eventually, the city did procure an increase in the appropriation of funds for unemployment relief of about $1 million.[238] These protests cum riots occasionally took on racial overtones, as unemployment and general misery stirred up divisions between racial groups, resulting in the targeting of minorities. On other occasions, the environment resulted in demonstrations of racial unity when labor faced off with police as symbols of the capitalist system that seemed to be the source of their troubles. A second large rally in Union Square in 1932 had over 50,000 demonstrators gathered, of which about a quarter was Black. When law enforcement authorities attacked, "Blacks and Whites fought together in solidarity to protect the march."[239] In addition to protests and riots, sustained unemployment and the forces of poverty and hunger contributed to hundreds of cases of mob looting across the country, including attacks on stores, distribution centers, trains, and trucks by very desperate Americans who presumably never would have previously imagined themselves resorting to such actions.

Over the longer arc of American history, there have been periods of substantial labor-related violence, often in periods of financial crisis following economic expansions that benefited one group (capital) at the expense of another (labor). When growth is not shared equitably with –

and technological progress doesn't benefit, or isn't affordable to – the working classes, social unrest, and violence is sure to follow. During the long US expansion that occurred from the 1870s through the turn of the century, which saw significant strides in urbanization, industrialization, and development of new technologies including the railways, oil extraction and production, and coal-mining, there was also substantial social unrest. The wealth created by these new technologies was highly concentrated in the hands of the "robber baron" capitalists and their elite management teams, the nineteenth-century version of our tech entrepreneurs and one-percenters, who saw vast accumulations of wealth at a scale previously unseen in history, at least until the advent of the winner take all capitalism prevalent in our own time in Silicon Valley. This saw highly violent confrontations between labor, capital, and government forces, which ebbed and flowed over nearly four decades. Numerous strikes, riots, and other industrial actions took place in the last three decades of the century, notably including the great railroad strikes of the 1870s, major strikes in the 1880s amongst the metalworkers' unions, the Haymarket Riot in Chicago, a labor protest which left eight dead, and the infamous Pullman Railroad Strike of 1894, which intervention by federal officers resulted in the deaths of 30 people, and finally around the turn of the century when there was significant social unrest for mineworkers, most well-known by the Anthracite Coal Strike of 1902. This strike was ultimately settled with president Theodore Roosevelt's unprecedented intervention in what was previously considered a private matter to be resolved between shareholders, board, management, and unions and explicitly outside the jurisdiction of the US government.[240]

America has benefitted from a near century-long period of industrial peace. This was evidenced by declining labor-related violence, corresponding with the long economic expansion that began during World War II and continued through the turn of the century. This long peace and prosperity, combined with internal corruption, ultimately led to the decline in the power of the labor unions themselves. We now face a situation in which this period of peace may be beginning to reverse itself. While it may not be the same type of organized labor groups that coordinated industrial action in the 1870-1940 period, we are at risk of renewed social unrest resulting from the same underlying causes, which include income and wealth inequality, rising unemployment, and an inadequate distribution to the lower-income strata of the benefits the wealth creation brought on by the technology revolution of the twenty-first century.

The United States is growing substantially less equal, and this can be proven by over fifty years of available comparative data. During this time, the GINI index[v] of income inequality in the US has increased from 0.36 in 1967 to 0.47 in 2019. This means that we've become substantially less equal as a society over a generation, and now compare more to an emerging market than to a mature, developed economy on this metric of social development. Going back further to the immediate post-war period shows an even greater historical degree of income equality in the US, and thus an even greater slide towards inequality. Within the developed world, a relatively equal society such as seen in the Nordic countries (Norway, Sweden, Denmark, and Finland), benefiting from small and homogeneous populations, would score between 0.25 and 0.30, while a moderately equal

---

[v] The GINI index is a model of income inequality in large populations widely used to compare countries and societies around the world and across time. Measured between zero and one, a score of zero would indicate everyone is perfectly equal, a score of one would indicate that all of the nation's wealth is in the hands of one person.

country like the UK, France, Japan, Germany, Canada, Australia, Russia, China or India would score between 0.3 and 0.4. Less equal societies such as Brazil, South Africa, Nigeria, or Mexico tend to be less developed and would score anywhere between 0.4 and 0.6.[241] At 0.47, the United States is not in the best of company.

On another metric, using the same census data going back to 1969, the proportion of national income shared with the bottom 60% has fallen from 34.7% to 27.2% in 2019.[242] The proportion of taxable income captured by the top 20% has risen from 42.1% to 50.5%, but the benefit has accrued mostly at the very tip-top. Middle-income earners are now taking home only 43% of aggregate income, compared with 62% in 1970.[243] Part of this decline is as a result of the middle class itself shrinking and no longer representing a substantial majority of Americans. A generation ago, 61% of Americans lived in middle-class households (in 1971), compared with only 51% today (in 2019), which implies that our society is pulling farther apart into groups of haves (upper incomes) and have nots (lower incomes).

An analysis published in September 2020 by the RAND Corporation indicates that the top one percent of income earners took home 22% of taxable income in 2018, compared with 9% in 1975. Over the same timeframe, the bottom 90% of income earners saw their share of national income fall from 67% to 50%. When compared with what would have happened with an equal rate of growth over the period (i.e. if each group had maintained their 1975 share of national wealth), this shift implies just under $50 trillion of aggregate wealth transfer from 90% of Americans to the top 10%.[244] Given the steadily increasing productivity of the United States over this time, the explanation for this has to be that the return on capital (financial assets) increased while the return on labor decreased. Over this period, providers of capital took an increasingly larger share of the economic pie that workers did.

The global financial crisis of 2008-9 resulted in a substantial setback to the wealth of American households. Even with the strong recovery in asset values over the past decade, average household wealth in America has only returned to mid-1990s levels and remains over 30% below pre-crisis levels.[245] The wealth gap between upper-income families and everyone else is rising. Upper-income families now comprise nearly 80% of all household wealth, compared with 60% in 1983, while the share held by middle-income families has fallen from 32% to 17% over the same timeframe.[246] This decline is likely attributable to the 2008-09 housing crisis, which wiped out much of the equity that middle-income homeowners thought they held in their homes, which in most cases was their primary store of wealth.

Increasing income inequality and the widening wealth gap, both reflected in particular in the returns on capital relative to the returns on labor, have clear racial implications, given that African-Americans tend to be greatly underrepresented in participation in the financial markets and ownership of financial assets. With wide gaps in initial wealth between the races a generation ago, wealth and income distribution have fallen out on broadly racial lines reflecting vastly different starting points of capital accumulation and a diminishing return on labor. Alexandre Tanzi of Bloomberg noted in July 2020 that "African Americans held only 1.6% of corporate stock and mutual-fund shares in the US as of March 31 compared with almost 91.6% by White investors, who have gained from the roughly 45% rise in the S&P 500 since then."[247] Whites hold over 80% of real estate holdings, and Blacks hold only $6 of financial assets for every $100 held by Whites. This is not surprising when less than half of

Black families own their homes (compared to 70% for White families) and only 16.7% (less than one in six) of Black Americans earn over $100,000,[248] leaving little room for a family of four representing the other 83.3% of Black earners to invest in savings and the capital markets.

Beyond income inequality and the wealth gap, there are several other symptoms that when looked at collectively imply a widening disease. In our country, the symptoms include divisive politics, lack of trust (deservedly or not) in government, a diminishing estimation of the value of democracy itself, and low participation in our political process. In our civil society, we see similar disturbing trends: the predominance of cancel culture and the inability for healthy and rigorous debate in the public square, the rise of extremists (both left and right), and gross indifference about the value of our national patrimony and one's role in it.

We've never been more divided politically as a country than we are right now. Berkeley's Greater Good Science Center recently pointed to 14 separate negative consequences of our political polarization and resulting social antagonisms. Some of those observed effects include that: we're segregated in our own communities; our political culture is more and more antagonistic; we judge and loathe members of other political parties; our families are being undermined; we're less likely to help each other out; we feel pressure to conform in our groups; deception is more likely; gridlock is damaging our government institutions and we're losing trust in them; violence is more likely.[249]

There has never been a lower level of trust in the federal government, and in a particular Congress, than there is today. Only 18% of Americans approve of the work Congress is doing,[250] up somewhat from an all-time low of 9% in 2013, but well off of the long-term trend lines of 30%-40% and the majority approval rates enjoyed in the first few decades of the twenty-first century.[251] Not surprisingly, these views are drawn on party lines. Only about half the nation believes that congressional districts are drawn in a "fair and reasonable" way,[252] which presumably colors the outcome. Presidential approval rates continue to hover in the 40s, also broadly drawn on partisan lines. According to Gallup, "President Donald Trump's prospects of winning a second term in office will be closely tied to the level of his job approval rating. Historically, all incumbents with an approval rating of 50% or higher have won reelection, and presidents with approval ratings much lower than 50% have lost."[253] Gallup's reference set here seems to be eleven post-war elections, which is hardly a large enough sample size to be determinative either way. Data used from those same elections did not predict Trump's upset victory in 2016 either.

Only 30% of American Millennials believe it's essential to live in a democracy, an even lower portion than their European age cohort peers, for which 44% believe it's essential, even though by and large these European countries tend to have more socialist characteristics that the US. Compare that statistic to the still living silver cohort which remembers the horrors of Communism and Fascism around World War II. For this group, 72% of them say that living in a democracy is essential. It gets worse. Nearly a quarter (24%) of American Millennials actually believe democracy is a 'bad' or 'very bad' way of running the country, up 50% from the previous same age cohort's immature views twenty years prior.[254] If we are not careful, this new generation is going to have the opportunity to experience for itself what the alternative paths look like, only to belatedly discover that they are on *The Road To Serfdom*,[255] with great economic and social cost and human suffering along the way. Perhaps as a result of this indifferent view, Millennials appear to prefer to volunteer rather than to vote.[256] But the Millennials are not alone here. In the 2016 presidential elections, only 55.7% of eligible Americans voted, ranking the US number 26 out of 32 in voting participation in the developed and democratic countries comprising the OECD.[257]

We see other coincidental factors affecting our society, some of which are disturbing. Participation in religion is declining, with less than half of Americans attending a church or synagogue, and over a quarter expressing no religious affiliation whatsoever.[258] This is unsettling given the predominant role that religion has played in shaping American public life and morality since its founding. Social media and pornography both plague our society by ensnaring, enslaving, and dumbing us down. Worse, it is impacting our children and how they view sex, violence, relationships, and gender, with "early half of children between the ages of 9-16 experience regular exposure to sexual images."[259] Among American teenagers, suicides have now become the second-leading cause of death.[260] The Washington Post noted last year that "for many years, suicide among youths was relatively rare and its frequency relatively stable. But from 2007 to 2017, the number of suicides among people ages 10 to 24 suddenly increased by 56 percent."[261] This increase correlates with the rising prevalence of pornography and social media, both factors which many believe may be a contributing factor, especially among girls. The next section looks at the rise and role of social media and the impact it's having on us as a society.

With Friends like these, who needs enemies? (the role of social media)

"Surveillance capitalism runs contrary to the early digital
dream ... Instead, it strips away the illusion that the networked
form has some kind of indigenous moral content, that being
'connected' is somehow intrinsically pro-social, innately
inclusive, or naturally tending towards the democratization of
knowledge. Digital connection is now a means to others'
commercial ends. At its core, surveillance capitalism is
parasitic and self-referential. It revives Karl Marx's old image
of capitalism as a vampire that feeds on labor, but with an
unexpected turn. Instead of labor, surveillance capitalism
feeds on every aspect of every human's experience."[262]
– Shoshana Zuboff, *The Age of Surveillance Capitalism*

When boys and girls love what they feel
they lick the earth, and swear it's real
With a silver syringe before bells chime
the devil entices the children of time.

Beware proud creatures of the night
who close eternal windows tight
With a triple cheer at the scene of the crime
the devil endorses the children of time.
– The Choir, *Children of Time*

When Pokémon Go came out amid much fanfare in 2016, my then
13-year-old son must have been amongst the first to download it. Within
hours, he was completely absorbed and wandering around its virtual
world, but his physical body still appeared to be somewhat tethered to the
physical streets and sidewalks of our town. He perambulated in what
appeared to the uninitiated eye to be some sort of aimless progression that
first zigged, then zagged, then stopped, hovered, and Go, like the non-
linear movement of a UFO. It didn't take long for me to observe that he
had lost all connection with the world around him other than what was

being shown to him on the screen, and as a result was putting himself and others at some degree of intersection, if not danger. He eventually learned how to navigate between the two worlds, avoiding trouble for himself, and inconvenience for others. What took me a lot longer to realize was that Pokémon Go was not simply an awkwardly interactive and 'social' game based on the characters, but was actually an insidious and cunningly devised behavior modification program within the rapidly evolving data gathering universe to be able to track, monitor, and ultimately persuade and manipulate its user to shop for and consume the various goods offered up by the restaurants and stores that paid to advertise in its virtual world.

What I wish would have also emerged in 2016, and thus better enabled me to understand what was happening to my children, was Shoshanna Zuboff's magisterial 2019 masterwork *The Age of Surveillance Capitalism: The Fight for a Human Future at the New Frontier of Power*, which must have landed with its 700-page heft like a warm pile of manure into the collective laps of Big Tech intelligentsia and the Silicon Valley wunderkinder. In her devastating critique, Harvard Business School professor Zuboff eviscerates and then dissects the digital economy and its ethos, laying out for us in gory detail the component parts of the industry: its motive power, its philosophy and morality, its behaviors, and most importantly, its deleterious impact and the horrendous cost that it is extracting on our societies, our communities, our families and our own individual humanity. Zuboff defines surveillance capitalism as "the unilateral claiming of private human experience as free raw material for translation into behavioral data. These data are then computed and packaged as prediction products and sold into behavioral futures markets – business customers with a commercial interest in knowing what we will do now, soon, and later."[263] Zuboff observes that surveillance capital "is the puppet master that imposes its will through the medium of the ubiquitous digital apparatus called Big Other: [the] sensate, computational, connected puppet that renders, monitors, computes, and modifies human behavior."[264] It is AI.

Zuboff points out that surveillance capitalism differs from what we would historically think of as market capitalism in three unique ways: 1) it insists on unfettered freedom and knowledge, specifically freedom to conduct business practices in the way it sees fit, while maintaining freedom from laws or regulations that would get in the way, and sees knowledge as total information that tends towards certainty and guaranteed outcomes (they know where you are, what you are doing, and importantly can accurately predict what you are going to do next, with the potential to modify your thoughts or actions); 2) it abandons long-standing organic reciprocities with people, no longer relying on people as customers but rather as products, and reduces human experience to measurable behavior without ascribing meaning or moral value; and 3) the "specter of life in the hive betrays a collectivist societal vision sustained by radical indifference and its material expression in Big Other, an orientation that is completely opposed to our values of democracy and capitalism (as it was once). For its ... "own commercial success, surveillance capitalism aims us towards the hive collective." It is amoral, in that "anything that allows us to connect more people more often is de facto good." Its objective is not to discover or reveal truth, but to keep the content pipeline full, regardless of meaning or truth, with the singular objective of attracting and retaining the most users and ensuring that their engagement time is maximized.[265]

Tristan Harris of the Center for Humane Technology explains it this way, "Just like a tree is worth more as lumber and a whale is worth more dead than alive – in the attention extraction economy a human is worth more when we are depressed, outraged, polarized, and addicted." Sounds bad, but what does it matter? "This attention extraction economy is accelerating the mass degradation of our collective capacity to solve global threats, from pandemics to inequality to climate change." Not good. Where will it lead us? "If we can't make sense of the world while making ever more consequential choices, a growing ledger of harms will destroy the futures of our children, democracy, and truth itself." His suggestion? "We need radically reimagined technology infrastructure and business models that actually align with humanity's best interests."[266]

What might that kind of reinvention look like? The first step on the road to recovery is always to admit that there is a problem. In this case, that awareness comes in the form of being constantly and consciously aware that one's online life is being monitored, tracked, recorded, and tested for the purposes of predicting, influencing, and ultimately modifying one's behavior through persuasion and manipulation. This is in itself the business model of Facebook and Google. Practically speaking, we need to delete as many of these apps as possible. From the government's perspective, the US needs to consider a new regulatory framework that is designed to deal with these issues, not try to adopt a legislative framework from a century ago originally constructed to deal with phones and radios.

This is not a Luddite prescription. I am not suggesting that we revert back to the era before the Internet, before AI, or before social media, any more than I'm suggesting that we go back to a pre-atomic age. However just like the use of atomic power and a particular nuclear weapon these forces in society have to be highly regulated and controlled. We cannot continue on in the current environment of a spaghetti western-style free-for-all, where there is no overriding legal and regulatory framework that protects the citizens of the town from the depredations of the black hats. This is not easy for anyone to say who has considered themselves a lifelong proponent of the free market system. However, the challenge has been that we have assumed these technologies are a purely human good and make our lives better in the way we'd expect of any other consumer product, as opposed to recognizing them for what they are – weapons with massive destructive potential. Even if these technologies and businesses are somewhere in the middle, for example in the category of a public utility, then there is a long history and precedent of being highly regulated to protect their users.

The US government is beginning to take action to address some of the concerns that have been raised by the rise of Big Tech and social media in recent years. The Department of Justice is expected to file a lawsuit in the coming weeks that will challenge Google's search dominance, in what would be the largest antitrust case in decades. One of the vectors of challenges likely to be addressed is the way that companies such as Google and Facebook charge different prices to different customers for the same product, which would be illegal on anticompetitive grounds in the offline world of retail, but is allowed for certain services such as airline ticketing. One of the big issues is whether there will be a repeal or partial roll-back of Section 230 of the 1996 Communications Decency Act, which has enabled websites to operate without fear of liability for content posted by their users. Social media companies have invoked Section 230 to be treated like media companies or advertisers that have no responsibility for the content they put out, on the basis that they only act as intermediaries. By being able to hide under the protection of Section 230, Big Tech has been able to avoid many of the restrictions that would have otherwise faced them and thus fueled the dramatic growth in online advertising revenue that we've seen over the past 25 years. In September 2020, the Department of Justice sent draft legislation to Congress that would have the effect of weakening parts of Section 230. The Department of Justice proposal follows previously announced efforts to reform the ways social media operates and to hold them more accountable for their content. This all sums up to an indication that we may be entering into another round of trust-busting, similar to what America went through in previous eras in which we saw heavy concentrations of economic and political power in industries such as oil, the railroads, and the production of steel.

In testimony before congressional lawmakers in 2018, Facebook founder Mark Zuckerberg repeatedly suggested that more and better AI would be the solution to address the pressing issues facing Facebook and similar platforms, such as fake news, discriminatory ads, hate speech, and propaganda on the one hand, and censorship, fairness and human moderation on the other.[267] From this author's perspective, while better technology will certainly be part of the cure, AI appears a long way off from being able to understand, interpret, and appropriately filter the subtleties of human intention, emotion, humor, or satire, let alone the core of what it means to be human, including our morality, values, and our hopes and fears. Nor does it appear reasonable that as a society should entrust itself to a faith that a more powerful and sentient AI would have humanity's best interest at heart.

In the Immolation Scene, the closing of the final act of *Götterdämmerung* ("Twilight of the Gods"), the fourth and last cycle of Richard Wagner's operatic epic Der Ring des Nibelungen, the heroine Brünnhilde sacrifices herself to the flames to ensure that the ring of power, which grants its owner mastery of the universe – and as a result has provoked every possible kind of evil in the heart and actions of the men and gods who pursued it –, is returned to its source to be purified in fire and then renewed in the waters of the Rhine. Only then, once the fire has cleansed it of its curse, may the ring be reclaimed from the waters to begin again on a new foundation. As the ring is returned to its source, the chaotic gods and dark heroes of Valhalla are seen going up in flames, symbolizing the end of the old world order and its decadent evils, a world in which those same gods bewitched and manipulated mankind into every form of sin and malevolence. The act signifies the expectation that redemption and renewal will arise with the birth of the new. This is dramatic but relevant symbolism for the level of change that is required to how Big Tech is allowed to operate in our society. We need a rebirth and renewal to a more humane and just technology world, freed from the short-termism, manipulation, and ensnaring of human free will that has resulted from the unsafe use of this potential destroyer of worlds.

#Cancelculture and the death of free speech

> "Refusal to draw inferences from negative signs … was
> recognized in … George Orwell's 1984, as what the author
> called 'Crimestop.' Crimestop means the faculty of stopping
> short, as though by instinct, at the threshold of any dangerous
> thought. It includes the power of not grasping analogies,
> failing to perceive logical errors, of misunderstanding the
> simplest arguments … and of being bored and repelled by any
> train of thought which is capable of leading in a heretical
> direction. Crimestop, in short, means protective stupidity.[268]
> – Barbara Tuchman, *The March of Folly*

Tightly linked to the rise of social media is the emergence of cancel culture and the death of free speech. We are in a strange moment in time in which it is no longer safe to hold or express ideas that don't fit nicely into the orthodoxy of a certain prevailing cultural view.

If one happens to have the temerity to stand up and say publicly something as blandly mild as "I'm proud of my English/Irish/French-German ancestry,"[269] or "I find value in Western Civilization," then one is immediately labeled a racist, a White supremacist or worse. If one bridles at these labels as unfair and untrue, then it proves that one is also an overly sensitive snowflake. This is madness. To accept other cultures or heritages does not require rejecting one's own. We have moved to a point where civil discourse and freedom of speech is not actually possible. There is no real discussion in the public square at this moment, only rancorous debate. If one doesn't tout the party line, then one is shouted down, canceled, unfriended, and in some cases increasingly shamed, harassed, intimidated, or worse.

To go further, it is impossible in this environment to make any discerning judgments between the cultural norms and values of different societal groups. Have we really come to a point in our civil society where we are unable to make judgments to discern good from bad, or better from worse, in cultural matters? Taken to an extreme, do we then have to say that the norms of societies and people groups that practiced cannibalism and incest as part of their 'civilization' are just as good as any other heritage, Judeo-Christian or otherwise? That a married couple with children provides no higher social good than a polyamorous tribe of childless Big Love enthusiasts?

I have spent the last 15 years walking out – with both my time and my money – a core belief that Black lives matter by serving as chairman of the board of charity: water (charitywater.org), a non-profit founded by Scott Harrison in 2006. Through this role and by financially supporting the organization, I have helped Scott and charity: water bring clean and safe drinking water to over 11 million people in sub-Saharan Africa (where water-borne illness accounts for a preponderance of disease) and elsewhere.[270] The positive impact of safe access to clean drinking water is most strongly felt in the lives of women and girls across the 19 African countries in which we've served. In particular, women and girls are now freed up from hours spent unsafely fetching dirty water and instead can invest their time in education, employment, and their own health and well-being. I have invested a good part of my heart, mind, and wallet here out of a love for people and real concern for poverty and justice issues around the world, only to be told recently that this life-long philanthropic effort simply proves that I'm a racist, because it shows I have a 'White savior complex,' even if subconsciously. I have filed this accusation in an already half-full cabinet in my office labeled No Good Deed Goes Unpunished and moved on, but perhaps this small anecdote illustrates the absurdity and madness of the cultural moment we are in.

The Editorial Board of *The Wall Street Journal* recently called out Facebook on the issue of cancel culture and free speech. It this case, specifically for taking down any favorable reference to Kyle Rittenhouse, including balanced sites that propose mitigating facts and circumstances, suggested his innocence of first-degree murder charges (which requires, among other things, premeditated intent) or offers to aid his legal representation to challenge the charges in what his lawyers assert was a case of self-defense.[271]

I am not here to defend Rittenhouse or try to explain what happened that night, but video evidence[272] of the situation appears to support his claims of self-defense in each of the three incidents (which shows him being attacked, then chased as he tries to flee, multiple other shots are fired, he's seen being hit on the head or neck with the edge of a skateboard after he trips, he's approached by someone with a pistol, etc.). One of the most foundational and sacred concepts of the American justice system is the presumption of innocence. We are, as it is commonly phrased, "innocent until proven guilty."

At a minimum, Rittenhouse deserves a fair hearing in the full daylight of a courtroom. Facebook "seems to have declared Kyle Rittenhouse's fatal shooting of two people amid riots in Kenosha, Wis., a mass murder," without affording him due process. Facebook appears to be allowing content that describes his guilt while shutting off any contradictory opinion. Facebook also said it had made an "operational mistake" in the day before the shooting in allowing posts from local groups asking citizens to help law enforcement defend the town of Kenosha from rioters and looters, a town which had suffered substantial violence and vandalism the night before.[273]

In early September, Facebook, Twitter, and other social media platforms announced that they will limit controversial content around the election, ostensibly in an attempt to help reduce false and misleading content from spreading online. Specifically, Facebook decided to not post any new political ads in the seven days before the election.[274] This is meaningless, as ads already placed before the cutoff will be allowed to run, which ensures that advertisers will be careful to hit the specified deadline. Moreover, mail-in ballot elections will have already begun several weeks before the cutoff date, so the move actually does very little towards its stated objective.

The Trump campaign's response was not surprising. The deputy national press secretary for the campaign, Samantha Zager, was quoted as saying: "In the last seven days of the most important election in our history, President Trump will be banned from defending himself on the largest platform in America. When millions of voters will be making their decisions, the President will be silenced by the Silicon Valley Mafia, who will at the same time allow corporate media to run their biased ads to swing voters in key states."[275] Some Democrats also took issue with the decision on the grounds that it would limit ability to encourage election day turnout. A week later, Twitter said it would take similar actions, including banning or labeling any content about election results or potential voting irregularities.[276]

So two of our largest social media platforms that are relied upon by tens of millions of citizens, will basically be offline around the election that is expected to be the most contentious and controversial on record. On the other hand, we know that Facebook and the other most influential social media platforms have been viral super-spreader hotbeds of campaign-related misinformation,[277] so it's hard to know which is the lesser of the two evils.

9. Social unrest and the elections

"The long-term threat to social stability today arises less from
those who feel themselves unjustly treated than from those,
especially the young, who simply do not feel part of society at
all and so defiantly turned their back on it. It is among such
people that chiliastic and unreasoning mass movements, ...
dedicated to the destruction of the existing order, have,
historically, always found their strongest support ... But
neither should we ignore the existence of a dedicated minority
which does not wish to see those strains contained; whose
object ... is to exacerbate them to the point at which the entire
social order disintegrates, and a new revolutionary élite can
seize power and implement their own ideological objectives.
Their strategy was originally conceived by Lenin ... "[278]
- Michael Howard, *The Lessons of History*

The Enemy is not Us

I recently paid a visit to my local large-format sporting goods
outlet and was curious about the long queue of customers I saw formed at
the back of the store. It turned out to be customers patiently waiting at the
counter to buy firearms (handguns, assault rifles, and defense shotguns
seemed most popular, and no one seemed to be paying much attention to
the sporting or hunting models) and ammunition from what I saw were
already nearly empty shelves. It was, of course, alarming to consider that
this group of Americans of all ages, genders, colors, and walks of life were
essentially panic buying weapons (the day I describe was after a
particularly bad night for protests and riots around the country) ...
potentially to defend themselves from the very same person queued up
next to them.

Since then, I have come to understand that this same store, along with every other one in the region, and indeed across the country, has been unable to keep popular lines of ammunition in stock. Firearm suppliers are on backorder and rationing is occurring nationwide due to similar situations across the country, which one manufacturer's CEO confirmed was "due to elevated demand and not related to supply chain disruption from the lockdowns."[279] While similar buying patterns occurred in 2013 and 2016 (in the run-up to the presidential election) this one has the makings of something different, particularly given what we are witnessing on our streets. This is an incredibly disturbing pattern that should give all of us pause.

I have seen the national conflict reflected in the microcosm of my own home and personal relationships. I have two teenage boys who have found themselves gravitating, in their own personal exploration of the issues, to what appears on the surface to be opposite (and opposing) positions. One son is very aligned with the messaging of Black Lives Matter, and cannot understand why anyone wouldn't support the movement or dare to say that Blue Lives, or All Lives, Matter in light of the unjust killings of Breonna Taylor, George Floyd, and others. The other son finds it equally unjust that underpaid and overworked police officers, who risk life and limb to protect our bodies and property, are wounded and blinded by pyrotechnic and other projectiles fired by rioters, while state and local officials stand idly by, or when police officers are shot in their patrol cars in cold blood.[280]

We have discovered how much language matters in the discussion, learning to use more precise words in our conversations to distinguish between legitimate and righteous protests, civil demonstrations and protesters, on the one hand, and illegitimate and unrighteous riots, rioters, looters, and agent provocateurs, on the other. We have grown to appreciate that what we thought was a fundamental disagreement and difference of opinion was largely a miscommunication or misunderstanding about what the other party was saying. Once we were able to align our language and words to have a common meaning between us, we could hear and understand the other's perspective and position and have often found that it is not so terribly far away from our own. This is not possible without a willingness to Listen, to Learn, and yes to Love, even amidst strong differences. This dinnertime conversation is going on all over our country, but unfortunately is often painfully dividing rather than uniting, in part because the discipline of the three "Ls" is not being practiced.

I have heard a similar story of our cultural confusion from a close friend who lives with his wife and four children in a typical NYC-commuter bedroom community in a New Jersey suburb. One day this summer, as the Fourth of July – Independence Day for the United States – was approaching, his wife planted a series of small American flags in the flower beds and front lawn of their home in anticipation of the weekend's celebration and commemoration of their country's independence and hard-won liberties. Their 17-year old teenage daughter, a committed TikTok-ker and fully "awoke" by BLM and other messaging, came home that afternoon and was quite upset by what she saw. She said to her parents, "You don't understand … You can't have those [flags] up. You have to take them down now! If the kids (her school classmates) see them they will knock them down and [vandalize] our house."

Religion and politics have always been very difficult and divisive topics in our culture. Something is very different now, however, in that we have completely lost our ability to have any kind of civilized discourse around very challenging topics. An Orwellian-like version of *1984*'s thought police has descended upon our culture, rendering free speech impossible and subject to shame, ridicule, and occasional violence. Until we can find a new forum and protocol to safely debate these issues, which will require re-establishing grounds of civility in public discourse, the situation will continue to worsen amongst ourselves as Americans.

Observations on the protests

We have seen three distinct types of groups participate in the protests witnessed across the country since May 2020. The first, representing the vast majority, has been comprised of peaceful demonstrators who have effectively used the protests to appropriately convey a sense of anger, sadness, and frustration, and to successfully communicate and advocate with local, regional, and national leadership the urgent need for real and sustainable change. Their approach and intent have been pacific and in the honorable non-violent tradition of Dr. Martin Luther King and others. The second, a small but damaging single-digit minority, is the criminal element, which has skulked in the shadows of the demonstrations for no reason other than to exploit the opportunity for looting and theft. The third group, perhaps also small and yet the most dangerous, consists of the fringe elements of extremists on both sides: White Supremacists, Anarchists, hard-core ANTIFA adherents, and similar groups. This faction is comprised of very dedicated radicals on the outermost margins of both Right and Left, who in many cases have come from elsewhere, whether imported in from organized groups or more often traveling miles on their own initiative to participate and influence the direction of the demonstrations according to their own objectives and beliefs.

These two fringe groups, criminals and fanatics, have been an unfortunate distraction from the urgency, importance, and rightness of the message that the peaceful demonstrators have carried, and they have in many ways effectively sullied the movement and limited its efficaciousness by keeping other willing but more moderate and peaceable participants home for fear of violence or of otherwise being caught up in dangerous mayhem. The criminal element is not worth discussing here other than to say that these individuals dishonor themselves, their communities, the victims of injustice, and every other person out there standing up for any hope of justice and truth. Fortunately, this element has received pushback and restraint from enough within the majority of peaceful demonstrators that, with some exceptions in June, we have not seen sustained bouts of wide-scale looting or mass destruction of property. Yet. The risk that we will remain extremely elevated going into the fall and election season, especially if law enforcement determines to err on the side of restraint in terms of their presence at the protests.

The radical political element is responsible for most of the violence and chaos that we have witnessed. Their members tend to be young, mostly but not exclusively male, and largely middle-class, with a jumble of ideological views that wouldn't stand up under rigorous thought. As Ayaan Hirsi Ali has recently pointed out, their leadership has managed to form an ideological cohesiveness around a few core ideas which seem to blend Marxist principles with Islamic absolutism, indoctrination, intolerance for debate or dissent, and "a fondness for iconoclasm." in the tearing down of both statues and existing historical narratives.[281]

The recently deceased historian and Professor Emerita at the Graduate School of the City University of New York Gertrude Himmebfarb was one of the most vocal of her generation to speak out against the various attempts to rewrite history on Marxist and postmodernist terms, reminding us that:

> "The defeat of Nazism and the collapse of the Soviet empire
> conclusively proved that Totalitarianism is not only oppressive
> and murderous; it is inefficient and fatally vulnerable. Now we
> must confront another problem: not how liberalism can defend
> itself against totalitarianism, but how it can defend itself
> against itself – against its own weakness and excesses. In the
> Marxist jargon that has survived the death of the Marxist
> regimes, this is the new "problematic" of liberalism. How can
> a society that celebrates the virtues of liberty, individuality,
> variety, and tolerance sustain itself when those virtues, carried
> to extremes, threaten to subvert the liberal society and, with it,
> those very virtues? The problem is not political but societal,
> cultural and moral; It is the ethics of liberalism that is at
> issue."[282]

The internal threat remains

When we talk about the internal threats facing the country we have to include the risk of domestic terrorism. The United States faces challenges from domestic terrorism in at least two varieties, although there may be shades of grey between them. The first category includes homegrown violent extremists, which are US citizens or at least residents who derive their inspiration, motivation, direction, and/or instruction not from other Americans, but by foreign terrorist organizations (sometimes officially state-sponsored, sometimes only tacitly acknowledged). The second group comprises domestic violent extremists, which are not directed by foreign organizations, but rather are internally motivated by racial, ethnic, national, or other factors, including ideologies such as Supremacism, Fascism, Marxism, Anarchism or Ultranationalism. Both White supremacists and true believer adherents to ANTIFA fall into this latter category of fringe ideologies on Right and Left (sometimes the ideologies can overlap weirdly and confusingly: one could be a radical Black Supremacist Fascist or a radical White Supremacist Marxist-Anarchist). Acting Secretary of the Department of Homeland Security, Chad Wolf, commented near the end of September 2020 that within the second category of domestic violent extremists, White Supremacists have been the most lethal threat over the past two years (2018 and 2019). However, he went on to indicate that the rise of anti-government, anti-law enforcement, and Anarchist extremists have been the emerging threat most impacting the country over the past four months. Specifically, Secretary Wolf noted that the criminal activity that had been observed occurring in recent weeks in Portland and elsewhere seemed to have an Anarchist ideology as the driving inspirational force behind it. It is not clear whether this Anarchist-mindset community is truly homegrown, or rather fertilized and funded by foreign government-sourced influences.[283] To date, the Department of Homeland Security has recorded 349 separate injuries to law enforcement officers in Portland, including 125 that have had eye injuries of one form or another primarily from lasers, and in some cases from incendiary or pyrotechnic devices. Inexplicably, however, a somewhat bland resolution before the Senate supporting the United States men and women in law enforcement was blocked by Senate Democrats.[284]

The related specific threat that our country faces in real-time is around election security. The US government identifies this as having two particular facets, the first being cyber-threats to the election systems, and the second being threats to the election infrastructure itself. It's important to note that to date, there has not been any specific evidence or allegations of attacks on either the election system or the election infrastructure from a foreign nation-state.[285] Since the government is focused primarily on systems and infrastructure attacks, they have not specifically addressed the question of influence campaigns.

We previously discussed the Microsoft detailed report saying among other things that they had evidence that there were cyber-attacks related to the elections coming from China, Russia, and Iran. The Department of Homeland security has confirmed, consistent with the Microsoft report, that with less than two months to run until the election, the United States is being bombarded with disinformation and propaganda campaigns coming from not only Russia, but also China and Iran, although they are operating with different motivations, modes, and tactics.

One specific risk is that the elections provide the stage on which bad actors can disrupt America's democratic process, whether through cyber-attacks and propaganda or through more direct acts of terrorism and violence. The next section looks at the topic of the November elections and some of the risks posed.

The November elections are a concentrated risk

It has been called the most contentious and controversial presidential election ever seen in the history of the American Republic. The nation never seemed more divided. Throughout the campaign, the Democrats called the Republican presidential candidate everything from a liar to a madman, a cheat, a traitor, an enemy of America, and a would-be tyrant. Firing back, the Republicans accused the Democratic challenger of being past his sell-by date and in ill health, of being corrupted by financial ties to industrial parties with conflicting interest with the United States, and as being a dull and lifeless prop for the dark forces conspiring behind him. Suspicion of voter fraud was rampant. Heavily armed and marauding White supremacists canvassed the country preventing minorities from voting. Election Day results in Florida and other states were deemed too close to call. The electoral votes were neck and neck, and the College needed resolution of those states to declare a victor. The media, for once, had almost nothing to say and were holding back conflicting information declaring the outcome of election results given the uncertainty, confusion, and questions abounding across the country. There were threats of another civil war and rumors of behind-the-scenes haggling.

As best as anyone could tell, it looked like one candidate would have the absolute majority of the popular vote, but a question arose in the Electoral College about the legitimacy of certain states' votes, and upon a recount, amidst accusations of ballot-box stuffing and the destroying of ballots, it was confirmed that in certain jurisdictions the number of votes exceeded the voting population. Then, when it seemed it couldn't get any worse, there were allegations of the election board in one state offering to certify the vote for a certain amount of future funding to that state. Similar accusations and reports of corruption and malfeasance were being launched back-and-forth from both Democratic and Republican trenches.

If this scenario sounds familiar, it's because it is … but perhaps not for the reason you assumed. This is not a prophetic picture of the November 2020 election between President Trump and Joe Biden. Rather it is a glance back past 150 years of American history to what has been called "the ugliest, most contentious presidential election ever,"[286] the epic battle between Rutherford B. Hayes and Samuel J. Tilden in 1876. The outcome of the election remains controversial. What is known to history is that although Hayes lost the popular vote by 48% to 51.5%, he won the election in part based on a shady backroom deal amongst the parties, which resulted in the Compromise of 1877.

While some compromises in political haggling are necessary and good, this one was diabolic, in that Hayes took the presidency in quid pro quo for agreeing to remove federal troops from the secessionist and vengeful South, which left the Black populations unprotected. It also brought an end to the process and dream of Reconstruction that President Grant had undertaken, and that so many millions of American souls had bled over years of war and strife. The Compromise allowed the slow process of the unwinding of the victory of the Civil War. It ushered in the Jim Crow era, allowing states to reimpose racial segregation, the rise of the KKK as a political and terrorist force, and for decades of inhumane depredations against Black Americans to continue unabated until the civil rights movement of the 1950s-60s.

The award of the most contentious and controversial election may not even deservedly go to Hayes vs. Tilden. The 1860 election of Abraham Lincoln, the nation's first Republican president, threatened to tear the country apart, and nearly succeeded. The newspaper *The Atlanta Confederacy* had this to say on behalf of its constituency in the days shortly after Lincoln's surprising election:

> "Let the consequences be what they may – whether the
> Potomac is crimsoned in human gore, and Pennsylvania
> Avenue is paved ten fathoms in depth with mangled bodies, or
> whether the last vestige of liberty is swept from the face of the
> American continent, the South will never submit to such
> humiliation and degradation as the inauguration of Abraham
> Lincoln." [287]

While Pennsylvania Avenue was spared this fate, the nation was not, and both North and South bled for the Confederacy's unwillingness to yield to the authority of the Constitution and the President of the United States of America. Atlanta itself would be a smoldering ruin just a few years later, and approximately 750,000 men, perhaps 5% of the total male population, would perish along the way.[288]

Following the Civil War, the nation made real progress towards greater justice in the Reconstruction years under President Grant. Grant, like President Lincoln before him, had over time become a true believer and advocate for the rights of Black Americans in the South and in the Union as a whole. Unfortunately, with Lincoln's assassination and Grant's eventual decline and passing from throat cancer, most of these hard-won and blood-stained victories were slowly but surely unwound by President Hayes and the Democratic Party in the decades to follow, using the cover of 'states' rights' as the dominant claim over federal sovereignty.

Over the following decades, the states and the federal government rolled back many of the Reconstruction-era laws, practices, and norms benefiting African-Americans that Republican Presidents Lincoln and Grant had put in place, and occasionally had had to enforce at the point of the bayonet. This regression probably reached a nadir under President Woodrow Wilson, who for all the good he sought to do at Versailles made the shameful policy of segregation the working practice, not just in the former slave-owning South, but also at the Federal level, including at the US Treasury, the War Department and the Department of the Interior.[289] Nonetheless, when called upon to assist on behalf of a county that had mostly snubbed and scorned them, these same African-American men and women continued to serve, fight and die in our various foreign wars as true patriots whose blood ran just as red as the child of England or Europe standing next to them.

Finally, during the Civil Rights movement of the 1950s and 60s, the country made real progress (although some of it was just making up for ground lost after Reconstruction was abandoned), again with the shedding of much blood and the assassinations of great leaders, and occasionally having to compel the states by federal force to achieve it. Just as the Civil War didn't end the conflict, the Civil Rights Act (or President Johnson's subsequent War on Poverty) didn't solve the issues, and the country again regressed and bled through a thousand cuts of unfair and discriminatory lending and housing practices, a broken criminal justice system, well-meaning but inherently bad government programming (that created dis-incentives for education and employment and led to perverse outcomes), redistricting, and generally making access to voting more difficult for the poor and minorities over the past two decades.

We are now at a third crisis point in our long and sad engagement with our fellow Americans ... who happen to be of African descent. We are once again confronted as a nation with the question of whether we will be able to live up to the commitment of "with liberty and justice for all." It is simply a statement of fact, not one of opinion or political propaganda, to affirm that with no justice, there can be no peace.

This third crisis point in our engagement with ourselves now comes to a head in the 2020 presidential elections. There has rarely been a period in time in American history where elections have not been highly controversial. Partisan political machines, which operated on the spoils patronage system, dominated American politics throughout most of the 19th century. Questions of ballot stuffing, secret vs. open ballots, out in the open voter bribery at polling stations, party corruption, and backroom dealing, all have played significant parts in the American election process. So what, if anything, makes the 2020 elections different?

One of the main reasons that there is so much controversy around this election is the concern and fear over whether President Trump would concede defeat and leave office peacefully if Biden stands elected. Statements that the President himself has recently made do not lend comfort to the issue. Beyond leaving the question outstanding and riven with doubt, the President has previously suggested that because of the risk of extensive mail-in ballot fraud the election results could be delayed for months. Both of these outcomes would range from severe to catastrophic.

Equally befuddling, President Trump lost a very easy opportunity to clarify his position on Supremacism during the first debate with Joe Biden at the end of September. As the Pulitzer Prize-winning journalist and former special assistant to President Reagan Peggy Noonan succinctly noted,

> "Condemning white supremacy is not only morally right, which is its own unarguable imperative; it is easy, a softball a competent demagogue could have hit out of the park. Americans disapprove of hate groups! They hate groups based on hating a race or religion or ethnicity. Such groups are un-American. It is scandal a president would not denounce them."[290]

Biden similarly lost an easy opportunity to be more clear-cut in denouncing the riots and violence that have ripped apart our cities in Portland and elsewhere. Both parties to the debate displayed puerile and unstatesmanlike behavior and left most Americans feeling saddened, discouraged, and disgusted with the whole thing. We have to do better as a nation, and it starts with our own leaders.

A number of the other potential issues facing this election have been the subject of this book. A confluence of extraordinary events, whether it be a combination of intervention by foreign actors in the form of cyber-attacks or other belligerence, continued disinformation campaigns that take on more virulent forms, a spike in COVID-19 related deaths and illnesses rendering voting stations and other public venues unsafe, accompanied by the resumption of lockdowns and other pandemic related effects, or perhaps other factors not covered here including confirmed and substantiated evidence of voter fraud. Attempts to make in-person voting safer by the introduction of new technologies at polling stations is itself not a cure. It is risky in that any new and unproven technology invites malfunctions, breakdowns, or other unforeseen glitches on systems that have not been tested and tried.

One thing appears fairly certain, which is that there does not appear to be any plausible Election Day scenario that does not raise very contentious and controversial issues that get to the heart of the legitimacy of the election and by implication our democratic process itself. If President Trump is reelected, nearly half of our country will believe that such a result was not legitimately possible and surely could only have come about by fraud or corruption, proving that Trump is a Fascist autocrat and not the legitimate leader of a democratic republic. Riots ensue.

If Biden wins, the MAGA crowd will similarly believe that such an outcome could only have come about by deep state conspiracy and fraud, proving Q right that there is indeed a shadow government led by a Clinton-Obama alliance of the damned. Counter-riots ensue.

Third path: the election is controversial, with results approximating a tie, there are many question marks and uncertainties that demand fact-checking and verification, and the results of the election are not certified for an extended period of time. The country enters into a phase of limbo that is not resolved for months. Legal challenges are lodged and rejoined. Demonstrations and counter-demonstrations by Left and Right continue on an endless vigil that slowly deteriorates into violence and discord, shaking to the foundations of our cities and communities, further breaking what little fraternity and civility remain between us as Americans. A National Emergency is declared and Emergency Powers evoked. The election result is declared invalid. Riots ensue. Blood is shed.

By the time the Supreme Court of the United States made its decision and final ruling in *Bush v. Gore* on December 12, 2000, nearly six weeks had passed since the election. Shortly thereafter, Vice President Gore conceded defeat, thereby avoiding a national calamity. The decision and the process of arriving at it were very controversial and continued to be the focus of the media through the first half of 2001.

It is not difficult to imagine that the issues and circumstances surrounding the 2020 election could be even more complicated than hanging chads and the validity of absentee ballots untimely received that were the controversies of 2000. As contentious and partisan as matters appeared at that time, there is little doubt that today's environment is even more divisive and rancorous some 20 years on. It is in fact quite difficult to see how this ends well.

Part V: The way forward

10. Countries will be forced to choose

What is of supreme importance in war is to attack the enemy's
strategy ...
Next best is to disrupt his alliances:
Tu Yu: Do not allow your enemies to get together.
Wang Hsi: ... Look into the matter of his alliances and cause
them to be severed and dissolved. If an enemy has alliances,
the problem is grave and the enemy's position strong; If he has
no alliances the problem is minor and the enemy's position
week.[291]
– Sun Tzu, *The Art of War*

Between a rock and a hard place

The Trump administration's foreign policy has in practice
repudiated the New World Order regime that prevailed since the end of
World War II. From the perspective of US foreign policy, multilateral
institutions such as the UN and its various agencies including the World
Health Organization, the International Monetary Fund, and World Bank,
which for well over half a century have been the primary venues for
dialogue amongst the nations, are receding into the background of
importance. There is a large question mark over the United States'
commitment to NATO, which has left the EU countries in an uncertain
and insecure position, as they reconsider their position in the world with a
more assertive Russian neighbor. Japan, Taiwan, and other Asian nations
face a similar question as to whether the United States will maintain its
previous defense and security commitments.

We can expect American trade, military, and other alliances to shift and to harden as the geopolitical environment worsens. Today, China's largest trading partners (exports plus imports) are the United States, the European Union (including the UK for this purpose), Japan, and South Korea along with Hong Kong and Taiwan.[292] These trading partners also represent significant diplomatic and military allies for the United States in any potential conflict with China. The trade wars, therefore, place these countries in an uncomfortable position of inherent conflict as between their economic objectives on the one hand, and their military and security needs on the other.

China has ratcheted up the pressure on foreign governments and companies in recent months through a variety of coercive means, primarily including state-issued threats, along with restrictions on trade, tourism, and travel. State-issued threats often involve the release of official statements threatening foreign governments and companies using terms like "countermeasures," "retaliation" and the like, often channeled through government-owned and controlled media companies.

In August 2020, an independent, non-partisan think tank, The Australian Strategic Policy Institute, put out a policy brief entitled *The Chinese Communist Party's Coercive Diplomacy*, in which it analyzed the CCP's use of coercive diplomacy over the past ten years, noting 152 cases of highly coercive tactics since 2010 (in which 100 targeted foreign governments and 52 targeted foreign companies). From 2010 through 2017, these cases averaged less than ten a year, but were often of high profile, such as when "the CCP enacted multiple coercive measures against Norway in 2010 in retaliation to the awarding of the Nobel Peace Prize to Chinese dissident Liu Xiaobo."[293] The report goes on to note that "after those measures were enacted, UN voting patterns showed closer alignment between China and Norway, and the Norwegian government supported the admission of China as an observer in the Arctic Council in 2013 and refused to meet with the Dalai Lama for the first time in 2014."

A very sharp escalation in the use of these tactics began in 2017-18, contemporaneous with the trade wars previously discussed. By the first eight months of 2020, there were already 34 cases logged for the year. Tactically, China seems to be deploying these tools by targeting and isolating an individual country in a classic divide-and-conquer approach. In our current environment, Western allies have been hesitant to back one another up in these challenges from China, presumably out of fear of enmeshment in the same controversy. This has left smaller and relatively weaker countries such as Norway, Canada, and Australia in a difficult and isolated position in trying to address the threats put forward by China.

The situation seems to come with a built-in and reasonably easy to find the answer, which is in greater cooperation and coordination among these trading partners under pressure by China, by working together to recognize, resist and respond jointly to the coercive tactics of the CCP. This is easier said than done, but it is the only path to be able to put up a staunch enough resistance. China needs to have a formidable opponent, of worthy stature and equivalent size and heft, before the challenge is taken seriously. That is one reason why the EU remains relevant in this environment as a significant trading block with adequate size and persuasive power, well beyond what each country in Europe would have on its own, and why the US needs to start rebuilding this relationship on mutually acceptable terms.

South Korea provides an interesting example of the essential conflict between economic, diplomatic, and military objectives. Uri Friedman pointed out in *The Atlantic* in July 2019 that South Korea relies on the US for its defense and security within the region, and in particular military protection from its unruly neighbor North Korea, but does more trade with China than with the US and Japan combined.[294] The South Korean government is thus caught between Scylla and Charybdis, navigating between the two perils as it struggles to keep each of China and the US happy. At best, South Korea has so far managed to leave each of them equally unsatisfied with the situation. But it does not appear long-term sustainable.

South Korea is only one of several countries, including Japan, Germany, Brazil, and Australia, which find themselves similarly trapped between their commitments under US defense agreements and China as their largest trading partner. Japan is a particularly troubling case for the US given its size and strategic importance as a forward base for the US military in the region. As the third-largest economy in the world (behind the US and China) it has been one of the US's most important trading partners since World War II, and the US has been exclusively responsible for providing Japan's defense. This relationship has come under strain in recent years as the US has appeared to wobble on its commitments to its partners in the region. As a result, Japan has begun to hedge the relationship by undertaking infrastructure and other projects with its ancient and now much larger historical enemy. With the resignation of Shinzo Abe and the installation of a new leader from the same dominant political party, the US will be well served to reconfirm and strengthen this relationship.

Revisiting the role of trade

When the Trump administration launched the first round of trade wars and started talking about tariffs, it applied the tool rather indiscriminately by not singularly targeting China as the obvious and primary adversary of the US, but instead applying similar regulations and restrictions on our neighbors and erstwhile allies including Canada, Mexico, and the European Union. To make the economic sanctions and measures effective against China, Russia, and Iran, the US is going to have to rethink how it engages with its proximate neighbors and allies in the European Union, along with Japan and South Korea, to be able to draw them into a closer alliance with the United States.

It does our country very little good to seek to make enemies of everyone at the same time. We're going to need allies, we're going to need their support, and we're going to need their help in creating trade patterns and supply lines that reduce our dependence upon China. In order for us to do that, we're going to have to have more favorable trade policies and lower tariffs and other barriers with those countries with which we want to strengthen and deepen our alliances.

Within the first year of President Trump's term, his administration went about aggressively withdrawing from free trade agreements around the world, including the North American Free Trade Agreement (NAFTA) with Canada and Mexico, the Transatlantic Trade and Investment Partnership (TTIP) between the United States and the European Union, and the Trans-Pacific Partnership (TPP), which excluded China but had fourteen signatories including Australia, Brunei, Canada, Chile, Japan, Malaysia, Mexico, New Zealand, Peru, Singapore, Vietnam and the United States, countries which in total represented 40% of global GDP.

President Trump had clearly signaled during his 2016 campaign that he intended to walk away from these agreements, including the TPP, as being 'bad deals' for the United States. But the application of the principle appeared indiscriminate, and in some cases may have weakened the US's position both in terms of trade and in the US's ability to use these agreements as geo-economic bargaining chips in its relationship with China and other nations. The United States has substantial opportunity to benefit from these relationships, but this will ultimately require cooperation, coordination, and the occasional compromise with the US's closest trading partners and allies in order to benefit from these very powerful tools. This may be exactly what the administration intended to do by applying a form of 'creative destruction' to undo and then redo these partnerships, but if so it has been a very disruptive and incomplete path towards achieving the objective.

Simply put, the US should reconsider its potential to use multi-national trade agreements to apply greater leverage in the trade relationship with China. By abandoning TPP rather than re-engaging on its terms, the Trump administration may have missed an opportunity to use the TPP in alliance with the other signatory nations to change the negotiating dynamic with China. George Mangus describes it this way: "Trump's insistence that the TPP was another useless multilateral agreement in which the US would lose out to others, and his failure to see the TPP as an opportunity for major nations to come together in ways that could wield leverage over China, were two sides of the same catastrophic coin."[295]

While the US has been busy withdrawing from multilateral free trade agreements, China has been working in the background to build up its own free trade networks and alliances. China has "nineteen bilateral deals under construction of which fourteen have been signed," including the Regional Comprehensive Economic Partnership (RCEP) which is intended to include sixteen Asian countries representing half of the world's population, 30% of global GDP, and 28% of world trade. The RCEP is much narrower in scope than the TPP and doesn't address contentious issues important to the United States but anathema to China, including "data and privacy, state enterprises, and protections for labor, human rights, and the environment."[296] While China is not the natural champion of globalization and free trade, the US risks missing the opportunity to recapture the advantage if it does not reassert itself as a leading force in these discussions with countries that are being pressed to make difficult choices.

The SCO as a proto-typical anti-American alliance

In addition to security and defense agreements on the one hand, and trade agreements on the other, the other force posed to challenge the existing Western multi-lateral establishment include multinational 'cooperation organizations.' These alliances provide a venue for discussion and agreement across a number of topics of relevance to countries in broader Eurasia but clearly have a pro-Chinese and anti-American orientation. One example of this is the Shanghai Cooperation Organization (SCO). Sponsored by China and Russia, the SRO is an eight-member organization of Central Asian powers (also including Kazakhstan, Kyrgyzstan, Tajikistan, Uzbekistan, India, and Pakistan). When first initiated at the turn of the century, both powers were of roughly equal weight. Since then, China has grown its economy (and thus its power) exponentially while Russia has stagnated under the weight of falling oil prices, an ossified, top-heavy and centralized economy, and kleptocratic corruption within the controlling elite aligned with Putin. Nonetheless, the alliance is important in having brought closer into the dialogue other nations hostile to the US and the West, including Iran and Turkey. The SCO provides a venue for discussion and cooperation in what one can reasonably conclude is an anti-US coalition.[297]

Both India and Pakistan were admitted as full members in 2015, notwithstanding their conflicts with each other and then each with China over Kashmir and other disputed regions in the Himalayas and nearby areas. India is walking a delicate tightrope here between its desire for stronger relations with the US (including the Quadrilateral Security Dialogue between the US, India, Japan, and Australia, intended to counter the threat of a rising China as a maritime power in the Pacific), and the practical realities of how to get on with its next-door neighbors. "India has explained its membership in both ostensibly clashing groups as a part of its principles of 'strategic autonomy and multi-alignment.'"[298]

While not a substantial threat today, the SCO illustrates a type of regional alliance that China is attempting to build as an additional geostrategic and geo-economic tool in its strategic arsenal toward the United States. While Iran is not part of the SCO, China, Russia, and Iran have been coordinating on several financial services and other infrastructure projects that pose a potentially more pressing threat to the US.

For example, China and Iran are in advanced stages of finalizing the terms of a 25-year strategic partnership between the two countries intended to align economic, military, and diplomatic agendas between the two regional powers. The plans would specifically include Chinese technical and other assistance in the development of the Iranian oil and gas sector, in exchange for the guaranteed provision of energy supplies to China over the 25-year term at highly favorable rates.[299] While not finalized, it is widely understood that the "Comprehensive Cooperation Plan Between The People's Republic Of China And The Islamic Republic Of Iran" entails a broader alignment well beyond economics into matters of mutual strategic interest in international affairs, and in particular regarding their relationship with the United States. The next section turns to the specific risk posed by Iran.

Iran poses a clear and present danger to America

> "Mr. Trump! Our revenge for martyrdom of our great general [Soleimani] is obvious, serious and real. … "We will hit those who had direct and indirect roles. You should know that everybody who had role in the event will be hit, and this is a serious message. We do prove everything in practice."[300]
> – Gen. Hossein Salami, Commander-in-chief,
> Islamic Revolutionary Guard Corps, September 2020

We've spent a lot of time talking about the rise of China and the inevitable risk of great power conflict between China and the US as they vie for global leadership. However, the near-term risk of escalation may first come from a different direction such as Iran, whether by proxy, coordination, or at least tacit consent with China acting in the background only. Iran's government, a sworn enemy of the US since the student-led revolution in the 1970s, now has an honor-culture revenge motive with the US's killing (by way of a drone strike in January 2020) of General Qasem Soleimani, the second most powerful person in Iran behind Supreme

Leader Ali Khamenei. Iran also has motive in a "revenge is dish best served cold" style retribution for the infamous Stuxnet cyber-attacks on their nuclear facilities in 2009,[301] which forced Iran to shut down its centrifuges for a period of time and substantially delayed the uranium enrichment program in its plants. While no one has claimed responsibility or been held accountable for Stuxnet, the malware has been unofficially attributed to the US and Israel, and this is the narrative that the Iranian government is working with as it bides it's time for a response.

As the United States faces off with Iran and its vow to seek "harsh revenge" against America for the killing of General Soleimani in January 2020, America finds herself standing alone. Her erstwhile European allies, sitting in London, Paris, and Berlin, have all backed away from the hard line that the US has drawn around economic and other sanctions against the Persian nation, specifically by refusing to extend an arms embargo against Iran past its October 2020 expiration.[302] This is not surprising as these nations, as part of the EU, have historically strong economic interests in reopening trade with Iran.[303]

Iranian President Hassan Rouhani spoke at the United Nations' General Assembly in September "to denounce American pressure and send a message of resistance and resilience to the United States, signaling no matter the pressure, the Islamic Republic will refuse to budge."[304] Over the past year, while sanctions have been in place, China has been Iran's top trading destination both in terms of exports and imports, followed by the UAE.[305]

In late September 2020, Iranian Revolutionary Guard Major General Hossein Salami, referring to the peace agreement that the US had brokered between Israel, the UAE, and Bahrain strengthening the anti-Iranian coalition in the region,[306] that the US has "reconciled reactionary regimes with the Zionists, causing the hatred of all Muslims. "Such hatred will not remain at the surface, but weapons and Jihad will come out of it," he said. "We are steadily increasing power here, never stopping, but increasing the range of our weapons and deepening the depths of our navigation."[307] This sort of bluster has gone one for years in the halls of Iranian power but we dare not ignore it now. There is legitimate, street-level anger at the assassination. US intelligence reports in mid-September 2020 asserted that Iran was plotting to assassinate a US ambassador. Gen. Salami denied the allegations and disclaimed the action on the grounds it was insufficient retaliation and not directed against those involved.[308]

The near-term risk posed by Iran should not be underestimated.

II. What should we do?

"Darkness cannot drive out darkness; only light can do that.
Hate cannot drive out hate; only love can do that."
– Martin Luther King, Jr.

The third little pig had it right

Every child is taught that there are wolves in the woods, but preparation can keep them at bay. Today, national preparation looks like creating redundancies, diversity, and flexibility in our supply chains, ensuring food security and healthcare continuity, replenishing both strategic national and household reserves, and hardening critical infrastructures such as telecommunications and energy resources. Preparation looks like deleveraging the balance sheets of our municipalities, corporations, and households, and increasing loss-absorbing capital buffers for our financial institutions. Preparation looks like fixing some of the flaws in the US-influenced global financial infrastructure, making these systems less unfavorable to other countries so that switching costs become prohibitive. Preparation also means finding common ground to unite as Americans, which must include addressing the very valid grievances of racial injustice and treatment of the poor, rather than letting our enemies exploit them as a means to weaken the fabric of our society and the country itself.

Our season of blissful ignorance is over. But, it's not too late to wake up, shake off our inertia, and better prepare for, and hopefully prevent, the parade of horrible potentialities outlined above.

One of the things that make America great is our free market system, which has included open and transparent governance, accounting, and access to capital, which has had the benefit of attracting both foreign capital and human talent. We also greatly value our First Amendment rights of freedom of speech, freedom of the press, and the right to assemble peacefully and address our grievances to the government. Over the years this has translated to one of the most vibrant, productive, and creative university systems in the world. We, and the world, benefit from talented professors and students from nations across the globe. Academic collaboration with other nations has led to massive advances in science, technology, and other fields that have helped alleviate poverty, improve the health and livelihoods of billions around the world. This must not change, but we need to be realistic and a bit more cautious about China's ambitions and the threat the CCP poses to us. This will require a reworking of how academic intellectual property is shared and better screening of the foreign nationals that are allowed to work or study on our campuses.

As the authors of Why Nations Fail point out, one of the main differences between economic institutions in the West and those in China or Russia that have the illusion of similarity based on external appearance, is the degree to which they are either inclusive or exclusive. Inclusive economic institutions provide built-in mechanisms for checks and balances as a result of a diverse group of stakeholders including shareholders, employees, management, customers, suppliers regulators, and independent auditors and the like, each of which has some form of a claim upon the integrity of the firm. While this doesn't work perfectly it does provide a strong directional signal that tends towards transparency, accountability, and sustainability over time and the mechanism of capital allocation provides self-correcting through losses, bankruptcy, divestiture, or winding down of entities that don't respond correctly to these signals. On the other hand, extractive economic institutions exist primarily for the benefit of the elite that controls them and generally fails to have the same kinds of checks and balances that would exist in an inclusive economic institution as is characterized by most firms in the West. As the name implies, this allows the extraction of financial and other resources including power for its own sake by the elites who run and control the institution.

As an investor in South Africa over the past decade, I saw firsthand under the Presidency of Jacob Zuma the horrible toll that state capture (infiltrating the apparatus of government, such as the treasury, judiciary, regulatory and other functions in order to seize power for the purpose of economic extraction) extracts on otherwise successful and performing economies. Over a long enough period of time, these forces can drain a nation of the very lifeblood of its strength and wealth (as we've recently seen in Venezuela, North Korea, and Zimbabwe) if not stopped along the way. The good and long-suffering people of South Africa finally stood up to it and voted Zuma out of office, but the difference there was that South Africa is a democracy (albeit young and therefore without deep roots) that nonetheless has very strong institutions such as a truly independent judiciary, a vocal free press that was able to be highly critical of Zuma and his cronies, and a highly competent national Treasury that was able to resist many of the more serious attempts at the seizure of economic assets.

We can see that this process is happening in Russia and China today. The difference for those nations is that the economic assets of the state have always been in the hands of a small ruling elite at the expense of the nation's people. Today, rather than the ideological tools of

Communism which were deployed in the past, the same elite uses the appearance of commercial free enterprise and capitalism as the facade to hide their actions. Over the long run, this leaves the state in a very fragile position because at some point the population – long under the thumb of economic repression through high taxes and other extractions – will organize, rise up, resist and potentially overthrow the powers of the elite. This is clearly the biggest fear that governments in any of China, Russia, or Iran face, each of which has gone through revolutions at various points in their histories, and why they take such authoritarian and brutal measures to restrain any signs of opposition or revolt that would threaten to undermine the power of the ruling elite. The authors of *Why Nations Fail* explain the process this way:

> Rich nations are rich largely because they managed to develop inclusive institutions …
> Under inclusive economic institutions there are more limited gains from holding political power, thus weak are incentives … to try to take control of the state.
> On the other hand, extractive political institutions create few constraints on the exercise of power, so there are essentially no institutions to restrain the use and abuse of power … and assuming control of the state … extractive economic institutions imply that there are great profits to be made merely by controlling power, expropriating the assets of others and setting up monopolies.
>
> When extractive institutions create huge inequities in society and great wealth and unchecked power for those in control, there will be many wishing to fight to take control of the state and institutions. Extractive institutions ... engender continuous infighting and civil wars ... This often starts a process of descent into lawlessness, state failure, and political chaos crushing all hopes of economic prosperity ... [309]

Some specific recommendations

There are certain specific things that the US government, companies, and individuals can and should be doing differently in this environment.

Each one of us should increase our general awareness of the tactics being used by China and other governments to undermine and destabilize US interests here and abroad. Those in government or corporate leadership should consider what are the best responses to each tactic in each particular situation based on the scope of influence and responsibility one has. At a national government level, the US needs to build or rebuild alliances that are better able to more effectively push back on state-sponsored intimidation and coercion. Responses should be coordinated and agreed in advance (i.e. response protocols for specific types of threats). They also may be possible at the private corporate or business level through industry sector trade groups and alliances where mutual interests can be identified and exploited. The US government needs to be willing to defend our alliance partners' interests by coordinating responses in a visibly aligned matter in resistance to CCP pressure.

Governments should be willing to take up their private company's defense and support when coercive foreign attacks come, so as to not leave these companies stranded in isolation. Western governments should capitalize on existing intelligence networks that already share information and other resources, and significantly expand their use in the economic (rather than just in military or diplomatic) realms. Western companies should recalibrate their relationships with Chinese businesses explicitly taking into consideration the geopolitical and geo-economic implications of their partnerships, supply chains, trade flows, and the like.

At the same time, US private sector corporations need to do deeper and better due diligence on the firms and people with whom they consider working or partnering. Supply chains need to be vetted, and board or executive team level discussions of potential commercial agreements or partnership transactions (JVs, mergers, or the like) need to more carefully consider the geopolitical and geo-economic realities of the current environment, recognizing that their potential foreign partners are playing by an entirely different rule book than they are. Companies need to be more "long-term greedy" and fully appreciate that trading away their sustainable competitive advantage through the loss of intellectual property for the sake of short-term gain is a losing proposition, not just for them, but for the nation as a whole. This will not be easy, especially given the temptations of the size of the Chinese market, but is critical to staunch the outward flow of the lifeblood of our economy.

Mandatory national service?

Great Britain is renowned for the national unity that it was able to achieve in the years leading up to the First World War, through the intra-war period and post-World War II. In light of its previous history, this was a rather surprising outcome, because during most of the first half of the 19th century Great Britain had seen "social disorders throughout the land which had sometimes approached the intensity of civil war," and in the second half witnessed grievous inequities and wretched poverty and decay in its large cities, arising from the rapid and chaotic industrialization and urbanization that took place during this time.

However, during the decade leading up to the First World War, the Liberal administration in which Winston Churchill served laid a foundation that led to " a far more orderly society than it ever been in the past." it was "the expectation of war before 1914 that made national fitness a serious political issue, and the war itself, when it came, speed the development of national community in two fundamental ways." The first was that the war effort was so dependent upon industrial productivity that it forced the British government and Victorian society to reconcile itself with its unruly labor element, putting aside classist grievances and ideological differences and finding a means to bring divergent views into the government and the administration of the economy and the war effort.

Second, and also a lesson for us today, was that "the experience of virtually universal military service forged, as it always had …, a sense of national identity and cohesion far deeper than any political or social programs could possibly have achieved." Among other benefits, this was very effective in bringing men from the wealthier classes in close proximity with all other manners and classes, allowing prejudices to be confronted and set aside, and revealing the inequities and injustices of their societies in ways that could not be ignored. This led to a commitment amongst enough of the elite leadership of that younger generation to make changes and bring about reform and a greater level of equality in their society, which they achieved to some degree in the 1920s and 1930s.[310]

Reflecting on the sad state of our Union, in which "Americans' civic discourse has all but disappeared, giving way to either pessimistic apathy or blind partisanship," General Charles C. Krulak (USMC Ret.), the former Commandant of the United States Marine Corps, wrote an opinion piece in May 2020 in which he made an appeal for a "mandatory, two-year, paid national service program to bring together Americans of different backgrounds and help break down geographic, racial, ethnic, religious, and socioeconomic barriers to a deeply felt and widely shared civic identity."[311]

This sort of program has been effectively implemented at various points in our national history, most remarkably during the New Deal era under FDR, in which a number of national civil works programs were implemented to get people back to work and productively engaged in the economy, and then during the early days of the Kennedy administration in which programs such as the Peace Corps and other national service programs were implemented. The momentum of these programs eventually and unfortunately gave way to the national draft that was reinstated as the Vietnam War continued to escalate. Gen. Krulak pointed out that the benefits to the participants would be substantial and broad-based:

> For many, this might be their first opportunity for on-the-job training. For all, national service would offer unique team-building experiences. Young people of all economic, social, ethnic, geographic, and religious backgrounds would find themselves thrust together in ways that simply don't exist today. Each participant would have opportunities to learn skills and gain experiences beyond what would otherwise be possible. And, to broaden young Americans' perspectives on issues facing communities beyond their own, half of each state's draftees should carry out their service in another state.[312]

This is a proposal to which the 2021-2024 administration should give serious consideration. While certainly not a panacea, there is good reason to believe that this type of program could go a long way in addressing some of the malaise that's afflicting our country and our society, imparting to a new generation a spirit of cohesion and camaraderie – and a sense of what it means to be an American – something that appears to be missing from younger generations today.

12. Concluding postscript

"In my opinion, it will not cease, until a crisis shall have been
reached, and passed.
A house divided against itself cannot stand."[313]
– Abraham Lincoln

I thought I'd awaken to a world in mourning.
Heavy clouds crowding, a society storming.
But there's something different on this golden morning.
Something magical in the sunlight, wide and warming.
. . .
We ignite not in the light, but in lack thereof,
For it is in loss that we truly learn to love.
In this chaos, we will discover clarity.
In suffering, we must find solidarity.[314]
– Amanda Gorman, Inaugural US Youth Poet Laureate

The COVID-19 pandemic reminded us that black swan events do occur, that they happen more often than one would expect, that they come unforeseen and unexpected, and often with devastating consequences. The silver-lining opportunity in such an event is it allows us to discover what lessons can be gleaned from the specifics of the event and apply them to other situations that may be analogous. This is the opportunity that has been presented to us in 2020. In his book *The Black Swan: The Impact Of The Highly Improbable*, Nassim Taleb describes three features of a black swan event: 1) it's so rare the possibility of it occurring is unknown (and possibly unknowable), 2) it has a catastrophic impact, and 3) it can be explained only in hindsight, as existing models would not and could not have included the possibility of its existence.[315] The black swan metaphor derives from history. From the time the Roman poet Juvenal first wrote about something being as rare as a black swan, implying it wasn't real, until the end of the 17th century, people did not believe the black swans actually existed.[316] The phrase was used at the time as a metaphor for something that was impossible to occur. It was only in 1697 when an actual black swan was discovered (at least by Europeans keeping records) in Australia, up-ending the previously held belief.

It is not exactly true that no one could foresee a pandemic or the global financial crisis of 2008-09. In fact, both these scenarios had many voices giving warning well in advance ... it's just that no one would listen. Taleb's point was not that if we try hard enough, we can predict and prevent black swans before they occur, but rather that our awareness that they do exist could enable us to build better and more robust systems to help withstand the impact of extreme events when they do occur. Our systems and processes can become less fragile than otherwise if we prepare for the unknown knowns[317] related to a wide variety of risks. We tend to not do this because such preparation and defensive redundancies cost time, money, and other resources that are hard to justify under the guise of "what if?".

Risk is always present in life. There is a lot of research, especially in the insurance world, which indicates that humans generally overestimate the probability of extremely rare but catastrophic events (e.g. commercial jet airliner crashes), and at the same time underestimate the probabilities of much more common and mundane events (e.g. automobile accidents).[318] We also tend to overestimate the probabilities of events happening if we have recently been mentally loaded with specific ideas, the same way a beach vacationer might overestimate the probability of a shark attack on her next dip in the ocean after just having watched several hours of Shark Week. This tendency to place more weight on recent information received is called Availability Bias.[319] For example, if you've recently seen several reports of police shootings, your estimation of how frequently they occur goes up dramatically.

Availability Bias has proven to be a big source of cognitive error, and we should watch out for it given how much new and unexpected information has come into and overloaded our minds in recent months as a result of the pandemic. I'm very aware of the risk of this error as I write this book. Having said that, what do I conclude?

One of the key messages of this work is that I believe that we are in a moment in history when the probabilities of experiencing one or more of the "tail risk" events I've described here has risen sharply. Secondly, those risks are reverberating in a way that may be creating constructive interference and amplifying both the probability of occurrence and the severity (i.e. how bad it might be if it does occur) of one or multiple events. The purpose of this message isn't to then try to predict in what form the event will manifest, or over what timeframe, even though I've given suggestive examples of both.

We do know that the days leading up to and following the elections pose a target for those who see potential to gain from our instability. Early November is thus a high-risk window for all Americans. While China may be the behind-the-scenes provocateur, the actual agent of an attack is unlikely to be China itself. China's leaders appreciate that the country and its people have no strong desire to further directly antagonize its relationship with the United States, which would be economically devastating and self-defeating. But China may be willing to provide covert backing and assistance to others more willing to take the lead here, so long as China is able to retain plausible deniability of its involvement.

An example of this scenario is one in which Iran acts as the agent that applies more aggressive active measures against the US in the coming months. This would be done in furtherance of its own interests but also as a willing proxy for China. There is real popular anger in Iran over the killing of General Soleimani, and a strong desire for revenge. Iran and its leaders are already economically and criminally sanctioned by the US and have thus pivoted to China, Russia, India, and elsewhere for trade and other alliances, meaning there is little further diplomatic or geo-economic downside so long as Iran can stay short of a full-on military confrontation.

Inflation is spiraling out of control, the economy is in shambles, and government risks losing the support of its people, swayed by the more radical elements of its Shi'a clerics. There is no animal more dangerous than one backed into a corner with no path of escape. If there were a vector through which a form of attack seems most likely to come, it would be an assault on our critical infrastructure. Very few things seem more suddenly destabilizing – and paralyzing – than if we were to have a critical failure in our telecommunications, information technology, or electrical infrastructure during this tumultuous time. I reach this assessment simply by putting myself in the shoes of those Iran who might wish to do his harm and have a motive, access, and means, and by and asking the question, where are the greatest weaknesses and how might they be exploited?

In this sense, the Trump administration was right to reduce our over-extended military presence and commitment in Afghanistan and the Middle East for several reasons. First, because these wars were unending and unwinnable, as anyone who knows the history of foreign invaders in Afghanistan (such as the Soviet Union or the British Empire before them) is aware. Secondly, these trillions of dollars of resources, both in men and materials, will be needed in other areas and against stronger, better-resourced enemies. The costs of maintaining the previous commitments were extremely high. Ultimately resources are scarce, they have to be allocated, and the country will have proven to be better off by moving these resources to other areas in anticipation of impending conflicts with more formidable opponents.

My objective beyond sounding a warning of such a possibly imminent event has been to encourage all of us, both as individuals and collectively as a nation, to reassess some of these risks and to ask ourselves, are we looking at the world in a realistic light? We should be asking ourselves if we were in China's / Russia's / Iran's shoes, what would we do? As Americans, what more should we be doing to prepare for what we now see is plausible? I'm starting with an assumption – which I think that the pandemic has proven out, especially with regard to health care, medical and food supplies – that our systems are not (in Taleb's terms) "anti-fragile" ... not resilient enough to absorb a significant magnitude event like the ones I've described.

As a nation, this preparation should therefore include the acceleration of timetables to harden our electrical, telecoms, transportation, financial, and other infrastructure. It should also include proactively creating redundancies and flexibility in supply chains, even at the cost of efficiency, and importantly, urgently creating or enhancing national stockpiles of food, fuel, pharmaceutical products, and medical supplies that could be drawn upon in an emergency. The cost (with no obvious payback, and thus not suitable for private enterprise), scale, and complexity of this is so vast that it can only be done in a coordinated and centralized fashion, i.e. by the federal government, with a bi-partisan willingness in Congress to allocate funds for something that may never be used. We have learned a lesson this year, which is that to rely on the individual states to independently do their own planning and work in this regard would only lend itself to the same patchwork of inconsistencies and inter-jurisdictional conflicts that we saw in responses to COVID-19.

At the individual personal level, many of these same principles can be applied. Households should think more carefully about how much debt they're carrying and what they can do to reduce it, the sources from which they get their food, and where vulnerabilities exist. At a minimum, they should reconsider and increase how much food and supplies they have on hand, ensuring access to prescription drugs and essential medical and other supplies during an emergency. Individuals should go through the unfamiliar mental exercise of considering what would be the impact on them of, and how they might cope with, a prolonged shutdown of electrical power. By prolonged I mean not just overnight or for a couple of days, but several weeks or even months. Almost anyone who goes through this uncomfortable process will quickly realize how dependent they are on the electrical grid, just how much they have taken it for granted, and how devastating it would be. On the other hand, the process will also lead to some very obvious, quick, and easy protections and contingencies that can be undertaken without adding significant cost. This would go beyond just having a couple of extra flashlights on hand, but it's beyond the scope of this book to outline in detail.

This preparation should also include the proactive dismantling of the gross disinformation machines that are now, under the guise of audience targeting using the tools of Big Data and AI, systemically leading this country away from any ability to see and sense what is true. We are being manipulated and deceived, and pushed into extreme ideologies on Left and Right, conspiracy theories (Pizzagate anyone?), and cognitive bias echo chambers in which we only hear viewpoints that reinforce our own existing and often mistaken opinions of "facts."

Here I hold the large social media companies just as responsible – if not more responsible – than any intervention by foreign actors. The motive of foreign political powers is clear, and in a way, we cannot blame them for taking active measures in pursuit of their own strategic interests, especially when the advertising revenue models of the social media platforms actually facilitate it for profit. We can blame ourselves not only for not properly defending against these attacks, but even worse for collaborating with systems with perverse financial incentives – by inviting them to track us –, like the business models of the social media platforms that are by design and intent about the targeting, segregation, and manipulation of their audiences.

In relation to our use of social media, we must remember the Silicon Valley adage, "if you are not paying for it, you are not the customer; you are the product being sold."[320] The social media companies have, I believe perhaps unintentionally and ignorantly, made a Faustian bargain and sold their souls and ours to the devil ... for the motive of profit, yes, but also because in their youthful hubris and a dream of the beautiful future they thought they were creating, they didn't see the trap until it was too late. In actuality they have facilitated the creation of a digital Frankenstein, an AI monster of our own making that, like the fictional zombies so popular today, are now eating out the brains and objective reasoning capacity of tens of millions of people, many of them so young that their minds aren't maturing in a normal way and who are unaware of what is happening to them.

We don't need tweaks around the margin, but a fundamental overhaul of how the large, influential social media and tech companies such as Facebook, Google, Twitter, and others are allowed to operate within this country. This is going to require change, and probably regulatory intervention, that will feel uncomfortable for those of us who do ascribe to the free market ideal of laissez-faire. However, such interventions are not unprecedented in times of crisis, and they are absolutely necessary if we have any hope of restoring the American democratic ideal and our sense of *E Pluribus Unum*, the model of the United States that envisions that one unified Union can be formed out of over 300 million people from many different states, ethnicities, cultures, and histories.

If we discovered that a large packaged foods company was offering a product that was immensely popular yet at the same time contained a poison that was slowly killing its unsuspecting customers, we would not hesitate to intervene and restrict that company's rights to continue to sell its product. This analogy has to be applied to how we think about the products and services that the social media platforms are offering to us, and how while perhaps not poisoning our physical bodies are indeed poisoning our minds as individuals, and equally importantly our social contract with one another as fellow citizens of this country. It took decades of litigation and regulation for the country to get to where it needed regarding the marketing and sale of tobacco products, and the ultimate solution still wasn't perfect. But here we don't have the luxury of time. The social media landscape has become dangerous, and we have to address it. Now. The threat to our Republic is so severe that urgent action is needed, lest we find ourselves further divided as a nation and beyond all hope of recovery.

I have argued that the imminent risks we see compounding in front of us come from the interplay of four categories: economic breakdowns, external Great Game conflicts, disease and natural disasters, and internal social divisions being distorted and manipulated from sources outside of ourselves. Each one of these has the potential to influence or amplify the others, but the most likely path of travel seems to be that any of the first three, whether economic crisis, nation-state conflict, or the natural world, could feed into increasing social unrest leading to wide-spread violence, up to and including massed armed conflict or perhaps even civil war.

We are at an extremely dangerous moment in history because of the increasing intensity and frequency of events related to these challenges and their potential to spill over into a broader conflagration. Conditions are now stacked up to be a perfect storm of events which, far from being unprecedented, have been seen time and again in the thousands of years of recorded history of the great powers which overextended themselves, from the Roman to the British empires in the West and the Qing dynasty in China and several in between. When crises came their weaknesses were exposed. External conflict combined with economic crisis almost always leads to internal social upheaval in the societies they governed, as students of the Roman Empire will recognize, and as the Weimar Republic example included here demonstrated.

The American economy started 2020 with a private sector that had strong companies and good prospects, but in the public sector, the US government was already stretched by years of widening deficits, unsustainably high and growing debt, and stubborn deflationary forces. Both the public and private sectors of the economy suddenly faced a gigantic demand shock in the form of the COVID-19 lockdowns, and in the case of the government - the sudden need to pay people trillions of dollars to not work - out of funds that did not exist.

An economic crisis may start in one of several ways, with the only certainly being that it won't look exactly like those of the past. Near- to medium-term risks for the US economy include a rout of the bond markets when the tide turns on investor sentiment about accepting negative yields, a substantial devaluation of the US dollar against other major currencies, improving our export competitiveness but weakening our purchasing power here and abroad, short-term deflation abruptly shifting to accelerating inflation; the consequence of all these factors being that the cash in our pockets becomes increasingly worthless. The knock-on effect of this is that foreign investors, who have been financing our consumption-driven lifestyles, suddenly lose interest in the dollar as an investment relative to other opportunities. Eventually, the US dollar loses its exorbitant privilege as the world's reserve currency.

If there is a take away from this on an individual or household level, it is the message that one can no longer assume that a dollar (of cash) in the pocket is worth a dollar (of spending power), and to the extent, possible households should rotate stores of wealth into reflationary assets that are more likely to retain value in an inflationary period. This would include assets such as precious metals, real estate, and equities of high quality, dividend-paying companies in industry sectors that are able to quickly reprice goods and services to keep up with inflation. This statement comes with a caveat that if any asset class is already overvalued due to recent monetary policy, then stay away. An example of this over-heating would include most real estate, which has benefited from easy financing with all-time low mortgage rates and with the government itself, through the effective subsidization of the government-sponsored entities such as Fannie Mae and Freddie Mac, as buyers of a substantial majority of all mortgages (nearly $7 trillion in aggregate).[321] In a case like this, where a reset is required, it may not be enough to avoid capital losses. But at least there will be a roof overhead. Whatever one's choices are, know that cash is no longer either a safe haven from short-term risk or a good long-term investment. Because we are likely to remain in a period of very high volatility, unless one is expert in financial markets, now is a good time to get out of most stock and bond markets and sit this one out on the sidelines until this dangerous period of time passes.

Outside of the US, several other situations simmer around the world, anyone of which could explode at any time, leading to a broader crisis. Turkey and Greece are facing off over oil exploration rights in the Mediterranean, with France now threatening to intervene, and as their warships bristle and maneuver dangerously around each other in uncomfortable proximity.[322] Russia is testing the mettle of NATO the Ukraine and Belarus, brazenly poisoning the political opponents of the Putin regime not only within its own country but on foreign soil. Chinese and Indian soldiers fight to the death in hand-to-hand melees over a patch of mountainous earth in the Himalayas, and the Chinese Navy is playing a dangerous game of chicken with US warships and planes in the South China Sea, and challenging the commitment of the West in places like Hong Kong and Taiwan. Any of these situations could go horribly wrong and lead to an escalation of conflict from a local skirmish to something much broader.

Will nations and multilateral organizations like NATO honor their alliances, as was the cause of the vast escalation of the First World War? We should not lose sight of the fact that on page one of the playbook for leaders of nations facing their own internal conflicts is the tactic of creating an external crisis, both as a distraction and as a unifying force for its domestic factions.

This confrontation will not be like the so-called Endless Wars in which the US has been engaged in the past twenty years in the Middle East and Afghanistan, which many Americans have been able to ignore as taking place "over there" in a faraway land and not touching them. Rather, this impending conflict will be brought in one form or another to American soil. I'm not suggesting that we will have a foreign military presence in the United States (but also not saying that we couldn't), but rather that the escalation of conflict – before reaching the stage of wide-scale military engagement – will come in the forms described in the chapters on War by any Other Name and Total Information War. The EMP threat and more intensive and destructive cyber-warfare are as good examples as any of how this escalation might manifest, as is the seeding of extremist groups with means (funding and weapons) and opportunity (another horrible killing, a contested election) to set fire to the tinder already laid.

As if all of this wasn't enough, we seem in 2020 to be inhabiting a world of biblical proportions with regard to natural disasters and mishaps. We have talked a good deal about COVID-19 and its effects, but at the same time, this has been a year of extraordinary naturally occurring disasters across the country. From the massively scaled wildfires on the West Coast to the extreme temperatures observed throughout the country this summer, and the tropical storms which season we are still in the middle of with more to come.

The situation on the West Coast appears to be moving to a magnitude and scale unrecognizable in the history of the state of California but not unheard of in geologic terms. As I write, smoke clouds from the Pacific states are covering the majority of the country, all the way from the redwoods of California, over the Rockies and Midwestern Plains to the airs above the skyscrapers of New York, releasing record-setting carbon-dioxide along the way. The data on global warming is definitive, regardless of cause. Temperatures are rising, and very quickly and we can expect that this will lead to more volatile and dangerous weather-related incidents in the coming months and years.

We have been fortunate in this country that through two centuries as a nation we have seen few massively scaled natural disasters, but as the other risks described here we have to start taking the possibility more seriously. Alongside the economic crisis of the Great Depression, the 1930s witnessed the worst series of droughts on record, impacting 70% of the country, leading to crop failures which exacerbated wide-spread bank and business failures. Some of the same potential effects that we've described around economic crises or external or internal conflicts could be present here in a severe natural disaster. These potential impacts could include disruption of supply chains including food, fuel, and medical supplies, electrical grid collapse, displacement of millions of individuals from their homes and communities, creating refugees trains of our own citizens migrating away from stricken areas, to the possibility of wide-scale famine resulting from crop failures or broken supply chains.

Any of these forces would tend towards increasing the social unrest that we've already seen evidence in 2020. We have weeds growing in the garden of our national character that we've left untended, and they've developed to such an extent that they threaten to crowd out our fruitful and natural produce. These overgrown weeds, especially of inequality and injustice, now risk providing ample fuel for the sparks of specific catalytic events that could erupt into flames.

These underlying existing conditions in our country are growing, evidenced by increasing income inequality leading to a widening wealth gap, persistent systemic racism seen in housing, employment, arrest practices, and incarceration policies, and are now being hard-coded and embedded into our AI-driven analytical tools. These issues are threatening to deepen the social divide, exacerbate inequality, and further disenfranchise the poor and marginalized. As Cathy O'Neil points out in her book *Weapons of Math Destruction*, when systems and processes have embedded and inherent prejudices, some of them based on policies and practices built over decades, and these get incorporated into the machine learning process, becoming the closest thing that AI can understand as an embodiment of truth, then the actual human beings involved don't have to be racist at all on an individual level for the system itself to function in a racially biased manner. Recent policy changes, including with regard to criminal justice reform, undertaken by the federal government and many states, are a step in the right direction, but much more needs to be done.

At this moment many African-Americans continue to feel excluded from – or at least second-class citizens in – the American experience, and this has to change. We see an overwhelming amount of evidence[323] that systemic racism still exists in this country and that it manifests in municipal and state governments, in private enterprises large and small, and in communities. It is a wicked, noxious weed, and it has to first be rooted out from the very hearts of the individuals in which it grows if it is to be more completely removed from our public and private institutions. Too many American men and women of all races and colors have sacrificed and shed their blood to protect our Union and the idea that all were created equal, and they and their children deserve the same opportunity to participate politically and thrive economically, to let this moment go to waste without real and lasting change. At some point, we have to get back to seeing each other in our humanity and our shared experience as Americans.

Today, there is a significant trust gap between African-Americans and law enforcement, and recent events have only made this worse. In many of our communities today, African Americans simply do not trust the police, and will not call on them for help out of fear of being wrongfully arrested or targeted. Unfortunately, this fear is not unfounded. There's an abundance of data that support the anecdotes that we've all seen in the media recently of prejudicial targeting, wrongful identification, and arrests of innocent by-standers (or mistaking victims for perpetrators on the basis of color) all the way up to wrongful arrests, convictions, and sentencing.[324] To be sure, some of these injustices such as wrongful convictions, mandatory minimum sentences, and asset forfeiture laws, cut across racial lines, but others are discriminatory.

In addition to identifying the specific risks the country faces, I've asserted that the heart of democracy itself is in jeopardy. As the longest standing constitutional democracy in history, we must not forget that democracy is itself incredibly fragile. History has shown throughout time and across societies that when conditions exist that dislocate and disenfranchise large segments of society, extremist movements abound, radical and dangerous economic and political ideas take root, and violence and demagoguery find a place in the public square. Our democracy is at risk in part because its citizens no longer esteem it. It is acknowledged but taken for granted as a nice-to-have rather than as cherished as the air we breathe. It is taken for granted because the generation that paid for it with their blood and toil is now passing from us, and their descendants have been too busy shopping and running social media popularity contests to take up the mantle.

Our media culture has become so toxic and so invasive that no one in their right mind would dare run for public office due to the scorn and disapprobation that is likely to be poured out upon them and their families. There is a very large segment of our culture that has grown weak and flaccid in a moment when other nations are strengthening and flexing their muscles abroad, and whose citizens still aspire to the more martial virtues of old including national honor. This is not a call to Nationalism, only to suggest that the same vigorous spirit may need to be resurrected in this country if we have any hope of defending ourselves and standing up to the threats we're faced with.

The value of democracy is diminished in part because a younger generation is unaware of its own history, and in many cases have never been taught it, as our public educational institutions are no longer providing proper instruction in civics. Mandatory national service may be one way to begin to restore a sense of patriotism and national community.

The word patriotism is itself now somewhat suspect, as it has somehow become shameful and uncool to be patriotic, to openly and avidly love one's country warts and all, and to take an active participatory role in the governance and improvement of our nation. To be patriotic doesn't mean to accept what is broken, or to ignore the very real issues that need to be addressed. It means caring enough about one's country to invest in seeing change, rooting out what is evil and unjust, and nurturing what is precious and good about preserving in our national patronage. Action is required. Is not the idea of America worth saving?

For our democracy to thrive, it is going to need rejuvenation. Many of our political and governance systems, including the way our elected representatives are appointed, needs re-working. The system is antiquated, and it's reasonably clear that it does not work to fairly represent the will of the people. There are several proposals out there for the reformation of the political system, and it is beyond the scope of this book to delve into them. What is clear is that in order for our democracy to remain strong, it will have to evolve to reflect the realities of the 21st century, not remain stuck in the 19th where it has been ever since.

I am an optimist at heart. But I'm described as a realistic optimist, or better still, as an optimistic realist. I believe that it is best to see the world as it actually is, not as we wish it were, and to work from there. Only by staring reality in the face can we begin the process required to identify and address the challenges that lay ahead of us. I'm not waiting for the apocalypse, and I think that the end of our civilization would, on balance, be a very bad thing. The purpose of discussing these difficult and unpleasant topics has not been to generate panic or to create the fear that leads to paralysis. Rather I believe that knowledge and awareness are the first steps towards being able to take action and to change the trajectory upon which we find ourselves. But I do believe that without course correction we will drive ourselves off of a cliff. The lights are flashing red, the danger is imminent, and it's time for us to take heed.

In this sense, COVID-19, as well as the wrongful killings of Breonna Taylor and George Floyd, among others, while each horrible in and of themselves, can be viewed as an opportunity for America to take a more honest assessment of where it stands in relation to its neighbors, and in relation to itself. Rather than cowering in fear, or taking a fatalistic view that it is too late for change, or adopting the ostrich strategy and singing along with Radiohead "I'm not here, this isn't happening," we need to find strength in our national backbone, and act with courage and vigor by moving quickly to address some of these challenges. In aggregate, these issues can seem overwhelming, but when disentangled from the whole, each one becomes approachable and manageable by the collective resources of our nation working together rather than tearing apart. All the more reason that we have to find a path towards national unity. This has been written primarily as a wake-up call and a warning which we should not ignore. To do so will be at our own grave peril.

Appendix: Significant recent State-sponsored cyber-attacks

The below list comprises a small sampling of the over seventy state-sponsored Cyber-attacks logged by the Center for Strategic & International Studies in the first eight months of 2020:[325]

- August 2020. Hackers for hire suspected of operating on behalf of the Iranian government were found to have been working to gain access to sensitive information held by North American and Israeli entities across a range of sectors, including technology, government, defense, and healthcare.
- August 2020. Taiwan accused Chinese hackers of infiltrating the information systems of at least ten government agencies and 6,000 email accounts to gain access to citizens' personal data and government information.
- August 2020. A Chinese cyberespionage group targeted military and financial organizations across Eastern Europe.
- August 2020. The Israeli defense ministry announced that it had successfully defended against a cyberattack on Israeli defense manufacturers launched by a suspected North Korean hacking group.
- August 2020. An Iranian hacking group was found to be targeting major US companies and government agencies by exploiting recently disclosed vulnerabilities in high-end network equipment to create backdoors for other groups to use.
- August 2020. Seven semiconductor vendors in Taiwan were the victim of a two-year espionage campaign by suspected Chinese state hackers targeting firms' source code, software development kits, and chip designs.
- August 2020. Russian hackers compromised news sites and replaced legitimate articles with falsified posts that used fabricated quotes from military and political officials to discredit NATO among Polish, Lithuanian, and Latvian audiences.

- July 2020. Israel announced that two cyber-attacks had been carried out against Israeli water infrastructure, though neither were successful.
- July 2020. Chinese state-sponsored hackers broke into the networks of the Vatican to conduct espionage in the lead-up to negotiations about control over the appointment of bishops and the status of churches in China.
- July 2020. Canada, the UK, and the US announced that hackers associated with Russian intelligence had attempted to steal information related to COVID-19 vaccine development.
- July 2020. The UK announced that it believed Russia had attempted to interfere in its 2019 general election by stealing and leaking documents related to the UK-US Free Trade Agreement.
- June 2020. The most popular of the tax reporting software platforms China requires foreign companies to download to operate in the country was discovered to contain a backdoor that could allow malicious actors to conduct network reconnaissance or attempt to take remote control of company systems.
- June 2020. North Korean state hackers sent COVID-19-themed phishing emails to more than 5 million businesses and individuals in Singapore, Japan, the United States, South Korea, India, and the UK in an attempt to steal personal and financial data.
- June 2020. In the midst of escalating tensions between China and India over a border dispute in the Galwan Valley, Indian government agencies and banks reported being targeted by DDoS attacks reportedly originating in China.
- May 2020. Businesses in Japan, Italy, Germany, and the UK that supply equipment and software to industrial firms were attacked in a targeted and highly sophisticated campaign by an unknown group of hackers.
- May 2020. The NSA announced that Russian hackers associated with the GRU had been exploiting a bug that could allow them to take remote control of US servers.
- May 2020. German officials found that a Russian hacking group associated with the FSB had compromised the networks of energy,

water, and power companies in Germany by exploiting IT supply chains.

- May 2020. Chinese hackers accessed the travel records of nine million customers of UK airline group EasyJet.
- May 2020. Two days before Taiwanese President Tsai Ing-wen was sworn in for her second term in office, the president's office was hacked, and files were leaked to local media outlets purporting to show infighting within the administration. The president's office claimed the leaked documents had been doctored.
- May 2020. US officials accused hackers linked to the Chinese government of attempting to steal US research into a coronavirus vaccine.
- April 2020. Suspected Iranian hackers unsuccessfully targeted the command and control systems of water treatment plants, pumping stations, and sewage in Israel.
- April 2020. US officials reported seeing a surge of attacks by Chinese hackers against healthcare providers, pharmaceutical manufacturers, and the US Department of Health and Human services amidst the COVID-19 pandemic.
- March 2020. Chinese hackers targeted over 75 organizations around the world in the manufacturing, media, healthcare, and nonprofit sectors as part of a broad-ranging cyber espionage campaign.
- February 2020. The US Defense Information Systems Agency announced it had suffered a data breach exposing the personal information of an unspecified number of individuals.
- February 2020. Chinese hackers targeted Malaysian government officials to steal data related to government-backed projects in the region.
- January 2020. An Iranian hacking group launched an attack on the US-based research company Wesat as part of a suspected effort to gain access to the firm's clients in the public and private sectors.
- January 2020. Mitsubishi announces that a suspected Chinese group had targeted the company as part of a massive cyberattack that compromised the personal data of 8,000 individuals as well

as information relating to partnering businesses and government agencies, including projects relating to defense equipment.

- January 2020. The FBI announced that nation-state hackers had breached the networks of two US municipalities in 2019, exfiltrating user information and establishing backdoor access for future compromise.

Endnotes

[1] <u>Parables of Keirkegaard</u>, edited by Thomas C. Oden, Princeton University Press, 1979, p. 3

[2] <u>Either/Or: Part I</u>, Soren Keirkegaard, edited by Howard V. Hong, Princeton University Press, 1987, p. 30

[3] <u>The End of History and the Last Man</u>, Francis Fukuyama, Free Press, 1992.

[4] <u>The Lessons of History</u>, Will & Ariel Durant, Simon Schuster Paperbacks, 1968, pg. 12

[5] <u>The Age of Surveillance Capitalism: The Fight for a Human Future at the New Frontier of Power</u>, Shoshana Zuboff, Public Affairs, Hachette Book Group Inc., 2019, p. 13

[6] Ray Dalio of Bridgewater Associates has done substantial work identifying, understanding and articulating these three forces, and in particular his analysis of the long-term debt cycle, in a way that provides a coherent framework. This will be detailed in his upcoming book, <u>The Changing World Order</u>, which is now is available online at https://www.principles.com/the-changing-world-order/#introduction

[7] <u>Destined for War: Can America and China Escape Thucydides's Trap?</u>, Graham Allison, 2017

[8] <u>War by Other Means: Geoeconomics and Statecraft</u>, Robert D. Blackwell and Jennifer M. Harris, The Belknap Press of Harvard University Press, 2016

[9] https://ftalphaville.ft.com/2020/05/12/1589294559000/The-Zimbabwification-of-Wall-St/

[10] <u>The Rise and Fall of the Great Powers</u>, Paul Kennedy, Vintage Books, 1987

[11] https://www.theatlantic.com/international/archive/2017/10/russia-facebook-race/542796/

[12] Ibid.

[13] <u>Destined for War: Can America and China Escape Thucydides's Trap?</u>, Graham Allison, 2017

[14] Personal Consumption Expenditure (USD billions) of $9,842.209 and $14,544.601 for 2009 and 2019 respectively. Source: https://fred.stlouisfed.org/series/PCECA.

[15] https://fred.stlouisfed.org/series/A006RL1A225NBEA

[16] https://www.census.gov/library/publications/2020/demo/p60-270.html

[17] https://www.shrm.org/resourcesandtools/hr-topics/compensation/pages/racial-wage-gaps-persistence-poses-challenge.aspx

[18] https://www.bls.gov/charts/employment-situation/civilian-unemployment-rate.htm

[19] https://www.pewtrusts.org/en/research-and-analysis/articles/2020/04/28/every-state-posted-economic-gains-in-year-before-the-pandemic

[20] https://www.statista.com/statistics/200410/surplus-or-deficit-of-the-us-governments-budget-since-2000/

[21] https://watson.brown.edu/costsofwar/files/cow/imce/papers/2019/US%20Budgetary%20Costs%20of%20Wars%20November%202019.pdf

[22] https://www.cbo.gov/publication/56517

[23] Ibid.

[24] The Deficit Myth: Modern Monetary Theory and the Birth of the People's Economy, Stephanie Kelton, Public Affairs, an imprint of Perseus books, LLC., a subsidiary of Hachette Book Group, Inc., 2020, pp. 234-235

[25] https://www.statista.com/statistics/1121448/fed-balance-sheet-timeline/

[26] https://www.treasurydirect.gov/govt/reports/pd/histdebt/histdebt_histo5.htm

[27] https://www.pgpf.org/national-debt-clock

[28] https://fred.stlouisfed.org/graph/?g=eUmi

[29] Ibid.

[30] Assuming 2.6 people per household based on Census bureau data.

[31] https://www.history.com/this-day-in-history/andrew-jackson-national-debt-reaches-zero-dollars

[32] In today's environment, the privilege of lending money to the US government for a few years will cost the investor over 1% per year in negative real interest. If one is willing to lock up one's investment for 30 years, like a mortgage, the investment will only lose 0.33% per year, or just under 10% of the initial investment over the term. *source: treasury.gov*

[33] https://www.newyorkfed.org/microeconomics/hhdc.html

[34] https://foreignpolicy.com/2020/04/29/federal-reserve-global-economy-coronavirus-pandemic-inflation-terminal-deflation-is-coming/ ; https://investors-corner.bnpparibas-am.com/investing/deflation-not-inflation-is-the-main-risk-now/ ; https://www.ft.com/content/6101eb0c-b63f-4b80-add4-b8ad20f94040; https://www.bloomberg.com/opinion/articles/2020-08-11/deflation-is-a-bigger-risk-for-global-economy-than-inflation

[35] https://twitter.com/WHO/status/1217043229427761152?ref_src=twsrc%5Etfw%7Ctwcamp%5Etweetembed&ref_url=https%3A%2F%2Fwww.foxnews.com%2Fworld%2Fworld-health-organization-january-tweet-china-human-transmission-coronavirus

[36] https://covid19.healthdata.org/united-states-of-america?view=social-distancing&tab=trend

[37] https://www.statista.com/statistics/1043366/novel-coronavirus-2019ncov-cases-worldwide-by-country/

[38] https://www.statista.com/statistics/1093256/novel-coronavirus-2019ncov-deaths-worldwide-by-country/

[39] https://www.bls.gov/charts/employment-situation/civilian-unemployment.htm

[40] https://www.ft.com/content/e2833ccb-b9ae-48dc-9c0a-a58b7182d8d3?shareType=nongift

[41] https://www.bea.gov/sites/default/files/2020-08/gdp2q20_2nd.pdf

[42] https://www.mba.org/2020-press-releases/august/mortgage-delinquencies-spike-in-the-second-quarter-of-2020

[43] https://www.fitchratings.com/research/corporate-finance/2020-global-corporate-defaults-to-date-top-2019-full-year-total-01-07-2020

[44] https://www.moodys.com/creditfoundations/Default-Trends-and-Rating-Transitions-05E002

[45] https://www.scmp.com/business/companies/article/3098498/defaults-chinas-us41-trillion-corporate-bond-market-could-hit

[46] When Money Dies: The Nightmare Of Deficit Spending, Devaluation, And Hyperinflation In Weimar Germany, Adam Ferguson, 1975. Quoted from 2010 PublicAffairs version, page 3

[47] Quoted at https://ritholtz.com/2016/09/triumph-keynesian-economics/ as being referenced from: "Bolshevist Lenine's [sic] View of Money," Commercial and Financial Chronicle, May 3, 1919, 1763. This quote is also referenced in "Lenin Pontificates," New York Times, April 26, 1919. Attributed to Vladimir Lenin by John Maynard Keynes in The Economic Consequences Of The Peace, 1919. Later affirmed by White & Schuler in the Journal of Economic Perspectives—Volume 23, Number 2—Spring 2009—Pages 213–222 Retrospectives: Who Said "Debauch the Currency": Keynes or Lenin? https://pubs.aeaweb.org/doi/pdfplus/10.1257/jep.23.2.213

[48] https://www.bloomberg.com/opinion/articles/2020-06-08/a-crash-in-the-dollar-is-coming

[49] https://fortune.com/2020/07/23/usd-crash-stephen-roach-alternatives-global-reserve-currency/

[50] Hyperinflation is typically defined as an environment in which prices increasing by greater than 50% month over month.

[51] https://www.thebalance.com/us-debt-by-president-by-dollar-and-percent-3306296

[52] https://ticdata.treasury.gov/Publish/mfh.txt

[53] https://fred.stlouisfed.org/series/W207RC1Q156SBEA

54 https://fred.stlouisfed.org/series/IEABC

55https://www.federalreserve.gov/monetarypolicy/files/FOMC_LongerRunGoals_guide.pdf

56 https://www.federalreserve.gov/faqs/about_12594.htm

57 https://www.nber.org/chapters/c11462.pdf

58 https://www.ft.com/content/facfe2cf-c78e-4085-882e-fdac59f1329d

59 The Economic Consequences of the Peace, John Maynard Keynes, 1919. Page [ ]

60 The Forgotten Man, Amity Shales, Harper Collins, 2007, p. 158.

61 The Downfall Of Money: Germany's Hyperinflation and the Destruction of the Middle Class, Frederick Taylor, Bloomsbury Press, 2013, pages 10-15.

62 https://www.bankofengland.co.uk/-/media/boe/files/quarterly-bulletin/1994/inflation-over-300-years.pdf

63 https://encyclopedia.1914-1918-online.net/article/war_finance_russian_empire

64 The Economics Of Inflation – A Study Of Currency Depreciation In Post War Germany, Constantino Bresciani-Turroni, translated by Millicent E. Sayers, George Allen & Unwin LTD, London, 1937, page 25

65 The Downfall of Money, Chapters 2 and 3.

66 The Economic Consequences of the Peace, John Maynard Keynes, 1919. Page 23

67 When Money Dies, page 33.

68 The Downfall of Money, page 173.

69Quoted from: https://www.frbsf.org/our-district/press/presidents-speeches/williams-speeches/2012/july/williams-monetary-policy-money-inflation/. Parenthetical mine.

70 https://www.bloomberg.com/news/articles/2013-11-03/mugabe-makes-zimbabwe-s-tobacco-farmers-land-grab-winners?sref=vKspbywX

71 When Money Destroys Nations: How Hyperinflation Ruined Zimbabwe, How Ordinary People Survived, And Warnings For Nations That Print Money, Philip Haslam and Russell Lamberti, 2015

72 Ibid, page 154.

73 https://www.theatlantic.com/ideas/archive/2020/02/venezuelas-suffering-shows-where-illiberalism-leads/606988/

74 Ibid.

75https://www.cnbc.com/2019/08/02/venezuela-inflation-at-10-million-percent-its-time-for-shock-therapy.html

76 https://www.theatlantic.com/ideas/archive/2020/02/venezuelas-suffering-shows-where-illiberalism-leads/606988/

[77] https://www.nytimes.com/2020/02/01/world/americas/Venezuela-economy-dollars.html

[78] Ibid.

[79] https://www.bloomberg.com/quote/XAU:CUR

[80] https://alerts.davispolk.com/10/5236/uploads/occ-confirms-that-national-banks-may-take-deposits.pdf?sid=2e2134d4-15e0-42a9-afff-ae48fe338b87

[81] https://www.wsj.com/articles/chinas-cdc-built-to-stop-pandemics-stumbled-when-it-mattered-most-11597675108

[82] https://www.aljazeera.com/news/2020/4/15/china-failed-to-warn-public-of-coronavirus-threat-for-days-ap

[83] https://www.theweek.in/theweek/cover/2020/10/01/made-in-china.html

[84] https://www.washingtonpost.com/climate-environment/2020/08/25/boston-coronavirus-superspreading-event/

[85] https://www.reuters.com/article/us-china-health-wildlife/chinas-latest-virus-outbreak-exposes-perils-of-exotic-wildlife-trade-idUSKBN1ZM0PE

[86] https://www.sciencealert.com/chinese-cdc-now-says-the-wuhan-wet-market-was-the-site-of-a-super-spreader-event

[87] https://www.whitehouse.gov/briefings-statements/chinese-communist-partys-ideology-global-ambitions/#_ftn6

[88] https://www.nytimes.com/2020/03/17/business/media/china-expels-american-journalists.html

[89] https://www.nytimes.com/2020/03/13/world/asia/coronavirus-china-conspiracy-theory.html

[90] https://zenodo.org/record/4028830#.X3mscS9h3GJ

[91] https://en.as.com/en/2020/09/18/latest_news/1600419725_620901.html

[92] https://web.archive.org/web/20200919003644/https://www.vox.com/2020/9/18/21439865/coronavirus-china-study-bannon

[93] https://web.archive.org/web/20200922194032if_/https://pubmed.ncbi.nlm.nih.gov/?term=limeng+yan&sort=date

[94] https://www.theweek.in/theweek/cover/2020/10/01/made-in-china.html

[95] https://www.independent.co.uk/news/world/americas/coronavirus-dr-li-meng-yan-twitter-account-suspended-wuhan-b454268.html

[96] https://thenationalpulse.com/breaking/dr-yan-mom-arrested/ ; https://twitter.com/Gnews202064/status/1312504834625425409

[97] https://www.telegraph.co.uk/news/2020/06/03/exclusive-coronavirus-began-accident-disease-escaped-chinese/

[98] *Where Did COVID-19 Really Come From?,* Lt. Col. (res.) Dr. Dany Shoham, BESA Center Perspectives Paper No. 1,664, July 28, 2020.

https://besacenter.org/wp-content/uploads/2020/07/1664-Where-Did-COVID-19-Really-Come-From-final-Shoham-3.pdf

[99] https://www.nytimes.com/2020/04/02/us/politics/cia-coronavirus-china.html

[100] Shoham.

[101] https://www.pbs.org/newshour/features/Uighurs/

[102] https://www.washingtonpost.com/world/europe/uk-public-tribunal-to-probe-Uyghur-genocide-claims/2020/09/03/58dab784-edc0-11ea-bd08-1b10132b458f_story.html

[103] https://www.statista.com/statistics/1043366/novel-coronavirus-2019ncov-cases-worldwide-by-country/

[104] https://www.statista.com/statistics/1093256/novel-coronavirus-2019ncov-deaths-worldwide-by-country/

[105] https://www.nytimes.com/2020/04/02/us/politics/cia-coronavirus-china.html

[106] https://www.cdc.gov/flu/about/burden/index.html

[107] https://www.census.gov/quickfacts/fact/table/US/PST045219

[108] https://covid.cdc.gov/covid-data-tracker/#demographics

[109] https://covid.cdc.gov/covid-data-tracker/#health-care-personnel

[110] https://www.england.nhs.uk/statistics/statistical-work-areas/covid-19-daily-deaths/

[111] https://www.cbpp.org/research/poverty-and-inequality/tracking-the-covid-19-recessions-effects-on-food-housing-and

[112] https://www.cbpp.org/research/poverty-and-inequality/tracking-the-covid-19-recessions-effects-on-food-housing-and

[113] https://tracktherecovery.org

[114] https://www.bloomberg.com/news/features/2020-09-24/harvard-economist-raj-chetty-creates-god-s-eye-view-of-pandemic-damage?cmpid=BBD092520_WKND&utm_medium=email&utm_source=newsletter&utm_term=200925&utm_campaign=weekendreading&sref=vKspbywX

[115] https://blogs.worldbank.org/opendata/impact-covid-19-coronavirus-global-poverty-why-sub-saharan-africa-might-be-region-hardest

[116] https://www.thelancet.com/journals/laninf/article/PIIS1473-3099(20)30568-5/fulltext

[117] https://en.unesco.org/covid19/educationresponse

[118] https://www.unicef.org/press-releases/unicef-executive-director-henrietta-fore-remarks-press-conference-new-updated

[119]

https://www.opensourceshakespeare.org/views/plays/play_view.php?WorkID=henry4p2&Act=3&Scene=1&Scope=scene

[120] https://www.medicaldaily.com/majority-americans-support-extended-lockdown-fight-covid-19-coronavirus-novel-452531 ; https://www.kansascity.com/news/coronavirus/article243788387.html

[121] https://www.foreignaffairs.com/articles/united-states/2020-09-16/coronavirus-america-needs-lock-down-again

[122] https://www.nytimes.com/2020/06/22/world/europe/sweden-coronavirus-pariah-scandinavia.html ; https://www.ft.com/content/5cc92d45-fbdb-43b7-9c66-26501693a371

[123] https://www.statista.com/statistics/1104709/coronavirus-deaths-worldwide-per-million-inhabitants/

[124] https://www.ft.com/content/5cc92d45-fbdb-43b7-9c66-26501693a371

[125] https://www.bloomberg.com/news/articles/2020-09-25/an-american-ceo-living-in-sweden-has-a-covid-lesson-to-share?srnd=premium&sref=vKspbywX

[126] https://rt.live as at September 21, 2020. Filter: Never Sheltered

[127] https://portal.ct.gov/Coronavirus/travel ; https://covid19.nj.gov/faqs/nj-information/travel-and-transportation/which-states-are-on-the-travel-advisory-list-are-there-travel-restrictions-to-or-from-new-jersey ; https://coronavirus.health.ny.gov/covid-19-travel-advisory

[128] https://rt.live as at September 21, 2020. Filter: All

[129] https://www.bloomberg.com/opinion/articles/2020-09-21/why-a-coronavirus-recession-in-florida-is-a-depression-in-new-york

[130] https://pfnyc.org/wp-content/uploads/2020/07/actionandcollaboration.pdf

[131] https://www.bloomberg.com/news/features/2020-09-29/new-york-city-bankruptcies-2020-pivotal-point-for-business-as-covid-cases-rise

[132] https://comptroller.nyc.gov/reports/comments-on-new-york-citys-fiscal-year-2021-adopted-budget/

[133] https://pfnyc.org/news/letter-to-mayor-bill-de-blasio-from-nyc-business-leaders/

[134] https://www.nytimes.com/2020/09/15/nyregion/business-leaders-nyc-de-blasio.html

[135] https://www.nature.com/articles/s41598-020-72798-7

[136] A Distant Mirror: The Calamitous 14th Century, Barbara Tuchman

[137] Why Nations Fail: The Origins Of Power, Prosperity And Poverty, Daron Acemoglu & James A. Robinson, Profile Books, 2013.

[138] https://www.bloomberg.com/news/articles/2020-09-09/lockdown-life-drags-on-for-singapore-workers-restricted-to-dorms

[139] The March of Folly: From Troy to Vietnam, Barbara W. Tuchman, Random House Trade Paperbacks, 2014, p. 5

[140] War by Other Means: Geoeconomics and Statecraft, Robert D. Blackwell and Jennifer M. Harris, The Belknap Press of Harvard University Press, 2016, p. 93

[141] https://www.theglobaleconomy.com/China/gdp_share/

[142] https://www.nytimes.com/1992/02/09/books/is-japan-out-to-get-us.html

[143] https://www.statista.com/statistics/270439/chinas-share-of-global-gross-domestic-product-gdp/

[144] https://en.wikipedia.org/wiki/Historical_GDP_of_China ; https://fred.stlouisfed.org/series/GDP ; https://fred.stlouisfed.org/series/RGDPCHUSA625NUPN

[145] Red Flags: Why Xi's China is in Jeopardy, George Mangus, Yale University Press, 2018, Page 6.

[146] http://statisticstimes.com/economy/united-states-vs-china-economy.php

[147] https://fred.stlouisfed.org/series/GDP

[148] Trade Wars Are Class Wars: How Rising Inequality Distorts The Global Economy and Threatens International Peace, Matthew C Klein and Michael Pettis, Yale University Press, 2020, Page 111.

[149] The Fatal Conceit: The Errors of Socialism, Friedrich Hayak, University of Chicago Press, 1988.

[150] Red Flags, p.161

[151] https://www.cfr.org/backgrounder/chinas-massive-belt-and-road-initiative

[152] Destined for War, p. 125.

[153] https://www.aei.org/china-global-investment-tracker/

[154] https://www.ft.com/content/9f5736d8-14e1-11e9-a581-4ff78404524e

[155] https://www.nationaldefensemagazine.org/articles/2020/3/9/eagle-vs-dragon-how-the-us-and-chinese-navies-stack-up

[156] https://www.worldpoliticsreview.com/trend-lines/28933/behind-china-s-military-build-up-an-effort-to-project-power-globally

[157] https://www.ft.com/content/9bf1c039-3222-4aa7-be37-6f01afc41ef2

[158] https://fred.stlouisfed.org/series/GFDEGDQ188S

[159] http://www.chinabankingnews.com/2020/05/20/chinas-total-domestic-debt-hits-317-of-gdp-for-record-quarterly-increase-iff/

[160] Red Flags, p. 77

[161] https://www.scmp.com/economy/china-economy/article/3084979/china-debt-how-big-it-who-owns-it-and-what-next

[162] The Rise and Fall of the Great Powers, Paul Kennedy, Vintage Books, 1987.

[163] Trade Wars Are Class Wars: How Rising Inequality Distorts The Global Economy and Threatens International Peace, Matthew C Klein and Michael Pettis, Yale University Press, 2020, Page 3.

[164] https://www.scmp.com/economy/china-economy/article/3096682/china-inflation-rises-27-cent-july-driven-higher-food-costs

[165] Destined for War, p.109

[166] The March of Folly, pp. 6-9

[167] Destined for War, p. xvii

[168] https://www.bloomberg.com/news/articles/2020-07-21/tiktok-hong-kong-and-more-u-s-china-flashpoints-quicktake

[169] https://www.bloomberg.com/news/articles/2020-08-27/china-s-missile-tests-warn-u-s-aircraft-carriers-to-stay-away

[170] https://www.theatlantic.com/ideas/archive/2020/01/china-sasse/605074/

[171] Red Flags, pp. 158-9.

[172] https://www.bloombergquint.com/global-economics/biden-trump-quit-praising-xi-to-feud-over-who-d-be-tougher

[173] https://www.ft.com/content/06047bc5-81dd-4475-8678-4b3181d53877?segmentId=645fb9d7-8d13-2a63-ff11-f5eb5a5882ed

[174] https://www.nytimes.com/2020/09/06/us/politics/biden-china.html

[175] https://www.youtube.com/watch?v=DcMT_QZN2xk

[176] https://www.foreignaffairs.com/articles/united-states/2020-01-23/why-america-must-lead-again

[177] https://www.ft.com/content/06047bc5-81dd-4475-8678-4b3181d53877?segmentId=645fb9d7-8d13-2a63-ff11-f5eb5a5882ed

[178] https://www.bloomberg.com/opinion/articles/2020-09-05/europe-just-declared-independence-from-china

[179] The War That Ended Peace: The Road To 1914, Margaret Macmillan, Allen Lane, an imprint of Penguin Canada Books Inc., 2013, pp. *xxix-xxxi*.

[180] The Economic Consequences of the Peace, John Maynard Keynes, 1919. Page 7.

[181] The War That Ended Peace: The Road To 1914, Margaret Macmillan, Allen Lane, an imprint of Penguin Canada Books Inc., 2013, page 545.

[182] https://abcnews.go.com/International/navalny-long-history-russian-poisonings/story?id=72579648

[183] https://www.ft.com/content/a1baaf54-dc5e-4bd8-84cf-ede02c7cf15f

[184] https://www.rt.com/business/472016-russia-india-china-swift/

[185] Philip Zelikow et. al., *The Rise of Strategic Corruption: How States Weaponize Graft*, Foreign Affairs July/August 2020

[186] https://www.aiib.org/en/about-aiib/financial-statements/.content/index/pdf/AIIB_H1-2020-Financial-Statements-sign-off.pdf

[187] https://www.aiib.org/en/projects/approved/index.html

[188] https://thediplomat.com/2019/05/what-to-make-of-indias-absence-from-the-second-belt-and-road-forum/

[189] https://blog.rsisecurity.com/the-many-cyber-security-threats-to-the-financial-sector/

[190] The Grid: The Fraying Wires Between Americans And Our Energy Future, Gretchen Bakke, Ph.D, Bloomsbury Press, 2016, p. xiv

[191] Ibid., p. xiv

[192] https://www.evwind.es/2020/02/19/eia-releases-2050-projections-for-energy-makes/73635

[193] https://www.ourenergypolicy.org/wp-content/uploads/2016/02/R42696.pdf

[194]

https://www.energy.gov/sites/prod/files/oeprod/DocumentsandMedia/DOE_SG_Book_Single_Pages%281%29.pdf

[195] The Grid, pp. 119-134.

[196] *Executive Order on Coordinating National Resilience to Electromagnetic Pulses,* March 26, 2019
www.whitehouse.gov/presidential-actions/executive-order-coordinating-national-resilience-electromagnetic-pulses/

[197] https://apps.dtic.mil/sti/citations/AD1102202

[198] *The new era of high-power electromagnetic weapons*, November 19, 2019
https://www.militaryaerospace.com/power/article/14072339/emp-high-power-electromagnetic-weapons-railguns-microwaves.

[199] https://www.thecipherbrief.com/column_article/north-korea-emp-attack-an-existential-threat-today

[200] https://www.lloyds.com/news-and-risk-insight/risk-reports/library/natural-environment/solar-storm

[201] https://link.springer.com/article/10.1186/s13705-019-0199-y

[202] https://www.census.gov/prod/cen2010/cph-2-1.pdf

[203] https://data.worldbank.org/indicator/SP.URB.TOTL?locations=US

[204] The Lessons of History, Will & Ariel Durant, Simon Schuster Paperbacks, 1968, pg. 12

[205] https://www.wincalendar.com/Calendar/Date/May-15-2019

[206] https://www.cbsnews.com/news/alabama-abortion-law-governor-kay-ivey-signs-near-total-ban-today-live-updates-2019-05-15/

[207]

https://twitter.com/BernieSanders/status/1128655854973128704?ref_src=twsrc%5Etfw%7Ctwcamp%5Etweetembed%7Ctwterm%5E1128655854973128704%7Ctwgr%5Eshare_3&ref_url=https%3A%2F%2Fwww.foxnews.com%2Fpolitics%2Fbernie-sanders-abortion-a-constitutional-right

[208] https://www.nbcnews.com/politics/justice-department/did-you-bring-your-handcuffs-ag-barr-ribs-pelosi-about-n1006121 ;
https://www.foxnews.com/us/alabama-passes-bill-that-would-make-almost-all-abortions-illegal-house-dems-target-trump-lawyers

[209] https://www.wincalendar.com/Calendar/Date/May-15-2019

[210] https://www.whitehouse.gov/presidential-actions/executive-order-securing-information-communications-technology-services-supply-chain/

[211] Ibid.

[212] https://www.whitehouse.gov/briefings-statements/chinese-communist-partys-ideology-global-ambitions/#_ftn2 ; John Garnaut, "Engineers of the Soul: Ideology in Xi Jinping's China," January 16, 2019, https://sinocism.com/p/engineers-of-the-soul-ideology-in

213

https://www.intelligence.senate.gov/sites/default/files/documents/Report_Volume2.pdf

[214] https://int.nyt.com/data/documenttools/senate-intelligence-committee-russian-interference/8cf58e574d235164/full.pdf

[215] https://www.bloomberg.com/news/articles/2020-09-10/microsoft-detects-foreign-cyber-attacks-targeting-u-s-elections

[216] https://thediplomat.com/2020/09/a-discussion-with-us-senator-chris-murphy-about-subnational-diplomacy-and-china/

[217] http://reports.weforum.org/global-risks-2018/executive-summary/

[218] https://www.wsj.com/articles/its-official-north-korea-is-behind-wannacry-1513642537

[219] https://www.nytimes.com/2018/12/20/US/politics/US-and-other-nations-to-announce-china-crackdown.html

[220] https://www.nytimes.com/2020/07/21/US/politics/china-hacking-coronavirus-vaccine.html

221

http://www.ipcommission.org/report/IP_Commission_Report_Update_2017.pdf ; http://www.ipcommission.org/report/ip_commission_2019_review_of_progress_and_updated_recommendations.pdf

[222] https://www.fbi.gov/news/speeches/responding-effectively-to-the-chinese-economic-espionage-threat

[223] https://www.who.int/news-room/detail/23-04-2020-who-reports-fivefold-increase-in-cyber-attacks-urges-vigilance; https://www.techrepublic.com/article/cyberattacks-on-the-rise-since-the-start-of-the-coronavirus-outbreak/; https://www.imcgrupo.com/covid-19-news-fbi-reports-300-increase-in-reported-cybercrimes/

[224] https://csis-website-prod.s3.amazonaws.com/s3fs-public/200901_Significant_Cyber_Events_List.pdf

[225] https://www.whitehouse.gov/briefings-statements/chinese-communist-partys-ideology-global-ambitions/

[226] https://www.reuters.com/article/us-tiktok-cfius-exclusive/exclusive-u-s-opens-national-security-investigation-into-tiktok-sources-idUSKBN1XB4IL

[227] https://www.whitehouse.gov/presidential-actions/executive-order-addressing-threat-posed-wechat/

[228] https://www.commerce.gov/news/press-releases/2020/09/commerce-department-prohibits-wechat-and-tiktok-transactions-protect

[229] https://www.reuters.com/article/us-usa-wechat/u-s-judge-halts-trump-administrations-order-to-remove-wechat-from-app-stores-idUSKCN26B0IY

[230] https://www.reuters.com/article/us-usa-wechat-ban/u-s-to-challenge-judges-order-that-blocked-u-s-wechat-app-store-ban-idUSKCN26C1QZ

[231] https://home.treasury.gov/system/files/206/CFIUS-Public-Annual-Report-CY-2019.pdf

[232] https://www.gibsondunn.com/cfius-developments-notable-cases-and-key-trends/

[233] https://www.clearytradewatch.com/2020/06/cfius-blocks-joint-venture-outside-the-united-states-releases-2018-2019-data-and-goes-electronic/

[234] https://news.cgtn.com/news/2020-08-27/How-Trump-was-able-to-leverage-CFIUS-to-block-Chinese-deals-ThgMQe1ndC/index.html

[235] https://supchina.com/2020/07/16/banning-tiktok-is-a-terrible-idea/

[236] *A Study of History*, Arnold J. Toynbee, Volume V. Cpt. XVII(5), "External Proletariats Of The Western World," Abridgement of Volumes I-VI by D.C. Somervell, Oxford University Press, p. 469.

[237] https://www.bls.gov/opub/mlr/1948/article/pdf/labor-force-employment-and-unemployment-1929-39-estimating-methods.pdf

[238] *NYC Then/Now: Great Depression & Great Recession*, Baruch College, Spring 2012 https://eportfolios.macaulay.cuny.edu/brooks12/then-protests/

[239] Ibid.

[240] *"Labor, Capital, And Government: The Anthracite Coal Strike Of 1902*, Democracy: A Case Study, David A. Moss, The Belknap Press of Harvard University Press, 2017, pp. 330-364

[241] https://data.worldbank.org/indicator/SI.POV.GINI/?most_recent_value_desc=false

[242] https://www.census.gov/content/dam/Census/library/publications/2020/demo/p60-270.pdf

[243] https://www.pewsocialtrends.org/2020/01/09/trends-in-income-and-wealth-inequality/

[244] https://www.rand.org/pubs/working_papers/WRA516-1.html

[245] https://www.pewsocialtrends.org/2020/01/09/trends-in-income-and-wealth-inequality/psdt_01-10-20_economic-inequality_1-3/

[246] https://www.pewsocialtrends.org/2020/01/09/trends-in-income-and-wealth-inequality/

[247] https://www.bloomberg.com/news/articles/2020-07-18/five-charts-that-show-the-extent-of-the-black-wealth-gap-in-u-s

[248] https://www.census.gov/content/dam/Census/library/publications/2019/demo/p60-266.pdf

[249] https://greatergood.berkeley.edu/article/item/what_is_the_true_cost_of_polarization_in_america

[250] https://news.gallup.com/poll/316448/congress-approval-drops-trump-steady.aspx

[251] https://news.gallup.com/poll/1600/congress-public.aspx

[252] https://www.pewresearch.org/politics/2018/04/26/3-elections-in-the-u-s-priorities-and-performance/

[253] https://news.gallup.com/poll/311825/presidential-job-approval-related-reelection-historically.aspx

[254] https://www.journalofdemocracy.org/wp-content/uploads/2016/07/FoaMounk-27-3.pdf

[255] https://press.uchicago.edu/ucp/books/book/chicago/R/bo4138549.html

[256] https://www.theatlantic.com/sponsored/allstate/when-it-comes-to-politics-do-millennials-care-about-anything/255/

[257] https://www.pewresearch.org/fact-tank/2018/05/21/u-s-voter-turnout-trails-most-developed-countries/

[258] https://www.wsj.com/articles/religion-is-on-the-decline-as-more-adults-check-none-11571320801

[259] https://aifs.gov.au/publications/effects-pornography-children-and-young-people-snapshot

[260] https://www.prb.org/suicide-replaces-homicide-second-leading-cause-death-among-us-teens/

[261] https://www.washingtonpost.com/health/teen-suicides-increasing-at-alarming-pace-outstripping-all-other-age-groups/2019/10/16/e24194c6-f04a-11e9-8693-f487e46784aa_story.html

[262] The Age of Surveillance Capitalism, p. 9

[263] https://news.harvard.edu/gazette/story/2019/03/harvard-professor-says-surveillance-capitalism-is-undermining-democracy/. Zuboff's full definition of Surveillance Capitalism is: 1. A new economic order that claims human experience as free raw material for hidden commercial practices of extraction, prediction, and sales; 2. A parasitic economic logic in which the production of goods and services is subordinated to a new global architecture of behavioral

modification; 3. A rogue mutation of capitalism marked by concentrations of wealth, knowledge, and power unprecedented in human history; 4. The foundational framework of a surveillance economy; 5. A significant a threat to human nature in the 21st century as industrial capitalism was to the natural world in the 19th and 20th; 6. The origin of a new instrumentarian power that asserts dominance over society and presents startling challenges to market democracy; 7. A movement that aims to impose new collective order based on total certainty; 8. An expropriation of critical human rights that is best understood as a coup from above: an overthrow of the people's sovereignty.

[264] Ibid, pp. 376-377.

[265] Ibid, pp. 495-525.

[266] https://www.humanetech.com/what-we-do#problem

[267] https://www.washingtonpost.com/news/the-switch/wp/2018/04/11/ai-will-solve-facebooks-most-vexing-problems-mark-zuckerberg-says-just-dont-ask-when-or-how/

[268] The March of Folly, p. 407.

[269] 23andMe also tells me that I am 3.9% American Indian, but like Elizabeth Warren I should probably keep that to myself.

[270] https://www.charitywater.org/our-work

[271] https://www.wsj.com/articles/facebooks-rittenhouse-mistake-11599260134

[272] https://www.youtube.com/watch?v=AbIQGLyz_O8

[273] https://www.facebook.com/zuck/videos/10112235089045271

[274] https://www.washingtonpost.com/technology/2020/09/03/facebook-political-ads/

[275] Ibid.

[276] https://www.washingtonpost.com/technology/2020/09/10/twitter-election-label/

[277] https://www.propublica.org/article/outright-lies-voting-misinformation-flourishes-on-facebook

[278] "Churchill and National Unity" from The Lessons of History, Michael Howard, Yale University Press, 1991, Page 161

[279] https://www.forbes.com/sites/aaronsmith/2020/08/18/amid-booming-gun-and-ammo-sales-arms-makers-aim-not-to-get-burned-again/#20897a0d4382 ; https://www.shootingillustrated.com/articles/2020/8/20/ammo-shortage-may-last-until-2021/

[280] https://www.latimes.com/california/story/2020-09-12/l-a-sheriffs-deputy-shot-in-compton-near-blue-line-station

[281] https://www.wsj.com/articles/what-islamists-and-wokeists-have-in-common-11599779507?mod=searchresults&page=1&pos=1

[282] On Looking Into The Abyss: Untimely Thoughts On Culture And Society, Gertrude Himmelfarb, Vintage books, 1994, from the essay *"Liberty: one very simple principle"?*

[283] https://www.rev.com/blog/transcripts/chad-wolf-dhs-secretary-senate-nomination-hearing-transcript-september-23

[284] https://www.rickscott.senate.gov/senate-democrats-block-sen-rick-scott-resolution-honor-law-enforcement-community-and-condemn-recent

[285] https://www.rev.com/blog/transcripts/chad-wolf-dhs-secretary-senate-nomination-hearing-transcript-september-23

[286] This section loosely drawn from https://www.smithsonianmag.com/history/the-ugliest-most-contentious-presidential-election-ever-28429530/

[287] Democracy, Cpt. 8. *A Nation Divided: the United States and the Challenge of Succession (1861)*, p. 244. Quoted in Richard H. Sewell, A House Divided (Baltimore: John Hopkins University Press, 1988), p .76

[288] https://www.nytimes.com/2012/04/03/science/civil-war-toll-up-by-20-percent-in-new-estimate.html

[289] https://www.theatlantic.com/politics/archive/2015/11/wilson-legacy-racism/417549/

[290] https://www.wsj.com/articles/a-bullying-president-at-an-ugly-debate-11601596545?mod=opinion_lead_pos8

[291] The Art of War, Sun Tzu, translated and with an introduction by Samuel B. Griffith with a forward by BH Liddell Hart, Oxford University Press, 1963, pp.77-78

[292] https://data.imf.org/regular.aspx?key=61726508

[293] https://www.aspi.org.au/report/chinese-communist-partys-coercive-diplomacy

[294] https://www.theatlantic.com/politics/archive/2019/07/south-korea-china-united-states-dilemma/594850/

[295] Red Flags, p. 157.

[296] Red Flags, 160.

[297] https://thediplomat.com/2019/06/the-shanghai-cooperation-organization-a-vehicle-for-cooperation-or-competition/

[298] https://www.thehindu.com/news/international/shanghai-cooperation-organisation-a-counter-coalition-of-eurasian-powers/article32589476.ece

[299] https://www.tehrantimes.com/news/452826/Zarif-to-visit-China-soon-to-discuss-long-term-agreement

[300] https://apnews.com/article/iran-iran-nuclear-international-news-baghdad-tehran-0f5efb8f2c00b538dea7ab44acc2f267

301 Countdown to Zero Day: Stuxnet and the Launch of the World's First Digital Weapon, Kim Zetter, 2014, Crown Publishers, an imprint of Random House LLC

302 https://www.nytimes.com/2020/09/21/us/politics/us-iran-sanctions.html

303 https://ec.europa.eu/trade/policy/countries-and-regions/countries/iran/

304 https://www.aljazeera.com/news/2020/9/22/iran-sends-message-of-resistance-to-us-at-unga

305 https://www.tehrantimes.com/news/447132/Iran-exports-goods-to-128-countries-despite-U-S-sanctions

306 https://www.cfr.org/in-brief/whats-behind-new-israel-uae-peace-deal

307 https://www.tehrantimes.com/news/452814/We-will-increase-range-of-our-weapons-says-IRGC-chief

308 https://www.politico.com/news/2020/09/13/iran-south-africa-ambassador-assassination-plot-413831

309 Why Nations Fail: The Origins Of Power, Prosperity And Poverty, Daron Acemoglu & James A. Robinson, Profile Books, 2013, pp. 366-7

310 The Lessons of History, Howard, pp. 156-159.

311 https://jheconomics.com/it-is-time-for-a-draft/

312 Ibid.

313 http://www.abrahamlincolnonline.org/lincoln/speeches/house.htm

314 http://www.amandascgorman.com/home.html ; https://www.cbsnews.com/news/amanda-gorman-youth-poet-laureate-coronavirus-pandemic/

315 The Black Swan: The Impact Of The Highly Improbable, Taleb, Nassim Nicholas (2010) [2007], London: Penguin, ISBN 978-0-14103459-1

316 https://www.wsj.com/articles/black-swan-a-rare-disaster-not-as-rare-as-once-believed-11584645612

317 "I don't know, but somebody does, and they ain't tellin'"; https://www.thepersimmongroup.com/how-to-use-the-knowns-and-unknowns-technique-to-manage-assumptions/

318 https://www.ncbi.nlm.nih.gov/pmc/articles/PMC5773401/

319 https://www.behavioraleconomics.com/resources/mini-encyclopedia-of-be/availability-heuristic/

320 https://www.metafilter.com/95152/Userdriven-discontent#3256046

321 https://www.urban.org/sites/default/files/publication/98669/housing_finance_at_a_glance_a_monthly_chartbook_june_2018_0.pdf

322 https://www.aljazeera.com/news/2020/09/east-med-crisis-greek-pm-raises-sanctions-threat-turkey-200910065201275.html

[323] https://www.businessinsider.com/us-systemic-racism-in-charts-graphs-data-2020-6#theres-a-similar-disparity-at-the-household-level-lower-incomes-mean-that-the-poverty-rate-for-black-families-is-over-twice-that-of-white-families-7 ; https://www.vox.com/2020/6/17/21284527/systemic-racism-black-americans-9-charts-explained

[324] https://www.washingtonpost.com/graphics/2020/opinions/systemic-racism-police-evidence-criminal-justice-system/

[325] https://csis-website-prod.s3.amazonaws.com/s3fs-public/200901_Significant_Cyber_Events_List.pdf

Made in the USA
Middletown, DE
30 December 2020

30472889R00159